A Child Shall Lead Them

A Child Shall Lead Them

Martin Luther King Jr., Young People, and the Movement

Rufus Burrow Jr.

Fortress Press
Minneapolis

A CHILD SHALL LEAD THEM

Martin Luther King Jr., Young People, and the Movement

Copyright © 2014 Fortress Press. All rights reserved. Except for brief quotations in critical articles or reviews, no part of this book may be reproduced in any manner without prior written permission from the publisher. Visit http://www.augsburgfortress.org/copyrights/ or write to Permissions, Augsburg Fortress, Box 1209, Minneapolis, MN 55440.

Cover image: USA. Washington D.C. August 28, 1963. Young men sing during the March on Washington. © Bruce Davidson/Magnum Photos

Cover design: Laurie Ingram

Library of Congress Cataloging-in-Publication Data

Print ISBN: 978-1-4514-8454-0

eBook ISBN: 978-1-4514-8762-6

This book was produced using PressBooks.com, and PDF rendering was done by PrinceXML.

For the four princesses of the Anderson, Dixon, Burrow, Wright, Waters, Burkhalter, Benson, and Joint clan: Sierra Lynn, Raven Lynn, Jade, and Bailey Reign. May you each strive to make the world a gentler and more just place, one in which every person will have equal opportunities to make a life worth living. May you lead the way in the honored tradition of black and white young people who boldly and courageously devoted their lives to the cause of civil rights and freedom in the 1960s. You honor your late father and all of us when you strive to make the world better than it is.

Contents

Foreword: Beyond Emmett Till   ix
The Hope of a New Generation
Michael G. Long

Preface   xv

Acknowledgements   xxxv

Introduction   1

1. Montgomery   17
   "Just to See Empty Bus, after Empty Bus
   Go By . . ."

2. Sitting-In and Taking a Ride for Freedom   55

3. Birmingham and the Children's Crusade   97

4. Mississippi   149
   Made to Disappear

5. Selma   217
   "What We Talk about Has Also to Do with the
   Children"

6. Who Will Carry the Freedom Struggle Forward?   271

Index   319

Foreward: Beyond Emmett Till

The Hope of a New Generation

Michael G. Long

If there's anything that shocks students in my civil rights course, it's the photograph of the mangled corpse of Emmett Till, the fourteen-year-old Chicagoan lynched by two adult thugs under the cover of night in Money, Mississippi in August 1955. Till, an African American, had broken local customs by whistling at a white woman, Carolyn Bryant, at a small grocery store she and her husband Roy owned and operated. In turn, Roy and his half-brother, J. W. Milam, self-appointed guardians of Jim Crow in Money, exacted revenge on young Till by pistol-whipping him, shooting him in the head, and dumping his body, tied to a cotton gin fan, in the Tallahatchie River.

Mamie Till Bradley, Emmett's mother, insisted on an open casket and permitted photography so that the world could see what the cowardly racists had done to her son.

Photographs of Till's brutalized and bloated head subsequently appeared in *Jet*, a national black publication, and these are the disturbing shots that give my students a small but significant glimpse into the indescribable brutalities suffered by African American children and youth in Jim Crow America.

I'm not exactly sure how to interpret my students' reactions when they see the image of young Till lying in the open casket. Are they upset and unsettled? Are they angered and outraged? Does the image make them want to close their eyes, turn their heads, and forget? Or does it inspire them to ensure such brutality never happens again? Do they see it as part of an ancient past never to be relived, or as evidence directly connected to contemporary racism and violence?

The *Jet* photographs infuriated African Americans across the country in 1955, but they had no similar effect on the all-white jury in Sumner, Mississippi. The male jurors needed little more than an hour to acquit both Milam and Bryant, and it took that long only because they stopped for sodas before returning to the courtroom. My students are incredulous when they see images of Bryant and Milam kissing their wives and chewing on fat cigars following the verdict. How could this possibly have happened in the land of the free?

We explore the reasons underlying the verdict, but I also make sure to tell them that the gross miscarriage of justice had a far more significant effect than incredulousness in 1955—that the case of Emmett Till actually helped to ignite the modern civil rights movement. The National Association for the Advancement of Colored People (NAACP) used the Till case to stage protests at the time, and just one hundred days after Till's death, Rosa Parks refused to surrender her seat on a bus in Montgomery, Alabama, launching a boycott that led to a full-scale movement.

Because of the lynching of Emmett Till, as well as countless other gross injustices, African American adults throughout the nation were primed for protest as 1955 drew to a close. Those adults included Reverend Martin Luther King Jr., who shortly after the return of the Till verdict, described the heinous case by saying it "might be considered one of the most brutal and inhuman crimes of the twentieth century."

The Till case also had a demonstrable effect on African American children and youths throughout Mississippi and other states where Jim Crow ruled with an iron fist. The lynching terrorized and traumatized them, of course, but it also made some of them angry as hell. That was the experience of Joyce Ladner, now senior fellow at the Brookings Institution, who was twelve years old and lived in southern Mississippi at the time of the lynching. "I cannot remember having felt more vulnerable, more frightened . . . but at the same time, more angry," she recalls, adding that she can remember her anger "very, very much."

Remarkably, the terror and fury that young people felt in the land of Jim Crow transformed into hope-filled action in the post–Till years. The sickening photograph of Till's mutilated face became a powerful image that inspired a generation of young African Americans to ensure that the same would not happen to them or anyone else. With Till's face burned into their hearts and minds, this new generation boycotted a racist bus company in Montgomery, sat at segregated lunch counters in Greensboro and Nashville, took Freedom Rides into the Deep South, filled the jails of Birmingham, marched on Washington, organized black voters in Mississippi, and demanded the right to vote in Selma, among so many other things. In the case of Joyce Ladner, she became a field secretary for the Student Nonviolent Coordinating Committee and, many years later, served as interim president of Howard University in Washington, D.C., where she inspired thousands of young African Americans.

This points to one of the main lessons of this powerful new book by Rufus Burrow: rather than despairing over Emmett Till, allowing his lynching to be the last and final word, a new generation of young African Americans organized themselves, grew powerful and, with hope against hope, tried to create a civil and political society marked by liberty and justice for all. It's so easy for us to focus stereoscopically on the gut-wrenching case of Emmett Till—his horrifying face, his mother's tears, his smirking killers, and their racist buddies—but Burrow's study sees Till's death as the beginning of an enlivening era of hopeful activism in which children and youths, particularly African Americans, stood tall, often taller than their parents, teachers, and mentors, and demanded the justice that had eluded Till and the first-class citizenship denied to millions of African Americans in the land of the free.

We are greatly indebted to Professor Burrow for sharing the inspiring story of these brave young activists. It's not an easy story to tell. For one thing, the young activists were not a monolithic block; they differed from one another in terms of strategy and goals, region and education, class and gender—and race-consciousness. Student activists from the corridors of power at Stanford and Yale, for instance, were radically different from young black leaders reared along the dusty roads of rural Mississippi. For another, the young activists were not a self-contained unit; they existed in relation to adults who, at different points, were insightful and clueless, courageous and fearful, helpful and obstructive. We can fully understand the energetic and brash Diane Nash of the Freedom Riders, for example, only by recognizing that while she took some cues from Martin Luther King Jr., she also plowed past his occasional reticence. In typical fashion, however, Professor Burrow tells the story with such nuance and clarity that by the end of the book we can only stand in awe of the masterly and compelling way in which he presents this understudied, underreported, and underappreciated part of U.S. history.

Burrow's book adds depth not only to our knowledge of the many roles played by courageous young people in the civil rights movement, some of whom died because of their daring work, but also to our understanding of Martin Luther King Jr. The interplay between King and young activists, so carefully depicted in the pages ahead, shows the great civil rights *leader* as a *follower* of young people—one inspired by their strategic ideas, their impatient attitudes, and their high-risk actions. It reveals America's prophet as an object of prophetic wrath unleashed by young people who found him too dependent on Washington. It depicts the Great Man of civil rights history as dependent upon imprisoned and beaten children and youth for the fulfillment of his dream—as part of a grassroots movement populated largely by young activists. And it shows the man who demanded so much of adults of all colors as generously supportive of young folks in need of their own inspiration and instruction.

I have been reading Professor Burrow's first-rate books for many years now, and I dare say this one stands above all others in the way it has captured my attention, fueled my imagination, and offered me a sense of hope for tomorrow. The generation of young African Americans who joined King in fiercely resurrecting the principles of equality, freedom, and justice to save the soul of our nation, as described so movingly here, leaves me with hope in the face of ongoing injustices related to race and ethnicity, including those which, like the Till case, end in murders crying out for attention—and for justice. The post-Till generation of young African Americans bore witness to the resilience of the human spirit like none other in U.S. history; the children and youths of this generation turned lynching into love—a tough love that pushed, even shoved, individual hearts and social systems far along the arc of the moral universe that King invoked so many times. We are better because of their unshakable witness, but we could be so much better if we tended to their hopeful stance anew, allowing their historic acts of courage to inspire us, no matter our age, to carry the freedom struggle forward.

Preface

Historically, in most black communities, it was thought that children have a certain place, and that they should be taught to remember it. There were certain things considered to be "grown folks' business," and children were taught and expected to remain in their place. As one of my students wrote in my course on King during the 2013–2014 school year: "We were expected to be silent in the presence of adults, and we were not to even ask questions." Strong, but loving parenting was necessary to ensure that children understood and abided by this code. This was all the more important during the time of blacks' enslavement in this country, since the failure of an enslaved child to keep the secrets of what was discussed or heard in the enslaved quarters could very easily lead to beatings and/or lynchings. In truth, then, the expectation that black children would keep their place, hold their tongue, and not involve themselves in grown folks' business is a carryover from slavery. But even after slavery, the period of Reconstruction (roughly 1867–1877) and beyond, blacks continued to believe that there were some things that simply did not concern their children, and that they should not be exposed to them. Whether intended or not, the practice slowly developed that required not only that black children not talk outside the home about matters pertaining to freedom, but they were to know that this was an adult matter, and adults alone would address it. In part, at least, this is the context for the stance of those blacks like Thurgood Marshall, Malcolm X, and many black residents in Birmingham and Selma, Alabama, in McComb, Mississippi, and numerous other places in the Deep South regarding the use of children and youth in the freedom struggle. Many adult blacks rejected the idea of utilizing black children and young people in this way, as we will see in this book. And yet, much to the surprise of many, but not all, it was the children and youth who boldly led the way in many of the civil rights campaigns, and who energized the movement at strategic moments. They asserted themselves, making it clear once and for all that they were fully aware of racial discrimination and its adverse effects on them.

This book focuses on the coming of age, self-determination, and role of black children and youths during the civil rights movement, and how their contributions aided the efforts of Martin Luther King and other civil rights leaders. We will see that at some points young people actually initiated and led campaigns for civil rights and freedom, such as the sit-ins, the Freedom Rides, and voter education-registration projects in Albany, Georgia, the Mississippi Delta, and Selma, Alabama. King exhibited deep respect and admiration for young people—from Montgomery, Alabama to Memphis, Tennessee. It was always his sense that because so much of the struggle for justice and freedom was about the future of these young people, and because they suffered the pain and agony of racial discrimination as much as black adults, they had every right to make their own contributions to eradicate injustice and to participate in the construction of a gentler and just society where the humanity and dignity of every person would be acknowledged and respected just because they were human beings.

To be sure, there was not always complete agreement between King and black youths regarding his increasingly staunch commitment to nonviolence as a way of life. This was particularly the case of those youths who were committed to movement goals, but did not undergo the rigorous training in nonviolence. This was the case of some Deep South youths, as well as many Northern black youths who went south to lend a helping hand. There were also instances in which some youths, particularly latecomers to the Student Nonviolent Coordinating Committee (SNCC), believed that King's actions sometimes did not go far enough, and that he sold out, as in the case of the second march to the Pettus Bridge in Selma after the "Bloody Sunday" tragedy two days earlier in March of 1965. But for all of this, the relationship between King and black youth was complex, and although there was often mutual cooperation between them, tension and divisiveness also developed regarding differences in strategy as well as ideology. To his credit, Martin Luther King made every effort to express his disagreements with youthful activists behind closed doors rather than publicly or through the media. He always wanted to give the public impression of a united front.

Martin Luther King always acknowledged that children and young people are human beings, and therefore are also adversely affected by racism and discriminatory practices. It affects how they think of themselves, just as it affects adults, King reasoned. In light of this, children and young people should be allowed to protest that which undermines their humanity and sense of dignity. If children and young people are old enough to understand that racism means that they should be treated as less than their white counterparts, they are old enough to do something about it. But just here, is where the responsible, guiding hand of adults comes into play. Even though young people may want to do something to end discriminatory practices against them, chances are they do not know quite what to do, or how to do it. This is a place where they can be taught the history of race relations, and God's expectation of human beings who face discrimination of various kinds. For King, this would also be the place at which young people can be taught the importance of nonviolence as the method for overcoming race discrimination and other forms of injustice.

During the civil rights movement of the 1960s, SNCC members and other youth activists were among the first to learn that children know more than adults are sometimes aware, and that they instinctively want to push back when their humanity is threatened or otherwise undermined. A King protégé, James Bevel, saw the wisdom of putting this idea to work in the Birmingham campaign of 1963. He and his wife, Diane Nash Bevel, had learned from their organizing work with black youth in Mississippi that young people tended to be less afraid than black adults. Moreover, even when they could not articulate it well on their own, black youths knew almost instinctively when they were being mistreated because of their race. James Bevel had the wherewithal to see how such youthful energy and desire to get involved in their own liberation process could be useful in pushing the movement forward.

From the 1950s through roughly the 1970s, black youth seemed to want to get involved in the struggle for civil rights and freedom because they were aware of its importance for themselves, for their parents and grandparents, and for those who would come after them. Since that time, however, things have shifted such that many black youth today seem to have little interest in such things, and seem to be content with what adults will do for them by way of social struggle. Very many seem content to pursue the elusive American dream, with no sense of the need for social critique. Let me give an illustration of what I am talking about here.

Several years ago, I was invited by a Midwestern university to give a lecture on King during a presidential election year. During the question and answer period, a black male student asked, "What can students do?" This was quite an appropriate question, since the conclusion of the lecture focused on implications of King's legacy and the role of young people today. The student's body language suggested that he was troubled when I responded that there are indeed things that students can do to contribute toward making a better society and world. The student seemed to suggest that this is adult work. Since he asked about what types of things students could do, I said that in a presidential election year, one thing they can surely do is to canvass neighborhoods in the immediate vicinity of the university to encourage people to register to vote, and if already registered, encourage them to actually go to the polls on electionday. I later heard back from the faculty member who extended the invitation to me. He informed me that the student had come to his office the next day and expressed his dismay that "adults won't do their job, but always seem to expect young people to do what they themselves should be doing." He apparently felt that since he was in college he should be permitted a kind of holiday from participating in any way in matters of social justice.

I took the young man's reaction very seriously, since I had heard similar comments made by young people before. I was particularly alarmed because more often than not, such comments are made by college students. My concern was not caused by any sense of these young people being among what W. E. B. Du Bois once termed the *talented tenth*. The alarm was triggered just as much by the fact that such comments are made by too many noncollegiate black students too. What occurs to me each time I hear such things is that such persons either have no sense of the history of race relations in this country, particularly during the civil rights era, or they just have no interest in knowing that history. Or perhaps they believe it has no relevance for their lives. While this is certainly the case with some, there is also good reason to suspect that more often than not, they just do not know the history; do not know that blacks' struggle against injustice and racism has historically been the concern of both adults and young people in the black community. They seem to have no sense of the large role that young people played during the civil rights movement, and that there is much that they themselves can do today.

It is therefore problematic to imply, as the aforementioned student did, that social justice work is adult work, and is not that about which young people should have to concern themselves. We will see that during the civil rights era many young people, mostly blacks, but some whites as well, actually dropped out of school to devote fulltime to the struggle, so important did they believe civil rights work to be. And yet, it was also the case that many students figured out ways to remain in school and to support the cause as best they could, sometimes participating in sit-ins and nonviolent demonstrations, passing out flyers door to door in neighborhoods near their college campus, and so on. But they did not, like the young man who asked the question, assume that they should be allowed to finish school, thus having a time for play, before being expected to contribute to the ongoing struggle for freedom. They knew that they and their people were in the fight of their very lives, and that every one of them had something to contribute; indeed, must contribute whatever they could. In my own experience, I find that far too many Afrikan American and other college students know little or nothing of that period of black history. There is therefore a need to learn this history and to begin appropriating it.

Now of course, some may be quick to say that the big advantage that young people had during the civil rights movement was that they actually lived through the events every day, and therefore could not pretend ignorance; could not pretend that what was happening had nothing to do with them. Because they were aware of what was happening, and were often directly affected by it, they were compelled to act in a way and to a degree that students today are not. The student who asked the question after my King lecture did not feel compelled to act. I want to think that to a large extent this had to do with his simply not knowing enough about the history of race relations in this country.

In any case, I am convinced that one of the sheer failures of the educational system in this country is that of teaching students the history leading up to and including the civil rights era, and beyond. This is important not only for Afrikan American students, but for all students, for this was history that U.S. citizens—regardless of race-ethnicity—all made together, for good or bad. It is *our* history together, and therefore it concerns us all. Educational curricula need to be altered so that students will be taught this history and how it is connected to many of the still-existing racial, cultural, political, and social problems that we face as a nation. The hope would be that through such teaching, some, at least, would see the relevance of young people's contributions to social justice struggles, particularly when educators help them to make the connections with current-day issues that may be adversely affecting them. Indeed, when fifteen-year-old Claudette Colvin's teacher, Mrs. Geraldine Nesbitt, was teaching her students about the U.S. Constitution in her Montgomery, Alabama classroom, she also helped them to make the connection between constitutional rights and bus segregation in that city. Because of this, Colvin, when subsequently ordered by a bus driver to give her paid-for seat to a white patron, refused, saying that, having paid the same fare as everyone else, she had a constitutional right to her seat. It seems to me that the educational component is a critical step as we think about how best to carry the struggle forward.

Reflecting on the civil rights era and the role played by herself and other young people, Diane Nash concluded that today's young people should be told about the struggle and the significant contributions made by their earlier counterparts; that it was not just adults who made contributions and sacrifices, including their very lives. "I think it's really important that young people today understand that the movement of the sixties was really a people's movement," said Nash. "The media and history seem to record it as Martin Luther King's movement, but young people should realize that it was people just like them, their age, that formulated goals and strategies, and actually developed the movement. When they look around now, and see things that need to be changed, they should say: 'What can I do? What can my roommate and I do to effect that change?'"[1] It might not be much that she and her roommate and others like them can do at the particular time, but the determination and courage to do *something*, matters, especially in the long sweep of things. Nash was remembering that during the civil rights movement, vast numbers of young people took it on themselves to actually fight for their rights; to contribute what they could. Her point was not to be unduly critical of King's role, for she was the first to admit that he was the symbol and beloved leader of the national movement. What Nash wants to convey to today's young people is that when she was a young college student, members of her generation jumped right in, wherever they were, and contributed what they could. They did not make excuses. They did not wait for the approval or permission of adults, including King, although they were open to sagely advice or counsel. They got involved, because they knew instinctively that their lives and futures, including that of the race, were at stake. Because it is often difficult for an

---

1. Juan Williams, *Eyes on the Prize: America's Civil Rights Years, 1954-1965* (New York: Viking, 1987), 131.

individual to step up to the plate, Nash reflected that it might be easier for such persons to seek out and join with a group or movement that may be trying to address a social issue that seemed particularly troubling. As for herself, Nash recalled that "[t]he movement had a way of reaching inside me and bringing out things that I never knew were there. Like courage, and love for people."[2] Her point is that everybody can do something, an idea that Martin Luther King stressed frequently during movement days. Even those who could not accept his nonviolent philosophy, and thus were not allowed to march in the demonstrations led by him, could run errands, do filing, make telephone calls, pass out leaflets, and so forth.

Young people today need to know that they matter, that what happens to them matters, and what they do about it matters. But they also need to know that the practical world is such that they dare not sit back passively and hope that someone else—adults or otherwise—will address the problems that concern them. Many young people (of all social classes) during the movement years figured this out. They decided that their involvement in the struggle for civil rights was their decision to make, and no one else's. Because many of the first youthful activists, e.g., SNCC youths, were trained in the method of nonviolence, they also understood that their involvement would be costly. They therefore braced themselves to face the consequences of their actions, including having to go to jail, and possibly even being made to disappear in one of the muddy rivers or an earthen dam in the Mississippi Delta.

Those who come to positive decision about carrying the movement forward will need fortitude and all that the term implies: determination, courage, endurance, strength, and stick-to-itiveness. During movement days, those who held the reins of power and privilege and benefited from injustices done to others generally did

2. Ibid.

not yield or share their power and privilege willingly, or out of a sense of morality, Christian or otherwise. It is no different today, which means that any struggle for justice will likely be a long and protracted one, with sometimes harsh consequences.

Although the primary focus of this book is on the contributions and sacrifices of Afrikan American youths, we will also see that many white youths made significant contributions and sacrifices during the civil rights struggle. Jim Zwerg was a white college student from Beloit College in Wisconsin, who had grown up in Madison. He volunteered to be an exchange student at the all-black Fisk University in Nashville. This was when he got caught up in the civil rights activism of the Nashville youth activists, many who were either in college, or had dropped out to devote fulltime to the cause. Zwerg joined John Lewis (now longtime U.S. Congressman) and other youth activists to continue the Freedom Ride in 1961 after another group of Riders had been brutally attacked outside Anniston, Alabama. Once the young people left the Birmingham bus terminal and arrived at the terminal in Montgomery, Zwerg and others were savagely beaten by racist thugs as they left the bus. Zwerg was likely beaten worse because he was white. In the warped minds of white supremacists, the worst thing a white person could do was to support and participate in the freedom struggle with blacks to make freedom and democracy a reality for all. Zwerg's injuries were such that he required extended hospitalization, and was unable to continue with his youthful Freedom Ride colleagues. From his hospital bed he displayed the fortitude that had already characterized his sister and brother Riders. He told an interviewer: "We will continue our journey, one way or another. We are prepared to die."[3] This was the motto of the youthful Riders. Diane Nash, leader of the Nashville

---

3. Quoted in John Blake, *Children of the Movement* (Chicago: Lawrence Hill Books, 2004), 33.

student activists, had said: "Mob violence must not stop men's striving toward right. Freedom Rides and other such actions must not be stopped until our nation is really free."[4] It must have taken a real sense of determination and courage for young Zwerg to continue in the struggle for civil rights and freedom for all. Indeed, these were kids who would not be deterred by violence; not even death.

In truth, the lives of blacks and whites continue to be so integrally intermingled in the United States that it is virtually impossible for either group alone to succeed in establishing the beloved community wherein every individual person is respected by virtue of being a person, and where the needs of all are met before any has the right to collect and store away surplus goods. But in order to establish such a reality, civil rights youths had a good sense that strong alliance building was needed. Somehow blacks and whites had to figure out how to build coalitions around strong common interests. Such efforts among black and white youth of the civil rights era did not go unnoticed by Martin Luther King, who was always quick to applaud their efforts in alliance building and to encourage them to keep at it. When black youth initiated the sit-in movement and also insisted on the need for the Freedom Rides to continue, white youth of conscience and good will quickly joined in coalition with them, an alliance, King recalled, that stirred and "aroused the conscience of the nation." This was all done by young people—kids—seeing the nation and world as it was, and making the decision to do something about it, with or without the support of adults. Neither blacks nor whites did a good enough job of addressing the racial aspects of the coalitions formed, which is why none of the alliances held together after the 1960s. And yet, it was a moment in history from which

---

4. Diane Nash, "Inside the Sit-ins and Freedom Rides: Testimony of a Southern Student," in *The New Negro*, ed. Mathew H. Ahmann (New York: Biblo & Tannen, 1969), 53.

youth of today can learn valuable lessons should they see the wisdom of building coalitions with groups that share similar goals.

Just months before he was assassinated, Martin Luther King declared that although he was not completely optimistic, neither was he ready to concede defeat.[5] To the extent that he trusted and had faith in God and the future, he had faith in human beings to do the things that make for a better society and world. The key, for King, was his faith in God, not in human beings as such. God was the source, the ground of any faith that King had in human beings. "I have faith in the future because I have faith in God," King said, "and I believe that there is a power, a creative force in this universe seeking at all times to bring down prodigious hilltops of evil and pull low gigantic mountains of injustice. If we will believe this and struggle along, we will be able to achieve it."[6] King's faith was in God, and through God, in human beings. Neither human beings nor God alone can abolish injustice and establish justice. Neither can establish the beloved community alone. Rather, King held, there must be ongoing cooperative endeavor between human beings and God.

Based on the youth activism that he witnessed from Montgomery to Memphis, Martin Luther King knew that if only because of those young people's contributions, there was reason to hope that the beloved community could be achieved, or more nearly approximated. He had witnessed with his own eyes what the imagination, determination, and courage of committed young people could accomplish. On the contrary, and but for a few exceptions, there was much less reason to be hopeful about what adults (the "oldsters" King sometimes called them) would accomplish

---

5. Martin Luther King Jr., "Impasse in Race Relations," in his *The Trumpet of Conscience* (New York: Harper & Row, 1967), 13.
6. Clayborne Carson et al., eds., *The Papers of Martin Luther King, Jr.* (Berkeley: University of California Press, 2005), 5:418.

toward establishing the beloved community, since many of them tended to be far too conservative and timid to contribute meaningfully in this regard.

Youthful activists, through their various coalitions, accomplished much during the sit-ins, Freedom Rides, and numerous voter education-registration projects, most notably the Freedom Summer Project in the Mississippi Delta region. So much negative history existed between black and white youths that even on their best days their alliance was difficult, at best, to maintain. There were issues of trust that constantly arose, as well as elitism among some whites (intended or not!). There was deep suspicion on the part of many black youth activists. Moreover, the specter of racism loomed large, such that when blacks and well-meaning whites called attention to this it led to added strain on the coalition. Some wondered, for example, how the federal government could launch such a massive search for Michael Schwerner, Andrew Goodman, and James Chaney when other civil rights activists—all black—had also disappeared in places like the Mississippi Delta and received virtually no attention. Indeed, some concluded that had Chaney, who was black, been the only missing civil rights worker, the federal government would likely have remained silent and uninvolved. Some, including white youths, voiced their concern that there was such a massive outpouring of grief throughout the country and within the federal government when white Unitarian Universalist minister James Reeb was clubbed to death in Selma, Alabama, while there was virtual silence outside the black community when Jimmy Lee Jackson, a black activist, was murdered by an Alabama state trooper in nearby Marion.

It was difficult for black and white youths to keep working together in common cause, but they did it better than most, until the alliance began to break down because of increased suspicion, as well as a sense among some black youth activists that they needed to do some work among themselves, without whites being present. In part, at least, this is what happened to SNCC, which, from its inception, had been an interracial organization that was open to whites being in positions of leadership. In late 1967, King's assessment was that the general alliance between black and white youth activists had fallen apart "under the impact of failures, discouragement, and consequent extremism and polarization. The movement for social change has entered a time of temptation to despair because it is clear now how deep and systemic are the evils it confronts. There is a strong temptation to despair of programs and actions, and to dissipate energy into hysterical talk. There is a temptation to break up into mutually suspicious extremist groups in which blacks reject the participation of whites and whites reject the realities of their own history."[7] That there was evidence that the old coalitions were breaking up did not mean, for King, that alliances were no longer important for those who had intention to continue the journey toward establishing the beloved community. Indeed, for King, coalition building for such people was all the more important, so much so, that what was now needed was a forging of even broader coalitions to include previously excluded groups, such as Hispanic youth and poor youth of all races that share common interests and goals, for example, civil rights, voting rights, healthcare, jobs that pay a living wage, reasonable immigration policies and practices, quality education, decent housing in relatively safe neighborhoods, and so on. Since Hispanics and Afrikan Americans are the largest and second-largest so-called minority groups in the country, respectively, it is most important that they commit to doing the very hard work of coalition building with each other. Together and together only, will they be a force to be reckoned with by the powers that be.

---

7. King, "The State of the Movement," Address presented November 28, 1967, at the Staff Retreat of SCLC at Penn Center, Frogmore, South Carolina, King Center Library and Archives, 7–8.

In the six chapters in this book, we will see that black children and youths made substantial contributions throughout the civil rights movement, beginning with the Montgomery bus boycott, the subject of chapter 1. Just like black adults, black youths were subjected to racist and disrespectful treatment on city buses in Montgomery. Moreover, we will see that the same year that Rosa Parks was arrested, black youths of Montgomery had also been arrested earlier in the year for refusing to give their seats to white patrons. When the black community agreed to a boycott of the buses, black youths were as supportive as black adults, willingly walking rather than riding the buses to and from school. Likewise, the training in nonviolence was provided for both adults and youths. Although a small number of white students exhibited support for the boycott, the numbers of white students who engaged in direct action swelled exponentially during the sit-ins, Freedom Rides, and voter registration projects throughout the Deep South.

Chapter 2 examines instances in which black youth actually led the way in the struggle for civil rights, with virtually no assistance from adults. This is what happened during the explosive sit-in movement that was ignited at the Woolworth lunch counter in Greensboro, North Carolina by four black male freshmen at North Carolina A&T. The sit-ins spread like wildfire in public places throughout the South and a few places in the North in the early months of 1960. Something similar happened in 1961 when student activists in Nashville, Tennessee, under the leadership of Diane Nash, insisted on the need to continue the Freedom Ride from Montgomery to New Orleans. As it turned out, the Riders got as far as Jackson, Mississippi before they were arrested and imprisoned for several weeks at the infamous Parchman state prison. The Congress of Racial Equality (CORE) originally initiated the Freedom Ride, but when the two busloads of riders were stopped at Anniston, Alabama and the riders were brutally beaten and one of the buses was bombed, CORE director James Farmer called off the ride. Student leader Diane Nash insisted that there would be long-term consequences for the "success" of the movement if they called off the rides because of violence. Nash reasoned that if they did not proceed with the ride, the message would be sent to every racist thug in the country that the way to put a halt to civil rights demonstrations of any kind is to subject the participants to violence. The students' argument won the day. Chapter 2, then, focuses on the youthful activists' contributions to the sit-ins and the Freedom Rides, which helped to push the movement forward. Here we see that the students' contributions gave new meaning to the biblical text that "truly a child shall lead them" (Isa. 11:6). A similar scenario would occur during the early weeks of the Birmingham struggle. The difference was that these were youths who were essentially under the supervision of the SCLC. In this case, as well as the sit-ins, Freedom Rides, and early voter registration-education projects, King and other adults were at best supporting cast. In these cases, young people were often more courageous than the adults in their communities.

We next turn to the Birmingham campaign in chapter 3. Birmingham was pivotal in King's civil rights ministry, for this would be the civil rights campaign in which the method of nonviolence was essentially on trial. When Martin Luther King and SCLC launched what they called Project C ("confrontation") in Birmingham, it did not take long before the campaign sputtered. Most of those who were committed to the demonstrations had been jailed already and the leadership was left wondering how best to give the campaign the shot of adrenalin that was needed to push it forward. Part of the aim was to fill the jails to overflowing, but they had essentially run out of bodies. It was at this point that SCLC staff member James Bevel suggested the idea of using massive numbers of black children and youths as nonviolent demonstrators. This not only had the potential for filling the jails, but it also had the important prospect of arousing the conscience of the nation. How would everyday American citizens react as they sat around their televisions and watched black children being carted off to jail for demonstrating nonviolently for their freedom? Bevel's idea led to the famous Children's Crusade, and proved to be yet another instance in which the children and young people literally led the way. Indeed, in this case, black children actually saved the Birmingham movement from collapse. The involvement of children and youths was illustrative of both determination and self-determination among young people to take their lives and futures into their own hands and to demand that they be treated as human beings with dignity; to demand that they be granted their God-given rights and those guaranteed by the Declaration of Independence and the Constitution of the United States.

It would be going too far to say that the Birmingham campaign caused the Civil Rights Act of 1964 to be passed. However, one is on quite solid ground when declaring that it contributed much toward the passing of that bill. As King, SCLC, and other civil rights groups pushed ahead in Birmingham, student activists in SNCC, along with youthful activists in CORE were breaking ground in the very dangerous Mississippi Delta, as they sought to organize and instruct rural and city blacks in voter education and registration. This is the subject of chapter 4. Youths such as Bob Moses, Chuck McDew, and Bob Zellner (SNCC's first white field secretary), were among the shock troops to enter Mississippi for the express purpose of helping to organize black residents for voter registration. The chapter examines the role of the amazing but dangerous Freedom Summer Project of 1964, which brought more than 600 mostly white student volunteers from colleges and universities of the North, and some from the South to work in the project. These young people established Freedom Schools and Cultural Centers, in addition to participating in the dangerous work of voter registration. Not all of the youths made it through Freedom Summer alive, including some local leaders. In addition, many were subjected to violence by the Klan and other white hate groups throughout the state. And yet, what is important here is that black and white youths led the way, even to the point of making the ultimate sacrifice. They possessed a healthy sense of fear for this most feared and dangerous state in the nation, and were determined that fear would not deter them from achieving their goal.

We will see in chapter 5 that the voter registration campaign in Selma contributed much toward the passing of the Voting Rights Bill of 1965. Not unlike the Freedom Summer Project in the Mississippi Delta, the Selma campaign was bloody and violent. We will see that the "Bloody Sunday" tragedy that occurred during the first attempted march from Selma to Montgomery was a significant contributing cause of the passage of the voting rights bill. Once again, we will see that at critical stages it was the children and young people who put their fears aside, and led the way. Because of the courage and determination of these young people, more adult members of the black community—parents, schoolteachers, and other professionals—got involved in the demonstrations and were also subject to violent treatment and arrests. They saw their children and students on the front lines; saw them being beaten. They could not remain standing on the sidelines, passively accepting what they witnessed. Martin Luther King never lost faith in young people and their ability and determination to help move this society in the direction of the beloved community. This is an important point to keep in mind in any discussion on King, youth, and the civil rights movement.

Chapter 6 is the last chapter in this book. It is an important chapter because it seeks to address the challenges to young people today, in light of the contributions of King and young people during the civil rights struggle. King seldom gave a speech, sermon, or wrote a book without inquiring and responding to the question, "Where do we go from here?" It is actually the question that no serious theological social ethicist will fail to address. The question is particularly relevant today when youth violence and homicides in black communities soar to astronomical numbers, whether on the Southside of Chicago, Illinois, or in the inner city of Indianapolis, Indiana. The question to be examined in chapter 6 is not: What would Martin Luther King be saying and doing were he alive today? Rather, the question is: What should those, particularly young people, who know and understand King's legacy and ideas, be saying and doing in the face of such a high incidence of youth violence and homicides, as well as the extraordinary numbers of youths who are undereducated, who drop out of secondary schools, and who are jobless, or appear to be condemned to working nonliving wage, dead-end jobs? The previous chapters reveal how youths of a generation ago stepped up to the plate and answered the call. This chapter challenges youth of today to do the same, and reminds them that doing so is the best way to ensure that theirs will be a future worth living—not dying!—for.

Acknowledgements

I have been teaching, writing, and publishing on Martin Luther King Jr. for more than twenty years. My primary focus has been on that area of King Studies that I refer to as the man of ideas and ideals genre. I have focused on this for two primary reasons. First, not as much has been written and published in this area, and second, once I read what had been written and published, I concluded that more needed to be said, and that the emphasis should not be placed merely on what King learned from European and European American thinkers, but on what he himself brought to the table. What did King bring from his black family and black church upbringing, as well as the influence of the black southern cultural tradition? How did all of this impinge on his formal intellectual development, and especially as he filtered it all through his own sociocultural lens and experience? How, for example, did his philosophy and practice of personalism differ from that of his teacher-mentors during his days as a doctoral student at Boston University? When I read the otherwise excellent works of Kenneth L. Smith and Ira Zepp Jr. (*Search for the Beloved Community: The Thinking of Martin Luther King, Jr.* [1976]), Ervin Smith (*The Ethics of Martin Luther King, Jr.* [1981]), and John Ansbro (*Martin Luther King, Jr.: The Making of a Mind* [1982]), I was, in each case, left wondering about King's own contributions to his formal intellectual development. Ervin Smith, a black scholar, had done some of this in his first and only book on King (to this point), but I concluded that it was not enough. Believing that more needed to be said about the family and church influences on King's intellectual development, I decided that this would be one of the areas of my own focus on King. At this point, I believe that we are a long way from exhausting the work to be done in this area of King Studies.

When I submitted the proposal for my last published book on King, *Extremist for Love: Martin Luther King Jr., Man of Ideas and Nonviolent Social Action* (Fortress Press, 2014), the editor, Will Berkamp, expressed strong interest in the project, but recommended that I remove part five, which focused on the mutual contributions of King and young people to the civil rights movement. I wrote Berkamp to state that I was agreeable to his suggestion. I went on to say that I would likely develop the deleted section of the manuscript into a book on King, young people, and the Movement. Berkamp responded immediately to say that based on what he had already read, Fortress Press would be interested in that manuscript as well. The gentleman's agreement was that I would complete *Extremist for Love* and get that into the production process. Afterward, a contract would be drafted for what we were tentatively calling *A Child Shall Lead Them*.

The truth is that I would not likely have turned my attention and energy to this book project had Will Berkamp not acted as quickly as he did, and then locked me into a contract with a deadline for completion of the manuscript. I am immensely grateful to Will for this. I am the first to say that the more I got into this project, the more clearly I could see the importance of such a book. Moreover, it was immediately clear to me that not very much had been written on the complex relationship between King and the social activism of children and young people, whom he loved and respected dearly. Moreover, King believed that virtually all that was happening in the civil rights movement had also to do with children and youth, and that they therefore had a right to offer their contributions to the struggle for freedom and civil rights.

As I delved deeper and deeper into the project, I could see that it was not the case that children and young people were only followers of the adult activists, but time and again, they actually led the way, at times when it seemed like the movement had stagnated, such as during the Birmingham, Alabama campaign in 1963. At other times, they led the way by virtue of their courage and their determination to not be stopped by violence and threats of violence from white racists. When James Foreman, Director of the Congress of Racial Equality (CORE) decided to call off the Freedom Ride when one of the buses was attacked and bombed and passengers savagely beaten just outside Anniston, Alabama in 1961, Diane Nash and other young activists of the Student Nonviolent Coordinating Committee (SNCC) argued passionately and persuasively that the Ride must not be halted because of violence. To do so, they argued, would communicate to racists that whenever they want to stop a civil rights campaign, all they need do is resort to physical violence. In addition, Nash and her youthful colleagues argued that *they* would continue the Freedom Ride. They were college students, but they were essentially just kids. Their action was but one of many that witnessed to the biblical truth that a child shall lead the way.

In my most recent annual class on King, I had occasion to share with students some of my excitement about the possibilities of young people and what they can contribute to making the world better than it was when they were born into it. Some students fed off of my own excitement about the possibilities, and began wondering out loud about ways they could tap into this in their day-to-day dealings with children and young people in their church and other activities. Many students were not aware of the contributions that children and young people made to the civil rights movement and the sacrifices they made—not least, severe beatings and death. What seemed to have caught my students' attention more than anything was the courage and determination of children and youths of the civil rights era to contribute toward their own liberation. Those young people did not always have the answers, but they knew they had to, and indeed could, try. They made mistakes, but they learned from them and forged ahead anyway. And when their peers and other activists were murdered at the onset of Freedom Summer in 1964, the vast majority refused their parents' pleas to return to the safety of their homes in the North.

I see the greatest hope and potential for youth involvement in struggles for justice and liberation, not in my generation and the generation behind it, but in the generation of my granddaughter, Bailey Reign Anderson. This is why I have dedicated this book to her and her three sisters (by different mothers). These are the ones, it seems to me, who will see the world as it is, and dedicate their lives to making it a better place than it was when they entered it. These are the ones who will most likely make real, and give new meaning, to the words of the prophet Isaiah: ". . . a little child shall lead them." In any case, this is the challenge to the generation of the four princesses—Sierra Lynn, Raven Lynn, Jade, and Bailey Reign.

Introduction

Because Martin Luther King Jr. was recovering from being nearly stabbed to death by Izola Ware Curry as he autographed copies of his first book (*Stride Toward Freedom*) at Blumstein's Department Store in Harlem on September 20, 1958, his wife delivered his written address to young people who participated in the Youth March for Integrated Schools in Washington, D.C. on October 25, 1958. King cheered, praised, and encouraged young people for what he considered a "great and historic demonstration" for freedom. Through his wife King told the youths:

> There is a unique element in this demonstration; it is a young people's march. You are proving that the youth of America is freeing itself of the prejudices of an older and darker time in our history. In addition, you are proving the so-called "silent generation" is not so silent. . . .
>
> Keep marching and show the pessimists and the weak of spirit that they are wrong. Keep marching and don't let them silence you. Keep marching and resist injustice with the firm, non-violent spirit you demonstrated today.
>
> The future belongs, not to those who slumber or sleep, but to those who cannot rest while the evil of injustice thrives in the bosom of America. The future belongs to those who march toward freedom.[1]

Not only did King welcome and applaud the youthful activists to the struggle, he urged them from the beginning to adhere to nonviolence. Even at this early juncture in his civil rights ministry, King was aware of what the youth of the nation could contribute toward achieving the freedom and civil rights of all people. He applauded their demonstration and encouraged them to keep the faith, to keep protesting and demonstrating for freedom.

In March 1964, Martin Luther King gave an interview to the seventh-grade English class at the George A. Towne Elementary School in Atlanta, Georgia. From the responses that he gave to the questions posed, it was evident that he took the interview by his youthful audience seriously. His answers revealed much appreciation for their concerns, as well as his respect for those asking the questions. All of this was quite consistent with his long-held stance that children and young people have much to contribute to the civil rights struggle, and therefore should not be expected to merely be passive onlookers as adults engage the struggle for freedom and civil rights.

Two of the questions asked by the students pertained to the subject of where King got the inspiration to engage in civil rights work, and what he believed to be the role of young people in the movement. With regard to the first question, King told the students that it was actually quite easy for him to work in civil rights because he had grown up the son of a minister who was committed to applying Christian principles and the Christian love ethic to the problems of injustice and other social maladies that adversely affected black people. He had grown up the son of a minister who believed blacks were morally obligated to fight for their freedom and right to live with dignity. In this regard, King said, he saw his father as an excellent ministerial role model. But more to the point of how he

---

1. Clayborne Carson et al., eds., *The Papers of Martin Luther King, Jr.* (Berkeley: University of California Press, 2000), 4:515.

came to be interested in civil rights work, King told the students: "My home influenced me because of [*sic*] my father as a minister, was always interested in civil rights and helping people who had been treated unjustly or unfairly."[2] He was further encouraged to move toward the ministerial vocation by the example of his Morehouse College teacher-mentors such as President Benjamin E. Mays and Professor George Kelsey. "As a young college student I was concerned about segregation and I always felt that one of the important roles of a minister is leadership in getting rid of segregation and discrimination."[3] The church and its ministers were not to be silent, passive backseat passengers in that struggle. Instead, wherever they were stationed they were to be vocal, aggressive, importunate leaders for justice, desegregation, and integration. King told the young students that his social conscience was near full bloom by the time he entered college, and thus at an early age he was concerned about the plight of his people and desired to do something about it. He was not satisfied to just sit back and wait to see what others might do. He wanted to make his own contribution. Consequently, he decided fairly early that education would be a primary means of preparing for such a vocation, although he did not blossom academically until he began seminary.

In addition to tracing his own interest in civil rights work to the example of his father and teacher-mentors at Morehouse, King was equally emphatic in telling the students that they needed to be open and willing to learn, as well as to be thoroughly trained in the fundamentals of nonviolent resistance. On this point he said: "Children suffer as much or more as a result of the existence of segregation as adults do, therefore, children have the right and a

---

2. Martin Luther King Jr., Interview by Seventh-Grade English Class at the George A. Towne Elementary School, Atlanta, Georgia, March 11, 1964, King Library and Archives, 1.
3. Ibid.

responsibility to participate in racial demonstrations if they are well disciplined. Those who participate in demonstrations must be disciplined in non-violence. . . . I do think children should be taught how to behave and what they are demonstrating for before they demonstrate."[4] Young people should be willing to be instructed and guided on the seriousness of the demonstrations and the importance of disciplined nonviolent resistance and what that entails. This is an important point, for we will see that while there were many youths along the civil rights trail who willingly abided by King's insistence on the need for disciplined nonviolent resistance, there were also many who rejected his unabashed, absolute commitment to nonviolence. For example, Nashville student activists (e.g., Diane Nash, John Lewis, James Bevel, and Bernard Lafayette) trained by James Lawson in Gandhian ideas and techniques bought into the idea of nonviolence as a way of life and took this attitude into the early phase of the work of SNCC. However, the increasingly strong contingent of Northern student activists who later joined SNCC exhibited less faith in nonviolence as the best means to social change, and had almost no appreciation for the idea of nonviolence as a way of life. In addition, many Deep South local black activists in the Mississippi Delta and Alabama also insisted on the need for self-defense, an ethic of which King himself adhered for a period during the early days of the Montgomery struggle.[5] At any rate, this attitude toward self-defense, particularly among youthful activists reared in the Deep South, contributed to the growing tension and division within SNCC itself, as well as with King, SCLC, and other traditional civil rights organizations. But for King's part, it was clear that nonviolence was not only the best, but the *only* reasonable

---

4. Ibid.
5. See Rufus Burrow Jr., *Extremist for Love: Martin Luther King Jr., Man of Ideas and Nonviolent Social Action* (Minneapolis: Fortress Press, 2014), 201.

way to solve interpersonal and group conflict. This meshed perfectly with his conviction that the universe itself is situated on a moral foundation and is governed by absolute moral laws, the chief of which is love. Love, King believed, is at the heart of nonviolence.

During the early 1960s, there was a tendency of many in the media to credit Martin Luther King with spearheading the student sit-ins, the student Freedom Rides, and the utterly dangerous voter education-registration work in Mississippi and in Selma, Alabama. To King's credit, however, he did all he could to correct this misconception. He never sought to take credit for what he did not do. Indeed, from the time of the Montgomery bus boycott, King often reminded people that *he* did not start the boycott, but just happened to be in Montgomery when a myriad of forces and events conjoined to ignite it. When the sit-ins began spontaneously on February 5, 1960 in Greensboro, North Carolina, King and other acknowledged civil rights leaders knew nothing about it until news of it was reported by both sympathizers and the media. In addition, when the Nashville student activists under the leadership of Diane Nash decided to continue the Freedom Rides in 1961 after CORE called them off because of the savage violence against the riders in Anniston, Alabama, King supported the initiative, but he did not try to take credit for the students' amazing and courageous decision to not allow any facet of the movement to be stopped in its tracks by violence. Much to the chagrin of the students, King did not accept their invitation to join the Freedom Ride. Reasons for this will be examined subsequently. For now, suffice it to say that the decision not to join the students early set the stage for mounting tension and division between the students and King (SNCC and SCLC).

Although Martin Luther King did not pretend to have anything to do with the start-up of the civil rights activity of young people, he was always willing to lend any support he and SCLC could. Indeed, it was under the auspices of SCLC, and then acting executive director Ella Josephine Baker, that black and white student leaders (mostly college students) from across the country were invited to Baker's alma mater, Shaw University, on Easter weekend 1960, to discuss how to coordinate their efforts after they burst onto the scene with sit-in demonstrations. Unlike Baker, who argued for the autonomy of any student organization that might develop out of the meetings, King, (and much more so) Wyatt Walker, and others argued that any such group should be under the authority and supervision of SCLC. Baker pushed very hard against this idea. She had few supporters among the all-male cast of SCLC board members, but there were a few, and she held her ground. Although the students respected King a great deal at this time and invited him to give the opening address, the Student Nonviolent Coordinating Committee was born out of the Shaw meetings as a separate, autonomous entity, with its own leaders. They chose a group or communal leadership style (reflecting Baker's influence), instead of the more traditional charismatic leader model of King and his black Baptist cohorts. Since King was, from the time of the Montgomery bus boycott, receptive to and supportive of the civil rights work of all groups (e.g., the NAACP, CORE, the Urban League, and the Fellowship of Reconciliation) that opted for nonviolent approaches, indicators are that he was less troubled by the idea of an autonomous SNCC than was Wyatt Walker and other SCLC board members who preferred a more controlling, leader-centered approach.

Without question, Martin Luther King loved children and young people. From the beginning of the movement, he displayed a good sense of their importance to the struggle for civil rights, acknowledging that the demonstrations that black adults were waging were also about the day-to-day lives of black youths, as well as their futures. He always told black children and youths that the nonviolent demonstrations that SCLC and other civil rights organizations were engaged in was about the futures of young people. Looking back, Jawana Jackson recalled "Uncle Martin" saying to her: "We're doing this to help you and all of the little children."[6] In addition, King was generally quite comfortable around children and young people, and they seemed often to gravitate toward him, a point that James Bristol made as early as 1959 during King's trip to India. In his tour diary, Bristol wrote that during a visit to one of the Ashrams King's popularity among the children was noticeably evident. Bristol wrote of what he perceived as King's "great love for children," referring to him as a "pied piper" who "moved about the Ashram with several children clutching his arm or holding his hand."[7] There were similar displays of his affection for children and King's popularity among them in various cities throughout the United States.

That King was so popular among many young people and understood that the struggle was also about them and that they had something important to contribute is no small matter. Although black youths respected and admired King for his leadership and contributions, we will see that many, particularly Northerners who joined SNCC and other youth civil rights organizations, disagreed with him at times and rejected his ideology, his integrationist ideas, and his unyielding commitment to nonviolence as more than a strategy or technique. While there was mutual love and respect between King and black youths, there were also generational, cultural, and even geographical differences that led to tension and division between them.

---

6. Ellen Levine, *Freedom's Children: Young Civil Rights Activists Tell Their Own Stories* (New York: G. P. Putnam's Sons, 1993), 131.
7. *The Papers* (2005), 5:210 n. 2.

The six chapters in this book focus on the contributions of primarily black children and youths in Deep South states who stepped up to the plate during a particularly dangerous period in the struggle against racism and racial discrimination in the United States. This was their way of showing that they wanted to do more than just passively exist in their present condition of deprivation and oppression; that they were somehow satisfied with second-class citizenship and race discrimination. They desired, instead, to have a life worth living. Furthermore, they were willing to struggle for such a life; a struggle that would at times include children as young as four years of age. The chapters in this book examine the contributions of black children and youths in Montgomery, the sit-ins and Freedom Rides, the events in Birmingham, and Mississippi, and Selma.

Although the focus is on the contributions of black youths, it would be an unforgivable error to be completely silent regarding the supportive role played by white youths, mostly from the North, but a few southerners as well. As important as the Freedom Summer Project was in 1964 when hundreds of mostly white college volunteers from the North descended on the Mississippi Delta, we will see that white youths were involved in earlier campaigns as well, not least the sit-ins, Freedom Rides, and Birmingham. Like their youthful black counterparts, white youth also suffered the inhumane and violent treatment of white hate groups. And yet we will see that in virtually every case the violence toward blacks was more severe. For example, it was not enough to lynch a black person. Racial hatred seemed to require that they be decapitated, that the body be literally cut in half, or that the face be disfigured beyond recognition. While to a large extent black youths had no choice but to fight for their freedom, white youths chose to put their own freedom on the line in order to fight for the freedom of blacks. Some of the volunteers figured out that because of the relational nature of what it means to be a human being, by fighting for the rights of blacks they were also fighting for their own rights. Like their black counterparts they too had a vision of a United States of America that was not, but could be; a vision of a truly democratic nation that was interested in the well-being, not of a select few, but of all citizens. We will see that to their credit, many understood that, historically, the country valued the lives of whites much more than those of Afrikan Americans, and that there was something fundamentally wrong with such a stance and the practices that ensued.

The witness and sacrifices of these young people—blacks and whites—is a tremendous lesson for youth of today, and is also an excellent reason for them to read, study, and reflect on the contributions of young people during the civil rights movement. Even today, young people in the United States have much to offer toward the achievement of a more just and humane society and world, but many are not aware of this, and one wonders whether they would know what to do about it if they were. What we learn in this book is that young people of the early and later civil rights era did not wait to be given either the permission or support of adults before courageously leaping into the fray. Many acted solely on the basis of their conscience and did not give much thought to whether parents, teachers, or other adults supported them. When they did think about such matters they were still not deterred from making their contributions.

Presently in King studies, I find that there is too little emphasis on discussions of his love and adoration for children and youths; his desire that they each have all of the things necessary for a life that is truly worth living; and his sense of their responsibility to help make this a reality. Although King never wanted to put children in harm's way, he discovered early in his civil rights ministry that it was virtually impossible to avoid this completely if they were to be allowed to make their own contributions toward the achievement of freedom and justice. Civil rights work in the Deep South was dangerous work for participants, regardless of age and race. Indeed, we will see that during the Birmingham campaign in 1963, it early became clear that from the standpoint of strategy there may be times when the children and youths can be more successful in accomplishing the objectives of the movement than the adults; can even *lead* the adults to deeper, more committed involvement in the struggle, or could even be the primary reason that some adults eventually found their way to involvement in the struggle. Sometimes, King learned, it is children and young people who lead the way for the involvement of otherwise passive, sometimes fearful, apathetic parents, teachers, and other adults.

During the Birmingham campaign of 1963, the Southern Christian Leadership Conference's progress stalled early when the jails quickly filled with the available committed adult demonstrators and there were too few remaining who could continue the nonviolent demonstrations on a mass scale in order to produce the impact that was needed to ensure media attention and that of the federal government. They did not have the numbers to accomplish what was desired. Although reluctant at first, King, at the urging of one of his close advisors, finally decided to allow massive numbers of black children and youths to participate in the demonstrations. It is important to remember that the decision to permit the involvement of children and young people was not simply a point of strategy for Martin Luther King. Rather, he respected the dignity and worth and the agency of the children as human beings,[8] and wanted them to contribute toward their own liberation as well as help to shape their own future. But not only this, King simply adored the children

---

8. Ibid. (2007), 6:212.

and felt a real sense of commitment to their present and future well-being.

There were times when Martin Luther King even appeared to be eager to be around children. And why would this not be the case for one who was a loving father and by this time had three young children and an infant of his own with whom he was not able to spend much time because (rightly or wrongly) he had given his life to his ministerial calling and the movement? King missed his own children in the worst way, and thus it should come as no surprise that he was so open, gentle, and patient with children in Birmingham, Selma, Atlanta, Chicago, and other cities. In a sense, many of these were King's surrogate children—his children away from home. There were times when, in a parental sort of way, he could be very protective of the children he encountered along the way.

Martin Luther King believed that everybody had something of value to contribute to the struggle for civil and human rights. He preferred that would-be demonstrators be willing to commit totally to the philosophy by which he lived, that is, that they be staunchly committed to nonviolence as a way of life. But he was a realist, and like Gandhi, he knew that most people would not be able to measure up, but that the "creative minority"—those committed to nonviolence in a thoroughgoing way and who viewed it as the only way of living in the world—would be able to encourage the less committed to at least use the methods of nonviolence pragmatically, or as a strategy. In any event, King made it clear that all volunteers could participate in some way in the direct-action campaigns of the nonviolent army under the leadership of SCLC, if not in the demonstrations themselves. Virtually anybody who wished to make a positive contribution was encouraged to join the nonviolent army. It was particularly important to encourage the involvement of the children and young people. Who would have thought that these, ranging from young children to young adults, would play such a vital role throughout the movement, especially in the Mississippi Delta, Birmingham, and later, in Selma?

To be sure, young people such as those affiliated with SNCC and others who were not under the watchful eye and supervision of SCLC also made significant contributions to the further advancement of the movement. Not only did they, more than any other civil rights activists, break ground in some of the most feared and dangerous areas in the Deep South such as the Mississippi Delta region and Alabama's Loundes County, but their refusal to give in to political expediency served to challenge King and other civil rights leaders to press for and hold out for more than they might otherwise have done in their negotiations with local white leaders, as well as federal authorities. Even the young people had a sense that it was naïve to think that they would get everything they demanded. But by demanding more, they also believed that they would get more. This brings to mind an idea expressed by social gospel proponent Walter Rauschenbusch in 1912: "We shall demand perfection and never expect to get it. But by demanding it we shall get more than we now have."[9] The young people seem to have understood this much better than their more conservative, cautious adult leaders. By demanding more, they put moral and political pressure on SCLC and other more traditional civil rights organizations to not settle for minor concessions. It was a reminder that the ideal of love demanded more than oppressors were generally willing to concede.

In the chapters that follow I focus on the contributions, creativity, energy, spirit, fearlessness, and the power of young people—from grade school through college—to the struggle for civil rights and

---

9. Walter Rauschenbusch, *Christianizing the Social Order* (New York: Macmillan, 1912 [1926]), 126.

freedom. In virtually every civil rights campaign, beginning in Montgomery, young people were involved and made their presence known and felt in positive—and at times negative—ways. In the earlier stages of the movement, essentially led by King, they were not formally included in the strategies for the civil disobedience campaigns, for example, in Montgomery. Youth activists led the way in the Albany, Georgia campaign of 1961 as a result of the leadership and work of SNCC, which sought to organize local blacks for what they knew would be a long protracted struggle for voter registration. SNCC activists essentially broke ground for the campaign that was later initiated by SCLC in Albany. SCLC failed to achieve its goals there, but King and his staff learned valuable lessons about how to carry out nonviolent direct-action projects in more efficient ways. After the Albany debacle, King was convinced that nonviolence was on trial and that they needed a test case, which, unknown to him at the time, would be Birmingham, Alabama.

To be sure, Afrikan American youths in Montgomery did not ride the buses to school and other places during the boycott. In this regard, they were significant participants in the boycott, although not much scholarly attention has been given at this point to uncovering any formal plans that might have existed as to how they were to be utilized in a strategic way. We know, however, that such a plan was in fact developed by SCLC leadership during the Birmingham campaign eight years later. But it is important to understand that young people made important contributions to the movement from Montgomery onward. Few understood better than King that young people were, like their parents and other adults, moral agents, self-determining beings who could decide for themselves how to respond to the racism, discrimination, and segregation that they too experienced each day of their young lives. Although not much has been written about it to date, we will see that King was not blind to the effect of the bus boycott on black youths in Montgomery. Moreover, black youths were not passive bystanders in Montgomery or any of the Deep South campaigns.

James Bevel, a younger protégé of King in SCLC, would argue in the early, but failing stage of the Birmingham campaign, that if it was reasonable to allow young children to make the decision to accept the Christian faith and to join the church (which was a common practice in black Baptist churches), it was reasonable to allow them to make their own decision as to whether to participate in the nonviolent demonstrations. What was happening to adults in southern black communities, Bevel convincingly argued, was also happening to the children. They were suffering right along with their parents, teachers, and other adults. They too experienced blatant and subtle forms of racism. They therefore *wanted* to participate in the struggle to eradicate racial discrimination and related forms of injustice. Indeed, Gwendolyn Patton told Charles Cobb Jr. that in 1952, when she was nine years old in Montgomery she made her first intentional protest against racism when a white counter boy called her a "pickaninny" at a drugstore. Her reaction was to deliberately spill water onto the counter.[10] A consideration of the recollections of some adults regarding the role they played when they were children and young people during the early movement years will confirm black youths' desire to protest the injustices done to them. For our purpose, the focus, in part, will be on reflections and contributions of a few black adults who grew up in Montgomery, Birmingham, the Mississippi Delta, and Selma, who share memories of the way it was. Attention will also be given to the contributions of youths who did not operate under the auspices of SCLC and other traditional civil rights organizations.

---

10. See Charles Cobb Jr., *On the Road to Freedom: A Guided Tour of the Civil Rights Trail* (Chapel Hill, NC: Algonquin Books of Chapel Hill, 2008), 208.

How did Martin Luther King and other local and national leaders react to and encourage young people? How did young people's fearlessness, sense of commitment, energy, enthusiasm, involvement in the demonstrations, sit-ins, kneel-ins, stand-ins, Freedom Rides, and distrust of the political process and the federal government influence King's thinking and action? These are some of the questions to be examined in this book. Since many of these young people, especially Deep South ones, had been reared in the church and were taught the same faith and religious values as adults, we will also look more intentionally at King's understanding of the role of the church in the face of injustice, as well as the positive contributions of local churches, prayer meetings, singing, and praying in preparation for and during the demonstrations. We will find that singing was particularly important for black youths, as well as many white youths involved in the Freedom Summer Project in 1964. We begin with a consideration of the struggles and contributions of black youths in the Montgomery, Alabama campaign to desegregate the city buses.

1

Montgomery

"Just to See Empty Bus, after Empty Bus Go By . . ."

The bus boycott (1955–1956) was not the first time that black residents boycotted public transportation in Montgomery, Alabama. Longtime black residents remembered that in August of 1900 (four years after the landmark ruling in *Plessy v. Ferguson* made "separate but equal" the law of the land) blacks organized a two-year boycott of segregated seating on city streetcars. "In response many of the city's African-American ministers urged their congregations to walk instead of ride. The protest forced the streetcar firm to suspend segregation, though Jim Crow seating resumed after the boycott died down."[1] Not only is this evidence that blacks in Montgomery, under the encouragement of their ministers, had boycott experience, it is also evidence that even before the bus boycott fifty-five years later,

---

1. Stewart Burns, *To the Mountaintop: Martin Luther King, Jr.'s Sacred Mission to Save America 1955-1968* (New York: HarperSanFrancisco, 2004), 460 n. 37.

they proved that they could in fact pull together in common cause. Black Montgomery residents were not simply a passive community that did not, at times, resist manifestations of racial segregation. When the bus boycott got under way, there were older black residents who knew something about the importance of sticking together in a common cause, and these very likely made important contributions in this regard during the more than yearlong protest.

Beginning with the bus boycott in Montgomery, and throughout his civil rights ministry, Martin Luther King Jr. was always quick to say that long before he arrived on the scene, human, divine, and cosmic forces had been at work preparing the stage for the protest movement he was chosen to lead. In this regard, King made it clear that even had he not come to Montgomery, the movement that was born there would have occurred anyway. He was under no illusion about being the cause of that movement, or even its most important leader. He did not, in this regard, have what he referred to as a "Messiah complex." Rather, he always knew that there was a need for many leaders to do the work of the movement.[2] In any event, the forces of history and the growing restlessness of blacks toward racial segregation and racism were such that the Montgomery struggle was nothing less than an idea whose time had come. None understood this better than Martin Luther King.

And yet, there is at least a grain of truth in James Farmer's observation that while it is true that many people and events were evolving and seeming to come together prior to the bus boycott, they congealed around none other than Martin Luther King. However, it seems to me that Farmer goes too far when he suggests that the emerging movement could *only* have formed itself around King. "It had to be the Montgomery bus boycott which had the charisma

---

2. Clayborne Carson et al., eds., *The Papers of Martin Luther King, Jr.* (Berkeley: University of California Press, 2005), 5:477.

to capture the imagination of people," said Farmer. "Other things happened that didn't capture the imagination of the nation. But King did."[3] True. But we humans can never know with certainty what God's plans are, and whether there is only one person who can carry them out. Farmer was right about much of what he said, but only in hindsight. No one could have known ahead of time of King's impact upon the stage of history. The signs were many that things were coming to a head in race relations in the South generally, and Montgomery, Alabama, in particular. In this sense, it is reasonable to say that a movement would have happened even if King had not been born, or arrived on the scene. I am always hesitant to say that if this or that person is not on the scene, God's will that justice be done will somehow be thwarted. The combination of outstanding qualities that were Martin Luther King's, were his alone, but this does not mean that God's will for Montgomery would not have been achieved had he not been present, or answered the call. King knew this better than most. And yet, the fact of the matter is that he was indeed present at that particular moment in the history of the United States of America, and he did not hesitate to answer the call.

Disregard for Black Personhood

Martin Luther King knew from personal experience and the experiences of numerous blacks, how demeaning segregation was to his people. He was surely aware of brutal acts of violence to which blacks had been subjected both before and after he arrived in Montgomery. Although the horrific lynching of Claude Neal occurred in 1934 when King was a five-year-old, it was the first of two such incidents that left an indelible mark on the minds and

---

3. Fred Powledge, *Free at Last?: The Civil Rights Movement and the People Who Made It* (New York: HarperPerennial, 1991), 82.

memories of blacks all over the country, but particularly in the South. Neal was brutally tortured and lynched in the north Florida town of Marianna, not far from the Alabama and Georgia state lines. Gene Roberts and Hank Klibanoff describe in gory detail the gruesome, torturous violation of black humanity.

> Neal, who was accused of having killed a white woman, was scalded repeatedly with a hot iron, castrated, and dragged through the streets before being stretched and displayed in a tree. This had not been an impulse lynching; newspaper and radio stories had given advance notice of it. As Neal was being hauled by a mob from an Alabama jail to Marianna, a crowd estimated at about four thousand had time to get to the scene. By some accounts, he was forced to eat his own genitals, and his finger [sic] and toes were put on display in the town. It was a story that haunted the Negroes of north and central Florida for decades.[4]

It is difficult to imagine that Martin Luther King and most black southerners of his generation were not made aware of this horrific crime against black humanity in particular, humanity in general, and the God of the Hebrew prophets and Jesus Christ.

Even if King was not aware of this particular heinous crime from childhood until young adulthood when he assumed pastoral responsibilities at the Dexter Avenue Baptist Church in Montgomery on September 1, 1954, an incident that was in some ways just as horrific occurred one year later in the Mississippi Delta on August 28, 1955 (eight years to the day before the March on Washington for Jobs and Employment). Fourteen-year-old Emmett Louis Till, a native of Chicago, was visiting a great uncle in Money, Mississippi when he allegedly made sexually implicit comments to a white woman named Carolyn Bryant. When Bryant's husband Roy, and his half-brother J. W. Milam, heard about the accusation they went

---

4. Gene Roberts and Hank Klibanoff, *The Race Beat: The Press, the Civil Rights Struggle, and the Awakening of a Nation* (New York: Alfred A. Knopf, 2007), 95.

under the cover of darkness to the home of Till's great uncle Mose Wright, forcibly removed the young boy, drove him some distance away, tortured him to the point that his face was not recognizable, shot him behind the right ear, barbed-wired a seventy-five pound cotton gin fan to his neck, and rolled his body into the Tallahatchie River where, three days later, his body was seen several miles downriver by some boys fishing. Although an indictment of Roy Bryant and J. W. Milam was issued quickly, and Mose Wright heroically and bravely testified that they were the ones who removed his nephew from his home at gunpoint, the two men were found not guilty by a jury of twelve white men after "deliberating" and drinking soda for sixty-seven minutes.[5]

We can be certain that Martin Luther King was devastated by the brutal murder of young Emmett Till by men who claimed to be Christians. He frequently referred to that tragedy and the culprits. In September 1955, not long after the jury issued the not guilty verdict, King said: "The white men who lynch Negroes worship Christ. That jury in Mississippi, which a few days ago in the Emmett Till case, freed two white men from what might be considered one of the most brutal and inhuman crimes of the twentieth century, worships Christ."[6] In February 1956 he said: "We have looked to Missippii [*sic*] and seen supposedly Christian and civilized men brutally murdering the precious life of a little child."[7] In April 1957, King queried God: "*Why* is it simply because some of your children ask to be treated as first-class human beings they are *trampled* over, their homes are bombed, their *children* are pushed from their classrooms, and sometimes little children are thrown in the deep waters of Mississippi?

---

5. See Dan Wakefield, "An Hour and Seven Minutes: Justice, in Sumner," in *Reporting Civil Rights: Part One, American Journalism 1941-1963* (New York: Library of America, 2003), 217–21.
6. *The Papers* (2007), 6:232.
7. Ibid., 6:253.

Why is it, oh God, that that has to happen?"[8] King believed that although young Till was not of voting age, his brutal murder was meant to terrorize local blacks in the Mississippi Delta and throughout the South as a means to keeping them from the polls.[9] In *Stride Toward Freedom*, King wrote of being skeptical that the white men accused of bombing his house would be prosecuted and found guilty. He wrote of the freshness of the Emmett Till case in their memories and concluded that, consequently, they had little reason to hope for a conviction.[10] All of this shows that King was deeply affected by the brutal racial murder of the child, Emmett Till.

Such blatant violence and total disregard for black personhood and dignity was most assuredly one of the key factors pushing blacks in Montgomery, and other places in the Deep South, to mount forces of resistance. Segregation ordinances and the day in and day out disrespect to which they were subjected by white bus drivers and police officers served only to fuel the fires of discontent growing within blacks. They had been pushed to the brink of no return. L. D. Reddick put it all in perspective in 1956.

> There had been a long history of abuse by the bus operators. Almost everybody could tell of some unfortunate personal experience that he himself had had or seen. Montgomery Negroes were fed up with the bus service in particular and, like Negroes throughout the South, with race relations in general. The outrage over the Emmett Till murder was alive in everybody's mind. The silence and inaction of the Federal Government, in the face of the daily abuse, beatings and killings of Negro citizens, was maddening. Negroes have no faith at all in Southern law-making and law-enforcing agencies, for these instruments of "justice" are in the hands of "the brothers of the hoodlums who attack us."

---

8. Ibid., 6:289.
9. Ibid. (2000), 4:369.
10. Martin Luther King Jr., *Stride Toward Freedom* (New York: Harper & Row, 1958), 179–80.

Negroes themselves wanted to get into action. Here and elsewhere they were willing to fight it out—if the fighting was "fair." . . . To remain human, the Negroes simply could not stand by and do nothing.[11]

Although King might not have known it, by the time he arrived in Montgomery, black residents were already poised to protest the injustices that many had borne passively for so long.

King's Ministerial Plan

When Martin Luther King was appointed senior minister of the Dexter Avenue Baptist Church in Montgomery, he was in the process of writing his doctoral dissertation, and was able to negotiate for reduced responsibilities that would allow him to complete that final requirement for the Ph.D. His plan for the first couple of years of his ministry included the completion and defense of the dissertation and receipt of his degree from Boston University the following year. While writing the dissertation, his intention was to effectively manage his pastoral duties as best he could, while also getting to know the members of the Dexter congregation. After receiving his degree he turned to those duties with an abandon, for he thought of himself first and foremost as a pastor, even though he also had aspirations to teach in a university or seminary setting someday. But this was a long-term objective, and he had no idea at the time as to what ministerial practice would bring.

King's aim was to get the ministry at Dexter on a solid footing, while also familiarizing himself with the city and its leaders in all areas. He told a ministerial colleague, Ralph Abernathy, pastor of First Baptist Church in Montgomery, that this would likely take

---

11. L. D. Reddick, "The Bus Boycott in Montgomery," in *The Walking City: The Montgomery Bus Boycott, 1955-1956* (Brooklyn, NY: Carlson, 1989), 72. Originally published in *Dissent* 3 (Spring 1956, ed. David J. Garrow): 107–17.

a few years. Consequently, he had no thoughts of leading a mass movement of any kind, and did not move too quickly to involve himself in too many nonchurch and community activities that might overcommit him to the point of detracting attention and energy from ministerial responsibilities at Dexter. He really wanted to focus his energy, attention, and talents on the church and its internal and outreach ministries. Toward this end he worked closely with the organizations and committees at Dexter, no doubt remembering the example of his father at Ebenezer Baptist Church in Atlanta. In addition, he was mindful of Abernathy's advice that he should make work with the church's committees a priority. Moreover, because of King's own interest in religion, its relevance and its application to social problems, he made a couple of moves toward creating and reviving internal ministries that clearly indicated his desire for the church to be involved in social and political activity. He established the Social and Political Action Committee (SPAC) that had the twofold responsibility of keeping before the congregation the importance of the National Association of the Advancement of Colored People (NAACP) and maintaining membership in it, as well as holding forums to discuss and address social problems that were adversely affecting blacks in Montgomery. This was also a good way of keeping the new pastor informed about major social issues affecting blacks in the city. The members of the SPAC already had a longstanding interest in and commitment to addressing and solving social problems. Some of the members, including Alabama State College English professors Mary Fair Burks and JoAnn Robinson, chair and co-chair, respectively, were also members of the well-organized Women's Political Council (WPC). Burks organized the WPC in 1946 and served as its founding president.[12] JoAnn Robinson joined in 1950. Houston Roberson contends that Robinson succeeded Jewel Lewis as president in 1952, making her the organization's third president.¹³ Having been disrespected and threatened by a Montgomery city bus driver when she was planning to visit relatives in Cleveland, Ohio during the Christmas holiday (not long after her arrival in Montgomery), Robinson remembered how utterly embarrassed she was over how she was treated, and vowed to not forget the incident. Moreover, she promised to make the city bus situation relative to her people a priority of the WPC.¹⁴

Burks and Robinson were not only leaders in the WPC, but as members of Dexter Avenue Baptist Church and also co-chairs of the SPAC, they kept their new pastor informed about bus and related incidents of segregation and racism throughout the city. In addition, King himself was a member of the local chapter of the NAACP, yet another way that he was kept apprised of problems faced by blacks in the city.

King unwittingly prepared the Dexter congregation for social and political activism in yet another way. In this instance, he revived and revitalized the church's youth ministry. This was one of three or four ministries to which the young pastor gave early attention and energy. He and the church organized the Baptist Youth Fellowship (BYF) to meet the spiritual needs of members from six to thirty-five years of age. In one of its early symposia the BYF presented a program on "The Meaning of Integration for American Society." This symposium mirrored and supported the work of the Social and Political Action Committee. Roberson helpfully observes that the significance of this is that we see early an effort on King's part toward

---

12. Mary Fair Burks, "Trailblazers: Women in the Montgomery Bus Boycott," in *Women in the Civil Rights Movement: Trailblazers & Torchbearers 1941-1965*, ed. Vicki L. Crawford, Jacqueline Anne Rouse, and Barbara Woods (Bloomington: Indiana University Press, 1993), 75.
13. Houston Bryan Roberson, *Fighting the Good Fight: The Story of the Dexter Avenue King Memorial Baptist Church, 1865-1977* (New York/London: Routledge, 2005), 140.
14. JoAnn Gibson Robinson, *The Montgomery Bus Boycott and the Women Who Started It*, ed. David J. Garrow. Sixth Printing (Knoxville: University of Tennessee Press, 1996), 16–17. See also xiii–xiv.

"the preparation for the church's active participation in the civil rights movement."[15] Another ministry that contributed significantly to this end was the revival of the spring lecture series. King believed this to be an excellent way to keep the members informed about major teachings and issues of the Christian faith, as well as the church's responsibility toward social issues. King invited Samuel DeWitt Proctor, an experienced pastor, as well as college professor, to inaugurate the newly revived lecture series. King's proposed topic for Proctor, "The Relevance of the New Testament to the Contemporary Situation," was consistent with his social gospel preaching at Dexter. King's hope was that the lecture series would encourage and energize the members "to become more aware and involved in the politics of their community, and to see a nexus between religion and civil life."[16]

We can see, then, that it was never the case that Martin Luther King did not want to be involved in directly addressing matters of race and other problems adversely affecting his people. As a young boy, in fact, he vowed to help his father to fight and eradicate such problems; to help him to fight racism.[17] In addition, influenced by his father's social gospel ministry and preaching, as well as the stories he heard about his maternal grandfather's social gospel ministry, as a first-term seminary student at Crozer Theological Seminary in Chester, Pennsylvania, King unequivocally and proudly announced in one of his first formal academic papers that he was a staunch advocate of the social gospel.[18] This was a significant claim, because an earlier generation of King scholars linked his social gospel leanings too closely to his studies at the predominantly white Crozer,

---

15. Roberson, *Fighting the Good Fight*, 136.
16. Ibid., 137.
17. Martin Luther King Sr., *Daddy King: An Autobiography* with Clayton Riley (New York: William Morrow, 1980), 109.
18. *The Papers*, 6:72.

implying that it was there that King developed an affinity for social gospel ministry through his study of Walter Rauschenbusch's classic work, *Christianity and the Social Crisis* (1907), and the encouragement of his white seminary professors. As scholars on King began gaining access to his unpublished papers, and as Professor Clayborne Carson, Director of the King Papers Project and his staff at Stanford University, began editing and publishing King's papers in what is hoped will be a minimum of fourteen large volumes, we now know with certainty that King was already a strong advocate of social gospel ministry when he arrived on the Crozer campus. This corrected the earlier view that while he had a strong social conscience when he arrived at Crozer, he only became formally committed to the social gospel once his white seminary professors introduced him to the work of Rauschenbusch. By King's own admission, his study of Rauschenbusch did indeed provide for him a formal theological foundation for his commitment to the social gospel and his early decision in seminary to devote his ministry to focusing on a trilogy of social problems: racism, economic injustice, and militarism.[19] Each of these issues was always on King's mind, even when his immediate focus was on one or the other of those issues. Increasingly, King had a strong sense that these three social problems were inextricably connected. Not only was King inspired and influenced by the social gospel ministries of his father and grandfather, but that of other southern black pastors, as well as the commitment to the social gospel that he saw in some of his professors and mentors at Morehouse College, including President Benjamin E. Mays and professors George Kelsey and Samuel Williams who taught him Bible and philosophy, respectively.

---

19. See ibid., 6:88, 126, 327.

Notwithstanding his commitment to social gospel ministry and activism, young King's decision as a new senior pastor to devote most of his time to focusing on internal ministerial responsibilities at Dexter for the first few years was quite reasonable. And yet, he seemed to be aware that other (unseen) forces—cosmic and divine—were at work in history and Montgomery that could trump his timetable and his best-laid plans. King could see God's Spirit working in pre–bus boycott Montgomery, and there is no indication that he desired to interfere with this in any way. He had no sense of what his responsibility or role would be in this, but he was vigilant in performing his ministerial duties and slowly familiarizing himself with the problems making the lives of black residents of Montgomery miserable.

Bus Incidents before the Boycott

Without question, Martin Luther King knew that Rosa Parks was not the first black woman to be arrested for not giving her bus seat to a white person. Historian Stephen B. Oates erred, therefore, when he wrote in his otherwise excellent and widely acclaimed biography of King (*Let the Trumpet Sound*, 1982) that Rosa Parks was in fact the first to be arrested.[20] It is known that even before the Parks bus incident King was very much aware of similar cases involving two young people, fifteen-year-old Claudette Colvin and seventeen-year-old Mary Louise Smith. Ironically, these two bus episodes occurred in March and October of the same year of the

---

20. See Stephen B. Oates, *Let the Trumpet Sound: The Life of Martin Luther King, Jr.* (New York: Harper & Row, 1982), 65. This was the most definitive biography of King to this point. To a large extent this was because it was the first biography that depended more extensively on unpublished papers by King as well as FBI and State Department files that had previously been unavailable to researchers and scholars. And of course, it didn't hurt that Oates was a talented and skillful writer-historian.

Rosa Parks arrest for a similar violation. Moreover, this is not to say that similar incidents had not occurred even before those of Colvin, Smith, and Parks. For example, in 1949 a number of other black women, including but not limited to Geneva Johnson, Viola White, and Katie Wingfield, were also arrested for refusing to give their seat to a white patron. In addition, David J. Garrow has written: "Earlier in 1949, two young children, visiting from the north and unfamiliar with Montgomery's practice of reserving the first ten seats on each bus for white riders only, even if black passengers were forced to stand over vacant seats, also were hauled in for refusing a driver's command to surrender their seats."[21]

Martin Luther King was, in fact, a member of the ad hoc committee that met with the police commissioner and bus officials regarding the Colvin incident. In his first book, *Stride Toward Freedom: The Montgomery Story* (1958), he recalled that the black community was in such an uproar about the violent treatment of Colvin by the arresting officers that there was talk even then of a boycott.[22] A tentative agreement was reached in that meeting that required bus drivers to be courteous to black patrons and to obey the segregation ordinance of the state of Alabama and the city of Montgomery that required that seats be filled by blacks from the rear of the bus and by whites from the front. Not entirely unexpected, the bus company attorney rejected the proposed agreement, which most likely would have been violated by bus drivers anyway. However, King observed that although the bus company and city officials once again failed the black community, something of momentous proportion had begun happening among blacks in Montgomery. He reflected on this, saying: "The long repressed feelings of resentment

---

21. David J. Garrow, "The Origins of the Montgomery Bus Boycott," in *The Walking City: The Montgomery Bus Boycott, 1955-1956*, ed. David J. Garrow (Brooklyn, NY: Carlson, 1989), 608.
22. King, *Stride*, 41.

on the part of the Negroes had begun to stir. The fear and apathy which had for so long cast a shadow on the life of the Negro community were gradually fading before a new spirit of courage and self-respect."[23] On the horizon for blacks in Montgomery was the emergence of a new sense of dignity; a new sense of somebodyness, as King called it. This not only affected black adults, but black students of all ages as well. In his memoir, James Forman acknowledged the effect that the Montgomery struggle had on blacks of all ages, but especially young blacks.

> The Montgomery bus boycott had a very significant effect on the consciousness of black people throughout the United States. In 1956 our people constantly said, "Well, black folks just can't stick together. We can never act as a unit, we can't unify to protest against this man. We're like a bunch of crabs—the minute one of us crawls through the top, the rest of us drag him back down." This idea had been instilled by the colonizing force of white society, which always played down the importance of the black man. . . .
>
> . . . The boycott had a particularly important effect on young blacks and helped to generate the student movement of 1960. I remember Ruby Doris Robinson, who became executive secretary of SNCC, saying that when she was about thirteen or fourteen and saw those old people walking down there in Montgomery, just walking, walking, walking, it had a tremendous impact. The boycott woke me to the real—not merely theoretical—possibility of building a nonviolent mass movement of Southern black people to fight segregation. . . . In Montgomery, you could see the real thing.[24]

Martin Luther King could see glimmers of black self-determination and a growing sense of pride and dignity even before December 1, 1955. Without question, then, King was aware of what was happening in Montgomery relative to racial incidents on city buses

---

23. Ibid., 42.
24. James Forman, *The Making of Black Revolutionaries: A Personal Account* (New York: Macmillan, 1972), 84–85.

and in other areas that directly affected the lives of blacks. He was also aware of what he described as a new sense of humanity and dignity emerging among black residents of Montgomery. Rev. Robert S. Graetz, a white pastor who was senior minister of the all-black Trinity Lutheran Church in Montgomery, also saw such a change take place not only in his parishioners, but in blacks across the city. For Graetz, this emergence of a new sense of dignity and worth was "the real victory" that blacks achieved during the bus boycott. "No court decision, no change in practices or regulations would have made any real difference in Montgomery, Alabama," he wrote, "if the Negro people themselves had not changed. They needed to recognize their own value as human beings. Only then could they step forward and appropriate their own value as human beings. Only then could they step forward and appropriate the legal victory they had won."[25] This change of attitude about themselves and their recognition and acknowledgment of their humanity and dignity was the real victory, according to Graetz.

Contributions of Black Youths to the Bus Boycott

What is interesting about the Claudette Colvin episode, but was not at all unique to her, is that she both refused to give up her seat, and physically resisted the police officers who sought to forcibly remove her from the bus. Her resistance went beyond mere words, although merely talking back to whites—regardless of age—in those days, or even refusing to do what they commanded, could have had severe consequences. Colvin went further, in that she did everything in her power, short of outright attacking the police officers, to keep from being removed from the bus. The police officers reportedly called

---

25. Robert S. Graetz, *Montgomery: A White Preacher's Memoir* (Minneapolis: Fortress Press, 1991), 107.

her a "black bitch" and a "black whore" as they literally dragged her from the bus. Colvin recalled that one of the police officers kicked her multiple times with his heavy boots.[26] It is also significant that, unlike others who were previously arrested for violating Montgomery's segregation ordinance, Claudette Colvin actually "pled not guilty and through her attorney, Fred D. Gray," she "challenged the segregation ordinances."[27] Another very important, though frequently overlooked, point regarding Colvin's resistance is that she was a black youth of Montgomery, which gave lie to any claim that what was happening in Montgomery and other places in the Deep South affected primarily or only black adults; or that it was only black adults who resisted and fought against racism and segregation. We will see momentarily that young Claudette Colvin's resistance was not at all unlike the earlier intentional spilling of water on a restaurant counter by nine-year-old Gwendolyn Patton in 1952, which was also evidence that the same injustices and inhumane treatment experienced by black adults were experienced by black children and youths, and that they were just as aware and resentful of it as were adults. Moreover, it was evidence that black youths, without waiting for guidance, counsel, and approval from adults, also found ways to resist the injustices done to them. This was also evidence of a growing, deepening sense of their humanity and dignity.

Claudette Colvin was taught about the Constitution of the United States and the Bill of Rights by her history teacher, Mrs. Geraldine Nesbitt, a black woman, who taught at the all-black Booker T. Washington High School.[28] Many of Washington High's teachers were members of Dexter Avenue Baptist Church where King was

---

26. Ellen Levine, *Freedom's Children: Young Civil Rights Activists Tell Their Own Stories* (New York: G. P. Putnam's Sons, 1993), 24–25.
27. Horace Randall Williams and Ben Beard, *This Day in Civil Rights History* (Cincinnati: Emmis Books, 2005), 76.
28. Burns, *To the Mountaintop*, 4.

pastor. The lesson on the Constitution was quite likely still fresh in young Colvin's mind when she boarded a city bus—ironically in front of the Dexter Avenue Baptist Church—for the return trip home after school on the day in question. Ordered by the bus driver to give her seat to a white patron, Colvin insisted throughout the ordeal that she had a constitutional right to her seat, "just as much as that [white] lady, she said."[29]

Colvin's resistance on the bus was also illustrative of the growing sense among black youths that they had a real stake in what was happening in their city, especially when they were being hurt and otherwise demeaned by the racist practices of whites. Therefore, even in Montgomery, many black youths figured out early that if they were old enough to recognize that they were being treated inhumanely and unjustly, they were old enough to resist such treatment and to take steps to overcome it. This was a lesson that Southern Christian Leadership Conference staff member James Bevel would later help Martin Luther King to appreciate (during the Birmingham campaign in 1963) much more than he had previously. Black children had a real stake in any organized efforts to resist racial discrimination. It is not that King did not understand this, and even acknowledge it. He did. Initially, however, he was hesitant to include massive numbers of black children and youths on the frontline of mass nonviolent demonstrations for fear that they would be harmed. However, we will see later (in chapter 3) that King came to see that violence was being done to black children and youths whether they were directly involved in the nonviolent demonstrations or not, and consequently, it made sense to allow them to march for their freedom and dignity. In addition, there is no doubt that in later

---

29. Levine, *Freedom's Children*, 24.

civil rights campaigns King remembered the contributions made by Montgomery youths such as Claudette Colvin.

The history teacher who taught Claudette Colvin and her classmates about the Constitution and about their Afrikan heritage made such a lasting impression on Colvin that she developed almost overnight a new sense of pride and dignity. She changed her entire outlook, including her appearance. At a time when blacks used hot combs and curlers and spent huge amounts of money on chemicals to straighten their hair, Colvin decided that she would no longer resort to this, but would wear her hair in its natural form. She would no longer be ashamed of her kinky hair, wide nose, thick lips, and other Afrikan features. Unknown to the young teen at the time, her ideas and actions actually anticipated the Black Consciousness Movement of the late 1960s and the declaration of many blacks that "black is beautiful." Colvin said that her teacher "really had pricked my mind, so I went home and I washed my hair and I didn't straighten it."[30] Some of her peers thought their classmate's new look to be a bit comical, but Colvin paid them no mind, preferring to listen to and react to the rhythm of her own conscience.

Looking back on the Montgomery experience after forty years, Colvin told Ellen Levine that she had grown up in that city and that her parents taught her about racial ethics and the racial divide that existed between whites and blacks. Essentially she was told by her parents and other adult blacks, that black people had their place and whites had theirs. Blacks were in every sense considered the subordinates of whites. Even as a child, however, Colvin knew that whites were the inventors of this line of reasoning. Her first memory of being angry about racism and segregation was when she was about nine years old and wanted to go to the rodeo with her sister. Like so many Deep South black parents, her father had the difficult

---

30. Ibid., 21.

task of telling his child that only white kids could attend the rodeo. Not unlike the boy King when his parents tried—unsuccessfully—to explain to him why the white parents of his boyhood friend refused to allow the two to play together, it is hard to imagine that Colvin's father had better luck. The closest that Colvin and her sister got to the rodeo, she reflected, was the cowboy hats that their father bought for them.

Claudette Colvin recalled being permitted to buy things at the downtown department stores, but not being allowed to buy and eat food at the lunch counter. Blacks could purchase items, but were not allowed to sit down to eat at the store lunch counter. They could spend their money anywhere in the store, including at the lunch counter, but they were not permitted the decency to sit down comfortably at the lunch counter and eat the food their money purchased. This realization angered and unsettled Colvin and other black youths in Montgomery. As if this was not enough, another dehumanizing practice was that some stores would not allow blacks to try on clothing before they purchased them. Essentially they had to already know their size, or had to guess at it. It is not hard to imagine that blacks frequently had to make multiple trips to a store just to purchase a single item of clothing. Since they were not allowed to try on clothing in the store, they would have to return the item once they got home and discovered that it was too large or too small. Or perhaps they simply did not like the way the item looked on their body. Although Colvin and other black youths rebelled against such practices, adult blacks told them that this was just the way it was, and nothing could be done about it, a response that many black youths found to be entirely unacceptable.

As a young high school student during the Montgomery bus boycott, Claudette Colvin was angry about what she saw and experienced every day of her young life. Other black youths across the city were just as aware and outraged. Not surprisingly, Colvin and her friends talked with each other about their experiences, essentially sharing notes and commiserating with each other. The sharing was also cathartic and provided support for their increasing sense of discontentment. It was also a way of reminding them that they were not alone; that other black youths were also increasingly disenchanted about such discriminatory practices. In addition, mutually sharing their experiences of racial discrimination served to enhance their sense of camaraderie, as well as their sense that they did not have to continue to passively accept such treatment. Moreover, younger Montgomery blacks concluded that "the older [black] people let white people get away with it. They never said they didn't like it," Colvin lamented. "Older black people were always respectful to white people. But the younger blacks began to rebel."[31]

Older blacks' failure to protest discriminatory treatment by racist whites was a major disappointment to younger blacks. Moreover, Colvin recalled that black youths at Washington High School were angered the most when a classmate, Jeremiah Reeves, was accused of assaulting and raping a white woman. Reeves emphatically and persistently denied even having consensual sex with the woman. White authorities kept Reeves in jail until he came of legal age, and then executed him on March 28, 1958. About one week later, after worship service on Easter Sunday, April 6, 1958, Martin Luther King led fifteen black ministers on a protest march to the state capitol, where he addressed approximately two thousand people in protest of the electrocution of Reeves, and "the severity and inequality of the penalty that constitutes the injustice. Full grown white men committing comparable crimes against Negro girls are rare [sic] ever punished, and are never given the death penalty or even a life

---

31. Ibid., 20.

sentence," King told the crowd.³² Shamefully, yet consistent with white church reactions to the boycott and virtually any organized efforts on the part of blacks to resist racial discrimination, about three hundred white ministers and church leaders in Montgomery published a statement of condemnation of the Easter Sunday protest "and recommending that such mass meetings, 'with exaggerated emphasis on wrongs and grievances' be replaced 'by conversations among responsible leaders of both races.'"³³ Although King, Ralph Abernathy, and Robert Graetz issued a public reply "accepting the ministers' invitation to dialogue and requesting that they propose a date and place for such a discussion," there was no reply, and thus no meeting occurred.³⁴ King was clear that miscarriages of justice such as that suffered by young Reeves and countless numbers of blacks was not a political issue, but fundamentally a moral issue, "a question of the dignity of man."³⁵

The NAACP hired lawyers to defend Reeves. This was around the time that Claudette Colvin first heard of that organization. She recalled that she and her peers at the high school decided to show movies and take donations to help pay for good legal counsel for Reeves. Colvin observed that the "rebellion and anger" of black youths in Montgomery was very much connected to what was seen as the wrongful accusation, arrest, prosecution, and execution of Reeves.

Young Jeremiah Reeves had already been accused, arrested, and put on death row just prior to Martin Luther King's arrival in Montgomery. King soon heard about this travesty of justice, and wrote about the case in *Stride Toward Freedom*.

---

32. *The Papers* (2000), 4:397.
33. Ibid., 4:397 n. 2.
34. Ibid., 4:398.
35. Ibid., 4:397.

Reeves, a drummer in a Negro band, had been arrested at the age of sixteen, accused of raping a white woman. One of the authorities had led him to the death chamber, threatening that if he did not confess at once he would burn later. His confession, extracted under this duress, was later retracted, and for the remaining seven years that his case and his life, dragged on, he continued to deny not only the charge of rape but the accusation of having had sexual relations at all with his white accuser.[36]

During King's tenure as president of the Montgomery Improvement Association (MIA), the organization made sizable financial contributions to the death penalty cases of Reeves, as well as Drewey Aron.[37] King saw that these cases were most typical when it came to blacks' experience in the criminal justice system in Montgomery and the rest of the state. For example, during the years that Reeves sat in prison, a number of white men in Alabama were accused of rape, but their accusers were young black women. Not only were these men seldom arrested, they were quickly released by an all-white Grand Jury (even when arrested), and thus were never brought to trial. "For good reason," King said, "the Negroes of the South had learned to fear and mistrust the white man's justice."[38] Blacks knew that more often than not, neither policemen nor court officials (generally nonfederal court officials) were on their side; that they could not expect justice from them.

Claudette Colvin and other black youths were well aware of the Alabama state segregation ordinance and what this meant on the city buses that many of them rode to and from school every day. Signs on the buses pointed to "colored" and "white" sections. Black young people were as much affected by such practices as black adults, a fact that often seemed to elude many parents and other grownups. Black

36. King, *Stride*, 31.
37. *The Papers* (2005), 5:335.
38. King, *Stride*, 32.

youths witnessed what happened to Claudette Colvin in the bus incident, and were as angry and traumatized as she was in some ways. And yet Colvin, like many of her angry peers, really did not know how best to vent her anger, frustration, and disappointment. She and other black youths knew they were angry and knew the source of that anger. And yet, Colvin spoke for many when she said that they simply felt helpless and "just wanted change."[39] We will see later that another way Colvin asserted herself in the face of the segregation ordinances was by agreeing to be one of the four plaintiffs in the case against Montgomery officials filed in the U.S. District Court.

Joseph Lacey was a thirteen-year-old Montgomery resident when the bus boycott began. In later years, he spoke of how excited he and other black youths were as they anticipated the first day of the boycott. They were even more excited while walking to school and were being passed by empty bus, after empty bus, after empty bus. "It was just a beautiful thing," Lacey recalled. "It was a day to behold to see nobody on the bus."[40] There was much camaraderie and togetherness among black youths and adults during the boycott, Lacey recalled. They all "walked and enjoyed walking," because they were walking for their freedom and the freedom of those who would come after them. "Everybody felt like a part of the struggle because everybody had a part."[41] It is also significant that black youths were not of the view that *all* whites were guilty of intentional acts of racism and discrimination. This was really quite amazing in itself, inasmuch as there was good reason for blacks to draw the general conclusion that all whites were responsible for racial segregation. For the truth is that most blacks only witnessed exceptional instances when a white person behaved in a humane and respectful manner

---

39. Levine, *Freedom's Children*, 26.
40. Ibid., 27.
41. Ibid., 27.

toward them. While there were surely instances in which black parents, reacting to the racism they had experienced their entire lives, taught their children that all whites were guilty of racist behavior, most black parents did not do this. Instead, they taught their children that even though it might seem that all whites behaved toward blacks like members of the Ku Klux Klan and the White Citizen's Council, individual whites should be judged on the basis of how they actually behave toward blacks. Young Joseph Lacey believed that some whites, including white youths, even boycotted the buses as a sign of their sympathy with the cause.[42]

Although most white youth in Montgomery were not involved in the boycott to the extent of their black peers, it is instructive to know that a few young whites likely stood with them, as Joseph Lacey implied. Some white youths, like some white adults, intentionally did not ride the buses during the boycott. This was likely their way of expressing support for the protest.[43] While most white youths did not volunteer to do work for the MIA as black students did—for example, many black female youths volunteered to work in the MIA office[44]—it is known that at least one white female youth (who was from the North) did indeed volunteer to work there. However, because there were so many violent threats and outbursts from racist whites, black leaders advised her against it, saying that it would put her life too much at risk.[45] Although at this writing I have seen no evidence that significant numbers of whites actively sought to support the boycott, it is of no small moment that a few did. It is a reminder that no matter what era of history being discussed, God always has a witness, even in the group deemed to be the oppressor.

---

42. Ibid., 27.
43. L. D. Reddick, *Crusader without Violence: A Biography of Martin Luther King, Jr.* (New York: Harper & Brothers, 1959), 76.
44. Ibid., 128.
45. Ibid., 128.

This, of course, says more about God than human beings as such. God has created human beings such that they possess an inherent sense of right and wrong, of what is just and unjust. The faithful and obedient ones will always protest wrong and injustice, regardless.

Black male youths also had active roles in the boycott. One such volunteer was Yancey Martin, a college freshman during the boycott. When Martin asked Ralph Abernathy, a family friend, what he could do to support the boycott, he was told that since drivers were needed, he could help to organize drivers to pick up boycotters near the bus stops and transport them to and from work. Martin told Howell Raines: "And so all the guys who were on my street . . . and a group of other folk whose parents had cars, we would all get up in the morning as early as we could. . . . And what we had to do was we had to know the names of everybody in there or else the police would stop and try to charge you with operating an illegal jitney service. And so what we would do is, by knowing everybody's name, we'd just say that these are my cousins or these are friends of mine I'm giving a lift."[46] Just here, it is of interest to note that the taxi service devised and managed by the MIA was applauded by a local white librarian and activist, Juliette Morgan. Morgan had written letters to the local newspaper supporting the boycott, for which she would pay a heavy price. In the matter of the MIA's transportation system, Morgan wrote a letter to the editor of the *Montgomery Advertiser* on December 12, 1955, a week after the boycott began. "Not since the first battle of the Marne has the taxi been put to as good a use as it has this last week in Montgomery," she wrote. "However, the spirit animating our Negro citizens as they ride these taxis or walk from the heart of Cloverdale to Mobile Road has been more like that of Gandhi than of the 'taxicab army' that saved Paris."[47]

---

46. Quoted in Howell Raines, *My Soul Is Rested: Movement Days in the Deep South Remembered* (G. P. Putnam's Sons, 1977), 58, 59.

Although it is not clear that a part of the formal strategy of the MIA was that of soliciting the volunteer assistance of black youths, there is no question that they provided assistance in a number of ways. Just as some Montgomery blacks recalled with delight how all class differences seemed to take a back seat in the mass prayer meetings, Yancey Martin marveled at how Montgomery blacks seemed to unify as one big family in support of the boycott. "I had never seen that happen in Montgomery," he said, "and I must admit that I have never seen that happen *anywhere* among black people. . . . Even the people who were not in attendance at the meetings, who are just sorta like people who don't get involved, decided to abide by the rules. . . ."[48] Martin Yancey witnessed and applauded the fact that black people in Montgomery were sticking together in a common cause.

In addition, a fact that often goes unnoticed is that the weekly mass prayer meetings (that started out as twice-a-week meetings) were actually open to all members of the Montgomery community. Boycott leaders placed no restriction on the race or ethnicity of participants. It is known that only a couple of whites, such as Rev. Robert S. Graetz, senior minister of the all-black Trinity Lutheran Church, and Rev. Thomas P. Thrasher, rector of a large Episcopal church in Montgomery, were openly sympathetic toward the bus boycott. Of these, Graetz regularly attended and contributed to the mass prayer meetings, and like a number of black ministers, his home was bombed. This was the price exacted for his commitment to the civil rights and freedom for blacks, and his unwillingness to be terrorized into silence and passivity. Graetz was in fact one of the more popular pastor-leaders involved in the boycott. In his memoir he wrote of how enthusiastically the massive crowds received him at

---

47. Quoted in Sanford Wexler, *An Eyewitness History of the Civil Rights Movement* (New York: Checkmark Books, 1999), 80.
48. Quoted in Raines, *My Soul Is Rested*, 59.

the prayer meetings whenever he was called upon to do something, for example, read scripture.[49] White media representatives attended the meetings, as well as a few whites whose purpose was merely to keep an eye on what blacks were doing. In addition, King and boycott leaders were aware that black spies also attended the mass prayer meetings and would report back to the white authorities. King said that the mayor's cook was a known spy who attended the meetings, and that police commissioner Clyde Sellars allowed three black prisoners to "attend the mass meetings so that they can tell him what has happened."[50] It might well be that some of the information that black spies reported to whites was in fact disinformation intended to throw white officials off track.

Sense of Terror among Black Parents

A number of instructive things happened during the bus boycott. For example, not all black youths who participated in the prayer meetings at local churches had the wholehearted support of their parents or guardians. Some had no support at all. Such parents demanded that their child not get involved. What was behind this? Surely it was not because they preferred the mistreatment and disrespect of blacks by white bus drivers to continue. Without question, they did want such practices to stop, but they feared for the safety of their children if they resisted the racist commands of bus drivers.

Many black parents had lived too long with segregation and racism in the Deep South and thus had vivid memories of terrorist acts committed against family members or other blacks by white racists who were often affiliated with the Ku Klux Klan, the White Citizens Council, and other white hate groups. These individuals were

---

49. Graetz, *Montgomery: A White Preacher's Memoir*, 106.
50. *The Papers* (1997), 3:112.

frequently members of the local police department and/or officers of the court, including judges and district attorneys, which meant that blacks could count on no protection whatever from law enforcement officers and the courts. Often it was the case that blacks knew who the Klansmen and/or White Citizens Council members were who sought to terrorize them. They knew that these people were frequently churchgoers, affiliated with the police, officers of the court, or businessmen; so-called respectable members of white society. Because these were the very people that black residents had to depend on for justice, most blacks were not naïve enough to believe that justice was forthcoming. Black parents knew that their involvement in the mass prayer meetings and the bus boycott could cause them to lose their job if their white employer found out. This very thing happened to Georgia Gilmore, who lived near the Dexter Avenue Baptist Church parsonage. She was fired from her cafeteria job because of her involvement with the boycott. Undaunted, and refusing to bow down and passively submit to white racist pressure and threats, Gilmore went out and organized the "Club from Nowhere," through which black women baked and sold pies, cakes, and other pastries to raise money to support the boycott. This proved to be a significant source of revenue for the MIA.

In addition to the fear of losing jobs, there was the fear among many black adults of losing their life, and even more terrifying, the fear of losing a child. It was the type of unsettling fear that was exhibited by Mississippian Anne Moody's mother in 1955 when Moody, then fourteen, asked her if she had heard about the brutal murder of fourteen-year-old Emmett Till in Money, Mississippi. The Moodys lived near where the abduction and brutal murder had taken place. In her book, *Coming of Age in Mississippi*, Moody wrote about her mother's reaction to her question about the Till murder.

"Where did you hear that?" she said angrily.

"Boy, everybody really thinks I'm dumb or deaf or something. I heard Eddie them talking about it this evening coming from school."

"Eddie them better watch how they go around here talking. These white folks git a hold of it they gonna be in trouble," she said.

"What are they gonna be in trouble about, Mama? People got a right to talk, ain't they?"

"You go on to work before you is late. And don't you let on like you know nothing about that boy being killed before Miss Burke them [the white family for whom Moody did domestic work after school]. Just do your work like you don't know nothing," she said. "That boy's a lot better off in heaven than he is here," she continued, and then started singing again.[51]

Just as it did during the period of American enslavement of Afrikans, singing often helped blacks to bear their fears and uncertainties, as well as lift their hopes for freedom and justice. Notwithstanding this, Moody's mother was clearly terrified out of her mind, not so much for herself as for her daughter. She therefore instructed her to pretend to know nothing, and to say nothing around white people about the murder of young Emmett Till. Moody was taught to lie and be untrue to herself in such matters when in the presence of whites. In order to escape racist violence in the Deep South, blacks frequently had to defy truth. How must it have affected their psyche when they were taught in church and school the virtue of truth-telling? Too many of them (and their parents) knew that speaking and telling the truth about certain things meant severe punishment, and too often, death.

Most black adults during that period in the Deep South lived in utter fear because of what they had either experienced firsthand, or

---

51. Anne Moody, *Coming of Age in Mississippi* (New York: Dell, 1976 [1968]), 123.

heard about regarding white violence against their people, for no other reason than they were black. Anne Moody reflected that before Emmett Till was murdered, she "had known the fear of hunger, hell, and the Devil. But now," she added, "there was a new fear known to me—the fear of being killed just because I was black."[52] Imagine that; a child living her day-to-day life in literal fear of being killed just because she happened to be born with black skin.

What is significant about Anne Moody's questioning of her mother is the clear evidence that black youths were not only aware of violent racist acts against blacks (as black adults were), but were as much affected by such awareness as their parents and other black adults. In addition, black youths were more apt to want to do something about it, as SCLC staff member James Bevel discovered when he did voter registration work in Jackson, Mississippi a few years after the boycott and two years before the Birmingham, Alabama campaign. Bevel had witnessed with his own eyes the willingness of black youths to take risks when black adults would not. From the Mississippi experience, Bevel knew that like young Anne Moody and her peers, Birmingham's black youths were less likely to be appeased by adult blacks' advice to pretend, when in the presence of whites, that they knew nothing about the violence and brutality being perpetrated against their people by whites.

Notwithstanding black parents' concern for their job or the safety of their children, many black youths, such as Fred Taylor and other students at Montgomery's Booker T. Washington High School, who wanted their teachers to discuss with them what was happening during the boycott would secretly attend the mass prayer meetings, against the instructions of their parents or guardians. Taylor lived with his grandmother who was terrified for his life, and would not give him permission to participate in the protest at any level,

52. Ibid., 125.

including the mass prayer meetings. Nevertheless, in complete defiance, young Taylor would sneak away to the meetings and then lie about where he had been.

Like many Montgomery black youths, Taylor remembered the new sense of pride and dignity he felt when Martin Luther King declared at the mass prayer meetings that black people are *somebody*. This led to a changed self-image, as well as his outlook on his family. "It was right during the boycott that I began to have a different assessment of myself as an individual and to feel my sense of worth,"[53] Taylor reflected. At that particular time, King might not have known the precise impact he was having on black youths of Montgomery, but some of the young people did know, and like Taylor, did not hesitate to acknowledge it.

A New Sense of Dignity

When on December 20, 1956, U.S. Marshalls officially served the Supreme Court order that the city of Montgomery's and the state of Alabama's segregation ordinance was unconstitutional, Martin Luther King intended to ride the first desegregated bus in Montgomery early the next morning. King, E. D. Nixon, Ralph Abernathy, and Glenn Smiley all boarded the bus that ran in front of his house at 6:00 a.m. However, it appears that King and company might not have been the first to break the boycott. L. Alex Wilson, a black reporter of the *Tri-State Defender* in Memphis, and his photographer, Ernest Withers, were present when King announced the end of the boycott and thus knew that King would be trying to board a desegregated bus early the next morning. Gene Roberts

---

53. Levine, *Freedom's Children*, 29.

and Hank Klibanoff tell the story of what happened after King's announcement.

> In his hotel room after the meeting, Alex Wilson was feeling too inspired and exhilarated to let the story pass by him routinely. He came up with a plan of his own. At four in the morning, he woke Withers up and told him to get dressed, Withers would later say. The two of them went out onto Montgomery's dark streets and waited for a bus. When the first one arrived, Withers began shooting pictures of Wilson boarding the bus, then took some more shots of Wilson sitting in the front of the bus. The driver, Withers recalled, was hiding his face.[54]

According to this account, Wilson and Withers boarded a desegregated bus, even before King did.

In any case, Fred Taylor and other black youths followed the instructions of King and other MIA leaders on how to groom, dress, and behave when they returned to the buses. Before the boycott, they had to seat from the rear of the bus. When they returned to the buses they could sit wherever they wanted on a first-come first-serve basis. On the first day of desegregation, Taylor sat proudly behind the bus driver. He would sit next to a white man, he recalled, but was quite intentional about not sitting next to a white woman. For him, as for many other black youths, the fact that Jeremiah Reeves was still on death row for allegedly raping a white woman was still too fresh and painful in his mind. In addition, the image of the brutal murder of young Emmett Till was still etched indelibly into his and the memory and psyche of all southern blacks. This meant, in part, that even though the Supreme Court eventually outlawed the segregation ordinance in Montgomery and the state of Alabama, whites and blacks in Montgomery were far from being a real community, let alone the beloved community that was King's goal.

---

54. Roberts and Klibanoff, *The Race Beat*, 142.

Princella Howard reflected on what it meant to be an eight-year-old in a household that was actually devoted to working with the MIA during the boycott. She and her six-year-old sister participated in the boycott and later became student leaders in the post-boycott movement in Montgomery in the 1960s. One of her fondest memories was how, during the boycott, the MIA succeeded in mobilizing and bringing together blacks of different social and economic classes and "who were generally at odds with each other." People who did not otherwise worship or socialize together because of class differences had no difficulty participating together in the prayer meetings. Howard mused: "It was remarkable to see the rich blacks and the poor ones at mass meetings interested in the same thing."[55] She viewed this as one of the seldom-mentioned victories among blacks in Montgomery; that blacks of all social classes were able to stand and fight together for a common cause. Montgomery blacks had proved conclusively that blacks could unite around a common cause and stick together until there was an acceptable resolution.

Martin Luther King certainly did not fail to notice the intermixing of the respective social and economic classes in the prayer meetings. After the Montgomery campaign, he often recalled how blacks in that city came together, organized, learned to get along in common cause, and learned to stick together, regardless of social and economic class.[56] This showed King not only the need for this very thing to happen in other black communities, but that it was in fact possible. He reasoned that if blacks could do it in Montgomery—and as we saw earlier, blacks had even done it in 1900 during the boycott of the public trolleys—they could do it anywhere else in the country. Generally, King applauded the emergence of the new sense of self,

55. Levine, *Freedom's Children*, 31.
56. King, *Stride*, 187, 190.

dignity, and destiny among Montgomery blacks. "The Montgomery Negro had acquired a new sense of somebodiness and self-respect," he said, "and had a new determination to achieve freedom and human dignity no matter what the cost."[57] In addition, and most significantly, King made positive observations about the youths of Montgomery, saying: "The children seem to display a new sense of belonging. The older children are aware of the conflict and the resulting tension, but they act as if they expect the future to include a better world to live in."[58] This is significant because it means that already, in the first major campaign of the civil rights movement, Martin Luther King was aware of its effect on black youths, even if he was not as aware of his and the movement's effect on them; even if formal plans had not been made by boycott leaders as to how best to utilize black youth in the boycott. Nevertheless, a seed had been planted in his mind, and would take root and germinate to full bloom in the early weeks of the Birmingham, Alabama campaign, although we will see that when the time came he actually had to be prodded to permit the involvement of children and youths.

Martin Luther King was not the only one to observe and acknowledge the positive influence of the Montgomery struggle on black youths. Earlier in this chapter, we saw that James Forman reflected on the strong impact that the boycott had on the outlook of black youths in particular, and blacks generally. In addition, Robert Graetz made a similar observation while reflecting on how the bus boycott, even in its earlier stage, positively influenced black youths.

> White people couldn't understand the changes that had taken place. Again and again I had heard the refrain: "Our niggers wouldn't act like this!" Indeed they had never seen "their niggers" demonstrate such self-confidence.

---

57. Clayborne Carson, ed., *The Autobiography of Martin Luther King, Jr.* (New York: Warner Books, 1998), 99.
58. *The Papers*, 3:451.

Early in the protest, a group of teenage boys stood on a corner watching empty buses roll by. A police car pulled up. "What are you boys doing here?" one of the officers shouted. "I want you all to get away from this corner!"

One of the teenagers calmly walked over to the patrol car. "Mister," he said, "I ain't done nothin'. I ain't goin' nowhere. I'm going to stand where I damn am!" The befuddled officers drove away.[59]

There was clearly a sense among boycott leaders that the self-image and self-esteem of blacks generally had been positively affected as a result of their part in the more-than-yearlong protest, but also that something positive had happened in the psyche of black youth throughout the South.

Early scholars on King seldom (if ever) referenced his admiration and praise for black children of Montgomery. We now know that even at that early period of his civil rights ministry he acknowledged the concerns of the children, how they were affected by the struggle, and their expectations for the future. King carried this memory with him when he left Montgomery and did not forget that the struggle for human dignity was as much about black children and young people as about adults. He would therefore welcome their contributions along the civil rights trail.

The Montgomery movement did much to inspire the passing of the Civil Rights Acts of 1957 and 1960, although both were much too watered down in comparison to the 1964 Civil Rights Act. The latter was inspired by the struggle in what was arguably the most segregated city in the nation, Birmingham, Alabama. Later, the Voting Rights Act of 1965 would be spurred by the voting rights campaigns and struggles in other Deep South states such as Mississippi, and in Selma, Alabama.

---

59. Graetz, *Montgomery: A White Preacher's Memoir*, 107.

Need for Multiple Approaches

Prior to the Montgomery bus boycott (a direct-action approach), blacks' primary method of addressing issues of civil rights was through the NAACP method of litigation in the courts. This was a very methodical, albeit very slow method. What the Montgomery movement taught not only King and other leaders of that campaign, but prospective advocates for freedom and civil rights all over the country, was that the legal approach of the NAACP was not the only approach; that increasingly what were needed were multiple approaches working together. Montgomery depicted the simultaneous use of direct action *and* the litigation approach. It was thought by many that the mass direct-action approach could lead not only to more far-reaching results than the legal approach, but would enable individuals to participate directly in the struggle for civil rights through direct action. This message seemed to reverberate throughout the South and the nation—wherever the civil rights of blacks were impeded or outright denied. Fred Powledge provides an instructive and important comment in this regard.

> There was . . . something deliciously inviting about the here-and-now nature of direct action that did not characterize the legal approach at all. Granted, the courtroom route, when finally followed to its ultimate conclusion in the Supreme Court, might result in a decision far more wide-ranging in terms of geography and political jurisdictions than a local boycott. (*Brown* showed, however, that court decisions did not necessarily insure speedy change.) Montgomery proved that there was nothing wrong, and a lot right, with using both approaches at once.[60]

Not entirely surprising, NAACP legal defense hardliners such as the venerable Thurgood Marshall and John Morsell reportedly declared that had the boycotters in Montgomery stayed home and waited for

---

60. Powledge, *Free at Last?*, 85.

them to get the court's decision they could have saved themselves a lot of marching and trouble; that it was not so much the long boycott, but an NAACP lawsuit that actually led to the desegregation of Montgomery city buses.[61] Always the dialectical thinker, and one who insisted on seeing and examining as much of the evidence as possible, Martin Luther King argued against an either-or approach to fighting for civil rights and freedom. The fact that he himself became a lifelong member of the NAACP when he arrived as pastor of Dexter Avenue Baptist Church, and frequently urged his members to join, indicated his appreciation for that organization's efforts. In addition, he was aware of the importance of the NAACP to his father and grandfather in their own efforts to achieve civil rights for blacks.

In 1958, King rejected the criticism that the NAACP was outmoded, arguing instead that it "has achieved excellence in the area of legal strategy and is doing an excellent job in that area."[62] King argued for an approach that included virtually any method that focused on nonviolence as the means to civil rights, for example, the legal approach of the NAACP, the nonviolent direct-action approach of the SCLC and CORE, as well as potential contributions of the legislative and executive branches of the federal government.[63] He was quite clear, however, that the legal method had to be supplemented with direct-action methods. King persistently rejected the idea that he and SCLC were competing with the NAACP, or that their methods and aims were somehow in conflict with each other. He urged blacks and others to continue to support the NAACP.[64]

Suffice it to say that the yearlong bus boycott helped create the opening for other approaches to the struggle for civil rights. It will therefore be instructive to provide at least a brief discussion on

---

61. Ibid., 86.
62. *The Papers*, 4:434.
63. Ibid., 4:435.
64. Ibid., 4:174.

contributions made by sit-ins as well as student activists who bravely continued the Freedom Rides. Black college students initiated the sit-in movement in the early weeks of 1960. White students were quick to join in support. By joining with black students at segregated lunch counters, white students were subjected to the same insults and verbal abuse as their black peers. In many instances, the abuses toward white students were even more severe because local whites viewed them as "nigger lovers," and in their narrow, perverted minds, there was nothing worse. White students also joined the Freedom Ride that was initiated by student activists from CORE that followed in the spring of 1961. When CORE activists were brutally attacked outside Anniston, Alabama its director, James Farmer, called off the rides. Diane Nash, a student at Fisk University and a youth activist, argued against this, saying that they must not allow violence to stop their efforts;[65] that if they did, opponents would always feel that in order to stop a civil rights demonstration in its tracks, all one need do is violently attack demonstrators. At Nash's pleading, however, they were allowed to resume the Freedom Ride. As expected, when white students joined the Freedom Rides, they were bludgeoned with pipes, clubs, and bottles, just like black students. This is what happened when young people decided to sit-in, and/or take a ride for freedom.

---

65. Powledge, *Free at Last?*, 258, 262.

2

Sitting-In and Taking a Ride for Freedom

The beginning of the sit-in movement pre-dated the founding of SNCC, but was a reason for that organization's birth. In addition, and most important for our purpose, the sit-in movement was not initiated and led by any of the already formally established civil rights organizations such as the NAACP, SCLC, and CORE. Rather, the sit-in movement was ignited on February 1, 1960 by four black male freshmen college students at North Carolina A&T College in Greensboro: David Richmond, Joseph McNeil, Franklin McCain, and Ezell Blair Jr. (who later changed his name to Jibreel Khazan). The four students had at one time been affiliated with the NAACP Youth Council, and thus had some awareness of formal efforts to address racism, albeit through the courts. Although Dr. George Simkins, head of the local NAACP affiliate in Greensboro, endorsed the actions of the young men, the same could not be said of the national office. Rather than support Simkins, national NAACP officials rebuked him for violating agency policy. We saw in the previous chapter that the method of the NAACP was to work through litigation and the courts for civil rights. Direct-action approaches such as nonviolent civil disobedience campaigns popularized by King and SCLC, and now the direct sit-in actions of A&T students, were not consistent with the NAACP's policy and methodology.

When his own organization did not support him, Simkins sought the support of other established groups.[1] He contacted Jimmy Robinson of CORE, and discovered that the students' sit-in protest was just what that organization had been waiting for, since it had been trying—unsuccessfully—to find a way to broadly transform the South. Robinson and others knew that CORE would have to find a way to "provoke a general crisis of conscience among white Southerners."[2] However, the leadership of CORE simply did not know, at the time, how to bring this about, nor did they have the financial, human, and other resources that would be needed to sustain such a project. Although national leaders of the NAACP did not approve of Simkins's move, leaders of CORE saw it as the opportunity they had been waiting for, and therefore directed all of their attention and meager resources to supporting the Greensboro sit-in, in addition to planning and sponsoring "sympathy demonstrations" across the country.

In any event, Ezell Blair had heard a speech that Martin Luther King delivered at Bennett College in Greensboro two years earlier in 1958. It is not clear whether or how much this played a part in what occurred two years later, but we can be sure that the teen was impacted by what he heard King say. King had long acknowledged the importance of youth involvement in the civil rights struggle. I cannot imagine that King said nothing about the role of youth in

---

1. Raymond Arsenault, *Freedom Riders: 1961 and the Struggle for Racial Justice* (New York: Oxford University Press, 2006), 85.
2. Ibid., 84.

his speech at Bennett. Although the sit-ins started at a Woolworth's lunch counter, it was only a matter of days before the idea spread like wildfire throughout the South as well as in other places of public accommodation, such as restaurants, movie theaters, courtroom seating, and public libraries.

A Clothing Store Owner and the Sit-In

There is strong evidence that prior to the initial sit-in, Richmond, McNeil, McCain, and Blair had periodically been in conversation with a local white proprietor of a clothing store in Greensboro who allegedly put the sit-in idea into the minds of the four youths.[3] Presumably these were not the first black youths that storeowner Ralph Johns had encouraged to protest Woolworth's segregated lunch-counter policy and practice. "Since 1949 Johns had been suggesting to students who frequented his store that they test and attack segregation at Woolworth's. He and the students met in the rear of his store to discuss the youths' moves. He promised to cover their bonds if they were arrested."[4]

However, not all agree on the extent of Johns's involvement and contribution to what ensued in early 1960. "At a ceremony in Greensboro on February 1, 1990, commemorating the thirtieth anniversary, Johns, now a resident of California, commented that 'I started' the demonstration. Franklin McCain remembered that Johns played a less central role."[5] It is quite possible that Johns was instrumental in putting the idea of the sit-in into the minds of the four youths. In fact, Joseph McNeil recalled having talked to Johns

---

3. Miles Wolff, *Lunch at the 5 & 10*, revised expanded edition (Chicago: Ivan R. Dee, 1990 [1970]), 15–17, 23ff.
4. Fred Powledge, *Free at Last?: The Civil Rights Movement and the People Who Made It* (New York: HarperPerennial, 1992), 199–200.
5. Ibid., 200.

a number of times, and said that he "was extremely helpful to us in getting things rolling, in giving us some ideas."[6] Indicators are that when it came to actually doing something about the segregated lunch counter, it was in fact the four students who took action; who walked into Woolworth's, sat at the lunch counter, ordered a meal, and refused to leave until the store closed. Although it is conceivable that Johns might have promised to pay the bail of the youths should they be arrested, he did not have to fork out bail money, since they were not arrested the first day. McNeil, Blair, and Richmond were arrested on April 21st along with two white female students from Bennett College, for by then a number of white students from local colleges had joined the sit-in. The five students were released without bail.[7] Perhaps this is what was in the mind of Franklin McCain when Johns reportedly said that *he* started the sit-ins. McCain did not deny that Johns contributed toward planting the idea in their minds, but beyond that he did not recall any substantive contributions from him. The four youths initially acted alone.

Although the extent of Ralph Johns's contribution to the Greensboro sit-in is not clear, there seems to be no question that he was genuinely concerned about how blacks were treated generally in Greensboro, and at Woolworths in particular. In addition, it is known that he supported the sit-in, which he praised in newspaper editorials. He wrote a number of these in the Greensboro *Champion*, the local weekly newspaper owned by blacks. Writing under his pen name, Ricardo Raffles, he said: "On last Thursday, the valiant sit-down warriors of Greensboro joined the immortal ranks of those martyrs who are being jailed all over the South while increasing

---

6. Quoted in Henry Hampton and Steve Fayer with Sarah Flynn, *Voices of Freedom: An Oral History of the Civil Rights Movement from the 1950s Through the 1980s* (New York: Bantam Books, 1990), 56.
7. Wolff, *Lunch at the 5 & 10*, 139.

their right of equal, just and equitable treatment in places of public accommodation. . . . For the sacrifices being made by our young people today will make our country a better place tomorrow."[8] Miles Wolff contends that once the sit-ins started, Johns did what he could, such as writing supportive editorials under a pen name. Johns reportedly felt that any open public support by him would discredit what the students were trying to do. According to Wolff: "The students still came by his store after each day's demonstration, but it was more out of respect than for guidance: they knew what they were doing. He advised the students to court arrest, but he was realistic enough to know that if he were a part of it the movement would be discredited."[9] Floyd McKissick, an activist who had been experimenting with direct-action methods in nearby Durham, offered to provide legal counsel to the four black youths. Suffice it to say, the story of Ralph Johns's role in the Greensboro sit-in is one that warrants deeper investigation.

The Nashville Connection: Nonviolence Training for the Sit-Ins

Unknown to the students in Greensboro, student activists in Nashville, Tennessee, under the guidance and tutelage of Rev. James Lawson, had been engaged in nonviolent workshops for several months in late 1959 as they trained for broad-scale sit-ins in restaurants and other public places in downtown Nashville. Their training included workshops in Gandhian nonviolent techniques, including the use of *socio-drama* to give them a realistic sense of how they would be treated by racist opponents and how they should respond. Using a mock lunch counter, some of the students would

---

8. Quoted in ibid., 139.
9. Ibid., 140.

portray those sitting-in, while others would portray racist white opponents engaging in name calling, cursing, spitting, and squirting mustard, ketchup, and mayonnaise on those at the counter. There would then be a critical discussion of how each sit-in demonstrator responded. Where needed, advice would be given about how one might have responded. In addition to the training in Gandhian techniques, the students also received instruction on the philosophy and basic principles of nonviolence. This, along with the training in techniques, easily made the Nashville students the best trained of the early student activists. As they approached the Christmas holiday season, the sense was that they would begin the sit-ins in downtown Nashville within a month or so. As it happened, the Greensboro sit-in occurred almost spontaneously, and within a very brief period of time it took off like a fire in dry brush and strong winds. Having begun with four students, there were twenty-nine on the second day, and around 350 the third day. It was at this time that the Greensboro students appealed to Simkins, sensing that they needed help. They had unwittingly started a mass movement.

As implied earlier, the advent of the sit-ins marked an important change in a number of ways. A more general shift was a movement from legal to direct-action approaches. At least from King's perspective, this did not mean that the NAACP's litigation approach was no longer viable or needed. Rather it meant that, given the complexity of the issues and the growing impatience of blacks—especially younger blacks—with racial discrimination, other methods were needed that would allow individuals and organized groups of freedom fighters to directly involve themselves in the struggle, rather than to depend solely on the approach of the NAACP. The sit-in also signaled that young blacks had had enough, and were now desirous of taking the fight to those who opposed a racism-free society and equality between the races. With such moves, black youths put the more traditional civil rights leaders on notice that there was a place for them in the struggle, and they intended to make their presence known and felt. They would no longer sit passively on the sideline while adults conservatively called the shots and took the lead. Black youths were increasingly coming to the sense that as moral agents they had not only the capability, but the right to act on their own behalf, in their own way, on their own timetable. Fred Powledge has put it in a helpful way.

> It could be argued, and sometimes was, that there was nothing new under this particular sun: that direct action of this sort had been employed since slave days, and that young people had previously been represented in the Movement through their activities in NAACP youth councils. But something different had happened with Greensboro-by-way-of-Montgomery-by-way-of-*Brown*. The rules of engagement, as military commanders say, had changed. The calendar had changed, too: All of a sudden there was a hollow sound to the exhortation that justice would come in the by-and-by. The schedule had been rewritten, compressed. What the demonstrators were saying, and meaning with all the impatience and assumed immortality of youth, was "Freedom *now!*" with the emphasis on the second word. And suddenly no other option seemed worth even considering.[10]

Everything had changed, seemingly overnight, almost unexpectedly and spontaneously. The sit-in initiated by David Richmond, Joseph McNeil, Franklin McCain, and Ezell Blair Jr. in Greensboro was a clear sign that black youths were no longer willing to merely follow the agenda of their elders and be instructed by them. From now on, they would not accept uncritically the instructions of their elders in matters of race and civil rights. Instead, they would read their own situation and experiences, talk among themselves, share information and ideas, and develop and implement their own agenda and timetable. Some elders, even when not opposed to black youths

---

10. Powledge, *Free at Last?*, 107.

having their own organizations, fought to keep them under the supervision of an adult-led civil rights organization. SCLC initially sought to do this when student leaders met on the campus of Shaw University in the spring of 1960 and decided to form their own organization. This desire that traditional established civil rights leaders had to essentially control the youths would, of course, lead to tension and conflict between the two generations. I return to this important point subsequently.

Many of the youthful activists were college students who hoped to become professionals of various kinds, e.g., teachers, ministers, lawyers, and doctors. As they increasingly sensed what was at stake, many made the decision to drop out of school, for what they imagined would be for only a brief period, to work fulltime in the movement. The student activists in Nashville were among the earliest to do this. The hope that through their efforts freedom would come soon was based on their youthfulness, lack of experience, and naïveté. Many would discover that despite their commitment, courage, and direct-action approaches, freedom and civil rights was a long way off. The problems were systemic and thus deeply entrenched. But they had stamina, and they were determined.

Students' Respect for Martin Luther King

We have seen that, to his credit, Martin Luther King had too much integrity and character to try to steal the thunder of the youthful activists or to take credit for what they themselves initiated and were suffering through. At the opening of the Youth Leadership Conference on the campus of Shaw University on Easter weekend of 1960, King told those gathered: "This is an era of offensive on the part of oppressed people. All peoples deprived of dignity and freedom are on the march on every Continent throughout the world.

The student sit-in movement represents just such an offensive in the history of the Negro people's struggle for freedom. The students have taken the struggle for justice into their own strong hands. In less than two months more Negro freedom fighters have revealed to the nation and the world their determination and courage than has occurred in many years."[11] That the students invited King to give the keynote address said much about their respect for his leadership and their sense of him as the symbol of the movement, but the fact that he accepted the invitation and said what he did, just as clearly indicates his admiration for their commitment and courage to make their contribution to the struggle for freedom and civil rights.

The first major SNCC meeting since its founding at Shaw University occurred in Atlanta from October 14 to 16. SNCC leaders Marion Barry and Jane Stembridge (daughter of a white Baptist minister from Virginia and a student at Union Theological Seminary) invited King to deliver a keynote address on the philosophy of nonviolence. Three days after the close of the meeting, King and several dozen student activists were arrested and jailed for participating in a sit-in at the lunch counter at Rich's Department Store in downtown Atlanta. Charges were dropped against many of the demonstrators, but King and thirty-five others chose to remain in jail, refusing to post bond.[12] When news media representatives attempted to credit King with igniting the sit-in, he immediately corrected them by saying that *it was the students who invited him to join them.* He was not willing to upstage the youths or to say or do anything to make it appear that they were not capable of initiating and engaging in responsible protests on their own. King was totally aware that young people had important contributions to make and

---

11. Martin Luther King Jr., "Statement to the Press at the Youth Leadership Conference in Raleigh, N.C.," April 15, 1960, King Library and Archives, 1.
12. Clayborne Carson et al., eds., *The Papers of Martin Luther King, Jr.* (Berkeley: University of California Press, 2005), 5:522, 524.

that they had very capable leaders among themselves. He would not allow anyone to lose sight of that fact.

When word came that King had been arrested, jailed, and refused bond along with others who sat-in at Rich's, he was urged by students in the Nashville Nonviolent Student Movement to remain in jail "for the sake of the movement."[13] King, in fact, drew strength and encouragement from the youths with whom he was jailed in Atlanta. He acknowledged this from his jail cell when he wrote a thank-you letter to the young women who were jailed, thanking them for their brave decision to refuse bail.[14] Among the female inmates were Carolyn and Wylma Long, King's cousins.[15]

When King was arrested and jailed for participating in the sit-in at Rich's, Marion Barry and Edward King of SNCC sent him a note essentially applauding him for his leadership and example, and encouraging him for his "jail no bail" stance. The note said: ". . . in thanks to you for your deep commitment to the concept of no violence, and your vision of a free society which makes possible this student movement. You sat in with us, you went to jail with us, [sic] we want you to know that the fight will not end for we have taken up the torch for freedom, [sic] we will not forget that you are behind iron bars. We ask that you remember us as we try to remove the bars that exist in the hearts of men."[16] It is not known at this writing whether King actually received the note.

When King appeared before DeKalb County judge J. Oscar Mitchell on October 25, he was found to be in violation of his probation for having been arrested for driving on an out-of-state license when he moved from Montgomery to Atlanta. Mitchell revoked his probation and sentenced him to four months hard labor

---

13. Ibid., 5:524.
14. Ibid., 5:527, 528.
15. Ibid., 5:527 n. 1.
16. Ibid., 5:531.

in the Georgia State Prison in Reidsville, more than two hundred miles from Atlanta.

Let's be clear. The revocation of King's probation was quite a serious matter, the gravity of which the Nashville students may not have fully comprehended and appreciated when King later declined their invitation to join the Freedom Ride. To have been sent to the state prison in Reidsville—where he was taken at three o'clock in the morning (a tactic intended to terrorize him)—could very well have been a death sentence for King, who honestly thought that he might not see his wife and children again. It is true that some of the student activists were also on probation for their role in the movement, but the truth is that because they were not as high profile as King, and although those of them on probation could have also had their probation revoked, it is unlikely that they would have been treated as heavy-handedly as King, who was shackled along the full length of his legs, taken from his jail cell in the wee hours of the morning in Atlanta, and driven to Reidsville prison over two hundred miles away, where he was held incommunicado. This was when aides of presidential candidate Senator John F. Kennedy suggested that he phone Mrs. King to convey his concerns and ask if there was anything he could do. It is believed that this small, seemingly insignificant gesture might well be what allowed Kennedy to carry the black vote and win a narrow margin of victory over Richard Nixon.

Early Tension between King and Student Activists

After the sit-ins swept across the South and various places in the North, SCLC executive director, Ella Josephine Baker, suggested that student leaders convene on the campus of her alma mater, Shaw University in Raleigh, North Carolina, on Easter weekend in April

1960. Approximately two hundred student leaders from across the nation—black and white, many who had participated in the sit-ins—attended the conference. Baker urged the gathering of student activists to form their own separate organization, thus combining their own energy, ideas, sense of courage, and determination. The leadership of the SCLC, NAACP, and the National Urban League strongly urged that whatever organization the students developed should be under the auspices of one or more of their organizations, an idea that Baker found repulsive, and strongly advised the students to retain their own sense of independence and autonomy. Baker's idea won the day, as the students voted to retain mainstream civil rights organizations' emphasis on nonviolence, in addition to forming the Temporary Student Nonviolent Coordinating Committee in May. "Temporary" was dropped during their October meeting. An interracial organization, the group elected Marion Barry as its first chairman, with headquarters in Atlanta. In its early weeks, the group primarily served as a channel through which to communicate and coordinate sit-in activities throughout the country. But also during this period the group was trying to determine next steps for student activism in the movement. As the year 1960 was coming to an end, a number of department store chains desegregated their lunch counters as a result of the sit-ins. In addition, some restaurants in various cities also desegregated.

Over the next few months SNCC members debated next steps. Some within the group favored continuing efforts to gain the sympathies of otherwise well-meaning whites by continuing the sit-ins and other direct-action tactics. Others preferred more political methods, such as taking steps to help empower Deep South blacks by engaging in voter registration projects. Ultimately, the group decided to focus on both ideas. Whatever they did must be based on nonviolence, they concluded. They also concluded that voter registration was critical, in that it would potentially open the way to black empowerment, since blacks would be able to elect their own leaders.

On the surface, it might have appeared that SNCC decided on a two-pronged approach: direct action (e.g., sit-ins), and voter education-registration. As it turned out, SNCC activists discovered long before much of the country, including the Kennedy administration, that in the Deep South, virtually anything that blacks did to gain their civil rights and freedom was perceived by white racists as direct action. Consequently, even voter registration projects were considered to be direct-action projects. There were such hatred, violence, lawlessness, and corruption among local and state officials in Mississippi and Alabama, for example, that voter education projects were perceived by whites as a direct threat to their segregated, white-supremacist way of life. In this regard, even voter education campaigns were perceived as direct action, as much as sit-ins and nonviolent demonstrations. Moreover, SNCC activists discovered early that demonstrations were frequently necessary accompaniments of voter registration work. It was often safer, for example, for the people to march to the courthouse in groups when they wanted to register to vote.

While SNCC activists were debating next steps, the Congress of Racial Equality was engaging in the Freedom Rides of 1961 to test the Supreme Court ruling in *Boynton v. Virginia* that segregation in interstate bus and rail travel was unconstitutional. James Farmer, CORE's director, knew that this was a dangerous, potentially violent venture. The participants underwent a week of intensive training in nonviolence. An interracial operation, seven blacks and six whites left Washington, D.C. on May 4 in two buses. They were bound for New Orleans. Encountering little resistance initially, one of the Riders' buses was surrounded by racist thugs with metal pipes and other weapons when they arrived at the bus station in Anniston, Alabama. Although the police were able to hold the mob off until the bus left town, the mob followed, shot out the tires, and broke the windows. They boarded the bus and beat black and white passengers savagely. Some required hospitalization and many stitches. James Peck, a white veteran of Journey of Reconciliation, was on that bus. Peck told of how racist thugs entered and beat them; that he was not beaten as badly, but that a white professor from Wayne State University in Detroit, Dr. Walter Bergman, was beaten so badly that he later had a stroke and never recovered from his paralysis.[17] Peck recalled that six Klansmen boarded the other bus in Anniston, and instructed the bus driver to drive on to Birmingham. When they arrived, the passengers noticed that a large mob had formed, and that they were wielding metal pipes, bats, bottles, and such. The passengers were attacked upon leaving the bus. Peck was beaten unconscious and required more than fifty stitches in his head. John Lewis, later chairman of SNCC, was among those who were attacked and brutally beaten. All of this occurred not far from the Birmingham police station. Although the police knew the Freedom Riders would be arriving on Mother's Day, an informant told the FBI that police commissioner Eugene "Bull" Connor had agreed to let the mob have at the passengers for some minutes before sending police to the scene. Some of the passengers were beaten so badly that this came to be known in movement lore as "the Mother's Day Massacre."[18] When asked why the police were not on the scene earlier, Bull Connor gave the lame excuse that most were visiting their mothers.

Some of the Riders who were injured in the Anniston attack were taken to the local hospital, but were denied treatment. All the

---

17. Hampton and Fayer, *Voices of Freedom*, 78.
18. Ellen Levine, *Freedom's Children: Young Civil Rights Activists Tell Their Own Stories* (New York: G. P. Putnam's Sons, 1993), 70.

while, a vicious mob was forming outside the hospital. When hospital personnel refused the Riders treatment and demanded that they leave the hospital, they wisely refused.

Word of the Anniston attack had reached the Reverend Fred Shuttlesworth, arguably the most fearless, courageous minister in Birmingham, sixty miles away. As president of the Alabama Christian Movement for Human Rights (ACMHR), Shuttlesworth phoned a number of the organization's members and was able to garner a fifteen-car caravan to drive up from Birmingham to get the stranded Freedom Riders. Shuttlesworth had instructed his fellow ACMHR colleagues that although they were about to embark on a very dangerous mission, they were not to carry weapons, but instead "must trust God and have faith."[19] As it turned out, Shuttlesworth's colleagues were not of the turn-the-other-cheek or nonviolence school of thought, but preferred to err on the side of self-defense. Hank Thomas, one of the stranded Freedom Riders in Anniston, told Howell Raines how the caravan arrived with Shuttlesworth in the lead car and without police escort. In addition, Thomas reported that every one of those cars had a rifle or shotgun in it. "And Fred Shuttlesworth had got on the radio and said—you know Fred, he's very dramatic—'I'm going to get my people.' He said, 'I'm a nonviolent man, but I'm going to get my people.' And apparently a hell of a lot of people believed in him. . . . And each one of 'em got out with their guns and everything and the state police were there, but I think they all realized that this was not a time to say anything because, I'm pretty sure, there would have been a lot of people killed."[20]

---

19. Quoted in Andrew M. Manis, *A Fire You Can't Put Out: The Civil Rights Life of Birmingham's Reverend Fred Shuttlesworth* (Tuscaloosa: University of Alabama Press, 1999), 264.
20. Quoted in Howell Raines, *My Soul Is Rested: Movement Days in the Deep South Remembered* (New York: G. P. Putnam's Sons, 1977), 115.

Black youths marveled, and in some instances were changed, when they saw how both white and black Freedom Riders had been beaten because of their courage and determination to test the Supreme Court's ruling that segregation on interstate bus and train systems was unconstitutional. James Roberson recalled being seventeen years old when the Freedom Riders came to Birmingham. He was at Shuttlesworth's Bethel Baptist Church when the Riders began arriving at the church, some in bloodied condition. They were black and they were white. Southern black youth had not seen whites who had been beaten up by other whites because they protested racial segregation. "White kids and black kids had been beaten," Roberson reflected. "That was the first time I saw human blood being spilled for the cause. I actually saw people hurt and scared. They were holding handkerchiefs to their heads to stop the bleeding. . . . I knew that the police would beat up black people, so that was nothing unusual for me. But white people beating up white folks . . . I did not believe a white would do that to their own kind. . . . To see the inhumane treatment of their own made me realize it was not the color of the skin, but the principle they believed in."[21] Southern black youths learned that although they had experienced and witnessed the racism of southern whites all their lives, not all whites behaved this way, a conclusion shared by Ricky Shuttlesworth, who saw Freedom Rider James Peck bleeding profusely from the severe beating inflicted on him. "Here was a man whose dad had to be rich since he owned the Peck and Peck department store. And he would give up perhaps his life to come and do this for me," said Shuttlesworth. "I had a lot of respect for him."[22]

Indeed, some blacks, for instance, Gwendolyn Patton, remembered being a student when the Freedom Riders came through

---

21. Levine, *Freedom's Children*, 72.
22. Ibid., 72.

Montgomery. When a mass prayer meeting was held a few days later, some of the Riders were present. Patton recalled taking a few of them to her aunt's house. They were all sitting in the living room when her aunt arrived. Clearly angered by the presence of white people in her house, she summoned her niece to the kitchen and made it clear that because of how whites had always treated her—because she could only enter their houses through the back door, and was disrespected and mistreated by them—she did not want them in her house. On reflection, Patton acknowledged that her aunt had a point; that southern whites had done all the things she said, and much worse. The difference, Patton reasoned, was that the white people in her aunt's living room that day were Freedom Riders from the North who had risked their lives for blacks' freedom. "Then I turned around and I said, 'Aunt Chick, these aren't the white people like that [those her aunt found repulsive because of their racism]. This is a different kind of white group."[23] This was a clear instance of black youths instructing black adults on the difference between the racist behavior of numerous white southerners, and the freedom-fighting spirit of many white northerners, who were willing to be beaten and to risk their lives along with blacks for the civil rights and freedom of black people, and ultimately for all U.S. citizens.

In chapter 3, we will see that Fred Shuttlesworth early taught his children the importance of resisting racial injustice, and supplemented their training in nonviolence by sending them to the racially integrated Highlander Folk School in Tennessee. Moreover, Shuttlesworth himself had a long history of protesting racial segregation in Birmingham. His church and home had been bombed, and he had persistently and courageously stood up to the racist police commissioner, Bull Connor, and other city fathers. In addition, it

---

23. Ibid., 76.

was Shuttlesworth who persuaded Martin Luther King and SCLC to come to Birmingham.

". . . Afraid *Not* to Continue the Freedom Ride"

Because of the violent attacks on the Freedom Riders, James Farmer thought it wise to cancel the ride. When word about his decision reached SNCC activist and leader of the Nashville Student Movement, Diane Nash, she and other student activists quickly responded to Farmer in an effort to convince him that under no circumstance should the Freedom Ride be canceled. Nash argued, convincingly, that to cancel the ride because of violence committed against the riders would send the message to every racist group in the country that if you want to stop the Freedom Rides or any other civil rights demonstration, one need only subject the demonstrators to violence of the most brutal kind. The student activists did not argue that CORE riders should continue the ride, however. Rather, they volunteered to put their own lives and bodies on the line. They themselves, a combination of SNCC activists and students in the Nashville Student Movement, would continue the ride from Birmingham to Montgomery, along with John Lewis and another of the original Freedom Riders who chose to remain in Birmingham as the other CORE riders flew on to New Orleans.

At this point, it became very clear that black youths—most especially the Nashville student activists, who were committed to nonviolence—were determined to continue the ride for freedom regardless of the potential violence they might suffer. They put everybody on notice that they were courageous and strong enough to receive the violence done to them without responding violently; that with or without police protection they would persevere; that they were willing to die for freedom, believing with Gandhi, King, and James Lawson that unearned suffering is redemptive when one fights for her freedom and puts her all on the line. Diane Nash later reflected: "I was afraid *not* to continue the Freedom Ride. If the signal was given to the opposition that violence could stop us . . . if we let the Freedom Ride stop then, whenever we tried to do anything in the Movement in the future, we were going to meet with a lot of violence. And we would probably have to get a number of people killed before we could reverse that message."[24]

The Nashville students and SNCC activists decided among themselves who would go to Birmingham to continue the Freedom Ride. It was a dangerous venture, and they had been warned by some of the original riders, as well as traditional civil rights leaders, not to continue the ride. "It's a bloodbath," they were told. "Be assured, someone will be killed if you do come."[25] Aware that it was a life-and-death matter, some of the students who were chosen decided to write out the equivalent of their last will and testament and left them in sealed envelopes with Nash (who was elected by them as coordinator). The envelopes were to be sent to their families should they not make it back alive. Although Nash would stay in touch with officials at the Justice Department, as well as local leaders in each of the cities through which the riders would travel throughout the remainder of the trip, she had been cautioned by James Lawson not to expect federal protection for the riders. Nash and the students had no such expectation, having already decided that they would persevere no matter what.

When the contingent of Riders got to Birmingham, they were arrested and taken to jail. In the middle of the night, around 2:00 in the morning, the Riders were rounded up and forcibly driven to

---

24. Quoted in Powledge, *Free at Last?*, 262.
25. Quoted in Diane Nash, "Inside the Sit-Ins and Freedom Rides," in *The New Negro*, ed. Mathew H. Ahmann (New York: Biblo & Tannen, 1969), 53.

the Tennessee-Alabama state line and dropped off at the side of the road. John Lewis recalled how afraid they were, since they knew no one in that part of Tennessee. Fortunately, they happened upon the home of an elderly black couple, who were initially afraid to let them in, but finally decided to allow them to enter, fed them, and allowed them to call Diane Nash. Although Nash offered to arrange for them to return to Nashville, the students refused, arguing instead that it was necessary that they continue the Ride. This was the beginning of what would be a significant pattern for the student activists. They would not be easily deterred from civil rights projects in which they were involved, and by no means would they let violence stop them. In any case, John Lewis reflected that Nash "sent a car to pick us up, and she informed us that ten other packages had been shipped by other means. She was telling us through a code that ten other Freedom Riders had left by train to join us in Birmingham."[26] Upon arriving in Birmingham they met with Fred Shuttlesworth and student activist Ruby Doris Smith, who had come over from Spelman College to join the ride. Much to the chagrin of her family, Smith, the only non-Nashville student, was able to raise the money from several sources in Atlanta to get to Birmingham to join other Freedom Riders. As the bus was pulling into the station in Montgomery, the riders saw from their windows what appeared to be a ghost town. In her important book, *Freedom's Daughters*, Lynne Olson tells what happened next. "Only when the Riders disembarked did people slip out of alleys and side streets and from around the corners of office buildings. There were hundreds of them, men, women, and children, carrying bats, chains, tire irons, bricks, and pipes. 'Git them niggers!' several women screamed. The crowd fell on the fleeing Riders and the reporters who were there to cover

---

26. Quoted in Hampton and Fayer, *Voices of Freedom*, 84.

them."²⁷ John Lewis and other men tried to help the women from the bus into the cab of a black cabby. Since the law forbade black cabbies to have white passengers, the driver would not admit the two white women riders, Susan Wilbur and Susan Hermann.²⁸ They were left behind as the cabby drove away with the other five female riders. Wilbur was beaten, but luckily she and Hermann managed to flee several thugs who pursued them to a church where they were given sanctuary. The male riders were beaten, as well as reporters on the scene, including John Seigenthaler, who had been sent down as an observer by Attorney General Robert Kennedy of the Justice Department.

King as Freedom Rider?

Not surprisingly, Diane Nash and other student activists invited King to join the Freedom Ride. They believed that because of his high-profile stature, his participation would lead to more media coverage as well as possible intervention by the federal government, should the Riders be attacked. The students did not think about the security implications that joining the Freedom Ride would have for King. By this time in the movement, there was considerable hatred of King among white supremacists in the Deep South. Martin Luther King Sr. (Daddy King) and others close to King were convinced that the Freedom Ride would have been a death sentence for him. Moreover, they had good intelligence that white hate groups planned to attack the Freedom Riders in Alabama. They knew what the youthful activists did not; that were King on one of the buses there would be no way that he could be protected. When the Freedom

---

27. Lynne Olson, *Freedom's Daughters: The Unsung Heroines of the Civil Rights Movement from 1830-1970* (New York: Scribner, 2001), 186.
28. Ibid.

Riders stopped in Atlanta, some of their leaders dined with King and some of his aides, and had conversation for several hours discussing matters of concern regarding the continuation of the Freedom Ride to Alabama and beyond. King reportedly quietly warned *Ebony* reporter Simeon Baker (who was traveling with the Riders) that they had credible information that the Riders might not make it through Alabama alive. The students resolved that they would continue the journey, "that the Freedom Rides should and must continue," although not before they engaged in a workshop on nonviolence in order to freshen up on techniques and to purify themselves, King reported the next day.[29] "King and his people, including King's quite conservative father, knew from their sources in Alabama, which were excellent, that the Klan planned a violent reception for the riders there. If Martin Luther King were aboard the bus, these sources warned, he would be killed."[30] The buses would be attacked, and there was good reason to believe that law enforcement authorities would do nothing to prevent it, and that some of them might even be among the perpetrators. Nor would the FBI intervene in any way, although they were aware of what was going to happen.

At any rate, although the student activists found King's refusal of their invitation to be unacceptable—and this was the first sign of tension and division beginning to occur between them and King—the concerns and apprehension on the part of King and his aides went beyond merely being the copout that the students imagined. The students' stance was a clear indication of generational tension and difference between themselves and SCLC. To some extent, King's decision caused an open wound among some of the student activists, including Diane Nash. The wound would be aggravated over the coming months and next few years as further

---

29. Martin Luther King Jr., "Freedom Rides," May 31, 1961, King Center Library and Archives, 1.
30. David Halberstam, *The Children* (New York: Random House, 1998), 259.

disagreements occurred between King and the students regarding strategy and the growing sense that in many Deep South contexts the students would do the dangerous groundbreaking work in voter registration campaigns, only to have SCLC come in and get all the media attention and the lion's share of financial contributions.

Some student activists undoubtedly wondered just how far King and other civil rights leaders were willing to go for freedom and civil rights. Was there a limit to what they were willing to sacrifice? On the surface this was a reasonable concern. However, it was reasonable only for those who did not know King well enough, and had little understanding of his level of commitment and sense of calling regarding his civil rights ministry. Long before the sit-ins and the Freedom Rides began, Martin Luther King had decided that the struggle for civil rights and freedom was worth dying for.

King's Encouragement and Praise for Student Activists

Even before the sit-ins and Freedom Rides, Martin Luther King was generous in his praise for young people for their participation in the struggle for freedom and civil rights. King delivered an address at the Youth March for Integrated Schools on April 18, 1959, in which he described the thousands of black and white youths present as *"the generation of integration."*[31] He applauded the fact that by virtue of their presence, young people were saying that they refused to take "No" for an answer to the problem of desegregation and integration. King told the youths that in their determination to organize and demonstrate for desegregated schools they had "awakened on hundreds of campuses throughout the land a new spirit of social inquiry to the benefit of all Americans." For those who were high

---

31. *The Papers*, 5:187 (my emphasis).

school seniors, he admonished: "Whatever career you may choose for yourself—doctor, lawyer, teacher—let me propose an avocation to be pursued along with it. *Become a dedicated fighter for civil rights*. Make it a central part of your life. . . . Make a career of humanity. Commit yourself to the noble struggle for equal rights."[32]

When on February 16, 1960, Martin Luther King addressed youths in Greensboro who started the sit-in movement at the local Woolworth store, he told them that many young people were involved in the leadership of freedom movements in Afrikan and Asian countries. Encouraged by this phenomenon, King told the students: "*What is fresh, what is new in your fight is the fact that it was initiated, fed and sustained by students*. What is new is that American students have come of age. You now take your honored places in the world-wide struggle for freedom."[33] King saw the sit-ins as part of the transition from the slow litigation process to direct-action methods sparked by the Montgomery bus boycott. To those who wondered why the student activists began sitting in at segregated lunch counters, King called their attention to the indignities and injustices that blacks faced when they had spent their money in other places in a business and were then denied the right to sit down and comfortably eat a meal purchased at the lunch counter of that same business. "Almost every Negro has experienced the tragic inconveniences of lunch counter segregation," said King. "He cannot understand why he is welcomed with open arms at most counters in the store, but is denied service at a certain counter because it happens to be selling food and drink. In a real sense the 'sit-ins' represent more than a demand for service; they represent a demand for respect."[34]

---

32. Ibid., 5:188 (my emphasis).
33. Ibid., 5:368 (my emphasis).
34. Ibid., 5:449.

Not as patient as their parents and many other black adults, King observed, the students began to take matters into their own hands. Many seemed to know instinctively that if they were to regain their sense of humanity and dignity, they would have to find ways to resist discriminatory treatment. In "The Negro and the American Dream," an address given at the Annual Freedom Mass Meeting of the North Carolina State Conference of Branches of the NAACP on September 25, 1960, King had even more praise for black students throughout the South who, by virtue of sitting-in, standing-in, and praying-in, challenged the powers that be and institutional racism and discrimination. By sitting-in, the students were in no sense being passive. Rather, by sitting-in, they were actually demonstrating for their freedom and the freedom of their people. They were, in effect, sitting-in for freedom. King told the attendees:

> These young students have taken the deep groans and the passionate yearnings of the Negro people and filtered them in their own souls and fashioned them in a creative protest which is an epic known all over the nation. For the last few months they have moved in a uniquely meaningful orbit imparting light and heat to distant satellites. Through their nonviolent direct action they have been able to open hundreds of formerly segregated lunch counters in almost eighty cities. It is no overstatement to characterize these events as historic. Never before in the United States has so large a body of students spread a struggle over so great an area in pursuit of a goal of human dignity and freedom. I am convinced that future historians will have to record this student movement as one of the greatest epics of our heritage.[35]

Elsewhere King said in a similar vein: "These students are not struggling for themselves alone. They are seeking to save the soul of America. . . . In sitting down at lunch counters, they are in reality standing up for the best in the American dream."[36] King

---

35. Ibid., 5:511.
36. Quoted in Sanford Wexler, *An Eyewitness History of the Civil Rights Movement* (New York: Checkmark Books, 1999), 135.

saw the sit-ins as a sound means of dramatizing the indignities and injustices suffered and endured by blacks. In addition, the sit-ins (no less than the Freedom Rides) gave lie to the notion that blacks were not opposed to segregation; that they welcomed segregated living. The sit-ins dramatized the "mass demonstration of the dissatisfaction of the Negro with the whole system of segregation."[37] King was convinced that the most "striking quality" in the student activists was the determination as well as "the intensity and depth of their commitment."[38] Sadly, we have not seen the likes of such a sustained spirit among youths in the United States since that exciting period in the 1960s.

Martin Luther King was almost constantly encouraging and cheering young people for their efforts to obtain equal rights, whether they were sitting-in or otherwise engaging in nonviolent civil disobedience. When students at Florida A&M University engaged in demonstrations and classroom boycotts after one of their own was abducted and raped by four white men while on a date, King sent them a telegram in which he cheered and applauded them for their "courageous, dignified and effective demonstration, protesting the mass rape of your schoolmate and warning against 'double standards of justice.'"[39] He praised the students for their nonviolent approach, as he cheered Alabama State College student Rebecca Dixon for her role in the March 8, 1960 civil rights protest that got her and thirty-six others arrested. He commended her for the courage that she and her fellow students exhibited by protesting injustice, and vowed to provide "absolute support in these difficult hours."[40]

---

37. *The Papers*, 5:434.
38. Martin Luther King Jr., "The Time for Freedom Has Come," in *A Testament of Hope: The Essential Writings of Martin Luther King, Jr.,* ed. James M. Washington (New York: Harper & Row, 1986), 161.
39. *The Papers*, 5:196.

Indeed, when Durham, North Carolina minister and SCLC board member Douglas Moore, a classmate of King's at Boston University, member of the Dialectical Society (of which King was a founding member), telephoned King and invited him to address the students involved in the lunch-counter sit-ins, he did so two weeks after the first sit-in. King told the students that they "have taken the undying and passionate yearning for freedom and filtered it in your own soul and fashioned it into a creative protest that is destined to be one of the glowing epics of our time. . . . You have taken hold of the tradition of resolute non-violent resistance and you are carrying it forward toward the end of bringing all of us closer to the day of full freedom."[41] He told them how deeply he himself had been impressed and encouraged by the participation and leadership of young people in human rights struggles as he traveled in Afrika and Asia. What was new and different was that oppressed youths in the United States had awakened. Their actions were a "deathblow" to the outmoded view voiced by many racist whites that blacks preferred segregation to integration. But their actions were also a response to the criticism of those black adults who believed that the firing line was no place for young people. In addition, by their actions, the youthful activists themselves made it clear that they were not buying the truncated notion that separate facilities in public accommodations and education were somehow equal. King urged all people of goodwill to support the efforts of the students, and reminded all who were present that any impending victory would be not for blacks only, but for all people. The fight was not against white people as such, but against injustice, oppression, and the absence of freedom and democracy.

40. Ibid., 5:388.
41. Ibid., 5:368.

In the spirit of his Christian faith and of Mahatma Gandhi, King reminded the students that they were in for a season of suffering, and that suffering was a necessity for what they were fighting for. He did not mean that suffering as such was a virtue. He was not so naïve. And yet, many have frequently and wrongly interpreted him to mean that suffering is a virtue. King's point, however, was that in the struggle for freedom and justice suffering must be *made* to be a virtue, and one does this by how she responds to the suffering. She must *choose* to make suffering caused by injustice a virtue by aggressively resisting it. Challenging, protesting, and trying to eradicate suffering through determined nonviolent direct action is what makes unearned suffering redemptive. *That* was King's point. The students were already suffering prior to their nonviolent direct-action protests. There is nothing redemptive about suffering that one does not protest and fight against with all her might. The suffering takes on a redemptive quality only when the youthful activists decide to take steps to liberate themselves from it. Only in that sense, can suffering be deemed redemptive in Kingian ethics. King challenged the students to be fearless about going to jail, and in fact urged, like Gandhi, that they fill up the jails.[42] "Maybe it will take this willingness to stay in jail," he said, "to arouse the dozing conscience of our nation."[43] King clearly had not forgotten the message from Nashville youths that he remain in jail, after being arrested for his involvement in the sit-in at Rich's Department Store in Atlanta.

Martin Luther King knew that by sitting-in, the students were really standing up, and saying and demonstrating with their bodies that they wanted white business establishments to respect them as human beings as much as they respected their dollars.[44] He reminded

---

42. See M. K. Gandhi, *Satyagraha in South Africa*, ed. Shriman Narayan (Ahmedabad: Navajivan Press, 1928), 3:206–7.
43. *The Papers*, 5:369.

the students that the sit-ins and other protests they were engaged in were among the most creative and significant efforts in the entire civil rights movement.[45] Their contributions were second to none, and in many instances the youths were actually showing others the way.

In a statement to the press at the beginning of the youth meeting at Shaw University that led to the formation of SNCC, King suggested five things that the students needed as they gave serious attention to mapping out a plan for the future and for how they would operate throughout the country:

- Set up a permanent organization.
- Call for a nationwide campaign of "selective buying."
- Train a contingent of volunteers who will go to jail with the determination to reject bail until their demands are met.
- Take the freedom struggle into every community in the south.
- Develop a deeper understanding of nonviolence, both as a strategy and a philosophy of life.[46]

The last point was taken seriously by the founders of SNCC, mostly southern black youths with deep religious convictions, and respect for the church and for their elders, but it became increasingly less important to the group as more and more northern student activists joined. Many of the latter lacked religious conviction and the deep respect for the church that was so important to many southern black student activists.

In any event, King knew without question that with the emergence of SNCC something novel and rather phenomenal was

---

44. Ibid., 5:393.
45. Ibid., 5:415.
46. Ibid., 5:427.

taking place in the movement, and that it was generated not by what he sometimes characterized as the "oldsters," but by youths who were fed up, fearless, and determined to usher in a new day. Some weeks later, King characterized theirs as "an electrifying movement of Negro students" that "has shattered the placid surface of campuses and communities across the South."[47] What they were learning from their protest involvements went well beyond what they were learning from textbooks in school. Many had in fact already been expelled, fined, jailed, and were subjected to other forms of violence. Putting the best spin possible on this, King said: "But with the punishments, something more is growing. A generation of young people has come out of decades of shadows to face direct struggle for its own liberation. These young people have connected up with their own history—the slave revolts, the incomplete revolution of the Civil War, the brotherhood of colonial colored men in Africa and Asia. They are an integral part of the history which is reshaping the world, replacing a dying order with modern democracy."[48]

As noted before, within just a few days after the Greensboro sit-in, black students found allies in some white university students. Among the very first of these were white women students from Bennett College and Woman's College in Greensboro.[49] King was not unaware of the involvement and commitment of growing numbers of white students in the sit-ins and other civil rights demonstrations. In a number of speeches, he commented about the importance of their involvement.[50] Moreover, he received many letters from white college students expressing their support for what he and others were accomplishing in the struggle.[51] Such efforts

47. Ibid., 5:447.
48. Ibid., 5:450.
49. Wolff, *Lunch at the 5 & 10*, 43, 127.
50. *The Papers*, 5:450, 483, 557.

by white students—mostly from the North—made it impossible to categorize all whites as racist bigots.

Not infrequently, King found himself in the position of having to defend the student activists and their methods. Former President Harry S. Truman was one of many white Americans who were at best misinformed about the students' motives and goals. For example, Truman told a news conference on April 18, 1960 that the student sit-ins were instigated by Communists. He later said: "If anyone came into my store and tried to stop business I'd throw him out. The Negro should behave himself and show he's a good citizen. Common sense and good will can solve this whole thing."[52] When this came to King's attention he wrote the former president the next day. He told Truman that what he said about the sit-ins revealed "a limited grasp and an abysmal lack of understanding of what is taking place. It is a sad day for our country when men come to feel that oppressed people cannot desire freedom and human dignity unless they are motivated by Communism."[53] He expressed his disappointment that Mr. Truman was not able to see that the students were not merely concerned about their own well-being, but were interested in saving the soul of the nation. King challenged the former president to produce public proof that the sit-ins were Communist inspired, and that if he could not do so, he owed the nation in general, and black people especially, a public apology. At this writing, the King Papers Project has not located a response from Truman.

In his debate with James Kilpatrick on "The Nation's Future" on a live nationally televised show, King once again found himself

---

51. Ibid., 5:526, 533. Indeed, as early as 1956, King received a letter from four white student activists who invited his endorsement of the "Enroll for Freedom" campaign that sought student and youth involvement in the civil rights struggle. The King Papers Project has not yet located any response King might have given, but it is likely that he responded (see *The Papers* [1997], 3:439).
52. Quoted in ibid., 5:437.
53. Ibid., 5:438.

defending the student sit-ins, saying that it was a movement seeking moral ends by moral means. While SNCC members who watched the debate were disappointed in how King responded to some of the questions, he told the segregationist Kilpatrick that the students "respect law so much that they want to see all laws just and in line with the moral law of the universe. They're willing to suffer and sacrifice in order to square . . . customs and local laws with the moral law of the universe."[54] Indeed, Diane Nash asserted that the students had chosen nonviolent direct action, which she distinguished from "passive resistance," as their means of fighting for freedom. Furthermore, she said: "We have decided that if there is to be suffering in this revolution . . . , we will take the suffering upon ourselves and never inflict it upon our fellow man, because we respect him and recognize the God within him."[55] This idea of willingly taking suffering upon one's self, rather than inflicting it on one's opponent, is a Gandhian idea that was adopted by King, as well as James Lawson and his young Nashville protégés.

Referring to the "thousands of courageous students electrifying the nation by quietly and non-violently sitting at lunch counters that have been closed to them because of the color of their skin . . . ,"[56] King unquestionably had deep admiration for their courage, determination, and commitment. It has been estimated that by the end of 1961 more than 70,000 black and white students had engaged in sit-ins, kneel-ins, pray-ins, and wade-ins in about fifty cities throughout the South.[57]

---

54. Ibid., 5:558.
55. Nash, "Inside the Sit-Ins and Freedom Rides," in *The New Negro*, 59.
56. *The Papers*, 5:501.
57. Arvarh E., Strickland, "Student Nonviolent Coordinating Committee," in *Encyclopedia of African-American Civil Rights*, ed. Charles D. Lowery and John F. Marszalek (Westport, CT: Greenwood, 1992), 506.

Martin Luther King's persistent and genuine support and encouragement of youths' involvement in the movement said a great deal about who he was as a person as well as his sense that because injustice goes against the grain of the universe and affects everybody, all members of the community, including and especially young people, have a stake in working to eradicate it. King undoubtedly saw that this must be a communal effort, with contributions coming from all segments of the community. Moreover, his strength of character and his integrity were such that he had no need to be perceived as the sole leader of the movement, nor the most significant one. The media and some of King's aides frequently portrayed him this way, at times even ignoring and alienating local leadership by doing so, but we have seen that King himself consistently rejected the idea that it was he who started campaigns such as the Montgomery bus boycott and the sit-ins. From the beginning, he acknowledged the leadership and contributions of local leaders, as well as youth.

The fact that Martin Luther King so frequently and willingly praised and applauded black youths for their contributions to the movement probably served in a way to both lessen and blunt—even mute—criticisms he might otherwise have received from the public for his decision not to join the Freedom Rides. In addition, the sheer power of King's oratory and dedication continued to inspire civil rights activists across the nation.

King not only praised black youth as a group for their contributions to the movement, but was also known to write character letters for individuals among them. On April 9, 1962, he wrote just such a letter praising Diane Nash Bevel, saying:

> When the original Freedom Ride bogged down in Birmingham, Alabama after the Mother's Day massacre, it was Mrs. Bevel who organized the continued ride that led to the ultimate nationwide support of the Freedom Ride and its concentration at Jackson, Mississippi. Mrs.

> Bevel was present during most of the mob violence that followed the attack on the Rev. Abernathy's First Baptist Church in Montgomery. Her courage and demeanor in such trying circumstances betrayed a maturity far beyond her years.
>
> Mrs. Bevel returned to Nashville and worked there as Coordinator for the Freedom Ride through Nashville and convenor of the Freedom Ride Coordinating Committee. When the necessity of Freedom Rides abated, Mrs. Bevel transferred her energies to Mississippi and voter registration work in the heart of the Delta.[58]

In addition to his praise for and encouragement of young people's civil rights efforts and his willingness to write letters of reference for some of them, King was not opposed to requesting monetary resources from potential donors to support student leaders. He did this for Atlanta student leader Lonnie King (no relation) in late September 1960, for example. The student had gotten behind in his bills, and creditors were calling for full payment. It was determined that the creditors took this tack because young King was known to be one of the leaders of student protests throughout the Atlanta area.[59] Knowing this to be the case, Martin Luther King sought financial donors to assist the youth, which also enabled him to continue in his leadership role.

Lessons of the Sit-Ins and Freedom Rides

The Montgomery bus boycott was essentially planned and led by black adults. We have seen that although the role of black youth was not merely incidental during that period, it was evident that they took their lead from their elders. By 1960 this would change. Black youth would take the initiative and enter the civil rights struggle

---

58. King, letter to Mr. Basil A. Paterson in behalf of Diane Nash Bevel, King Library and Archives, April 9, 1962, 1–2.
59. *The Papers*, 5:512.

on their own terms. Nowhere was this more evident than in the Greensboro sit-in, and in SNCC activists' decision to continue the Freedom Ride from Birmingham to New Orleans. Indeed, going forward, a number of important lessons may be taken from the youthful sit-in movement and the Freedom Rides.

One of the most important lessons—a carryover from the Montgomery bus protest—was that there is more than one way to resist racial discrimination. Historically, the primary method of protest had been the litigation approach of the NAACP. Although fairly effective, it was also a very slow process. One could surely find isolated instances of direct action, but prior to the Montgomery bus boycott one was hard pressed to find examples of *sustained* mass direct-action campaigns implemented by blacks. The more than yearlong bus boycott put everybody on notice that while also retaining the NAACP's method of fighting for civil rights through the courts, blacks would also engage in direct-action methods, and would be open to other approaches as well. Engaging in simultaneous methods of social change only enhanced the possibility of success. From the beginning, Martin Luther King was open to multiple approaches, although nonviolent direct action was the preferred one for him. The sit-ins and Freedom Rides were further examples of the direct-action approach, which, in the minds of student activists, was here to stay as long as blacks were denied their civil rights.

Another lesson learned from the sit-in movement and the Freedom Rides is that they were evidence that black youths and their white allies not only had something positive to contribute to the struggle for civil rights and freedom, but were more than capable of implementing and carrying out their own plans. No longer did they feel the need to defer to their elders. They might need to periodically confer with these and traditional civil rights organizations in an advisory way, but they were confident in their own abilities to carry out their projects. They were determined and fearless. As noted before, when youths entered the struggle through the sit-ins and Freedom Rides, the rules of engagement, as well as the timetables, changed. There was more of a sense of urgency among the youthful activists, such that they made it clear that they were not willing to wait interminably for whites to make up their minds and for change to come. The unmistakable, unequivocal message of black youths was that they wanted their freedom, and they wanted it *now*. They had neither the fear nor the patience of many of their elders. Young people presented their own agenda, and saw no need to seek the permission of either their elders, or white sympathizers. Indeed, as King himself frequently observed, the courage and energy of the youthful activists served also to energize many of those who had been on the battlefield for a long time and were perhaps weighed down by battle fatigue and a discouraging sense that they would not see the changes in their lifetime.

Fred Powledge offers a helpful comment about how the sit-in movement marked a shift in the civil rights movement, in addition to being quite different from the Freedom Rides. "The sit-ins incorporated the experiences of the Montgomery bus boycott and moved the effort a significant step forward—from depending on arguments in the courtroom to throwing down a moral gauntlet before the perpetrators of segregation, and doing so with the rest of the world looking on. The sit-ins were the essence of passive nonviolence; all the demonstrators had to do was walk into a place of public accommodation and sit down, and the system did the rest."[60] Martin Luther King saw that when those young people sat down at segregated lunch counters they were not being passive at all. Instead, by sitting down they were in fact standing up for their humanity,

---

60. Powledge, *Free at Last?*, 287.

dignity, and freedom. In this sense there was nothing passive about their sit-in action.

Although the Freedom Rides also marked a significant change in the movement, not least establishing black youth as much more aggressive than their elders, they were different from the sit-ins. The Freedom Rides "dealt with a question of law, and they dealt with the moral question of public accommodations, but in a much more aggressive manner. The demonstrators compelled their tormenters to pay attention to their demands. They rode into a community—'invaded' was the term the segregationists used, and it was not all that far off the mark—and, striding past the signs and symbols that the community had long erected to separate the races, they insisted on their rights."[61] What might have been most unsettling for white segregationists is that the Freedom Riders were fully aware that they would meet with the violence of terrorists, but they continued on their Rides for freedom anyway, in sheer defiance. The Freedom Riders refused to be incapacitated by attempts to intimidate them. I would say that the racist segregationists on the Freedom Ride routes in Alabama towns such as Anniston, Birmingham, and Montgomery, as well as Jackson, Mississippi, were infuriated by the determination and courage of the riders, who knew what to expect but kept coming anyway, and actually resisted and humiliated them by refusing to return violence for violence. In a strange sort of way, this might have contributed to the utter viciousness of the segregationists' attacks on the Freedom Riders. This brings to mind something that King wrote in *Stride Toward Freedom*, while reflecting on the Gandhian influence on his philosophy and practice of nonviolence.

---

61. Ibid.

> Men are not easily moved from their mental ruts, their prejudiced and irrational feelings. When the underprivileged demand freedom, the privileged first react with bitterness and resistance. Even when the demands are couched in nonviolent terms, the initial response is the same. Nehru once remarked that the British were never so angry as when the Indians resisted them with nonviolence, that he never saw eyes so full of hate as those of the British troops to whom he turned the other cheek when they beat him with lathis. But nonviolent resistance at least changed the minds and hearts of the Indians, however impervious the British may have appeared.[62]

Similarly, it might be that the racist segregationists on the Freedom Ride trail responded so viciously toward the Riders precisely because they did not strike back, but essentially welcomed their blows. Subconsciously, the attackers were thrown completely off balance morally, which, in the moment, caused them to blame the Riders themselves for the beating to which they were subjected. This is part of the dynamic of what King, influenced by Richard Gregg, called "moral jiu-jitsu." What is most important here is the observation made by Raymond Arsenault that at least "for a time the Freedom Riders' victory over fear and violence became an object lesson in itself."[63] Indeed, by any measurement it was no small matter that the Riders continued on their journey, even when they received intelligence reports that they would be savagely beaten.

Although the Freedom Rides served to radicalize the movement, establishing black youth as its most aggressive proponents, they quite unexpectedly did other things that were important contributions to the movement in the coming days. For example, intentionally or not, black youth accomplished a feat that would prove to be of inestimable value as the struggle continued. Their efforts exposed the hypocrisy of Deep South elected officials, as well as the depth of

---

62. Martin Luther King Jr., *Stride Toward Freedom* (New York: Harper & Row, 1958), 218–19.
63. Arsenault, *Freedom Riders*, 514.

racism in local police departments, courts, white churches, and the federal government. Second, in addition to putting traditional civil rights leaders on notice, the Rides also put white liberal and moderate allies on notice, as well as exposing their moral weakness and level of commitment to the struggle for justice and civil rights. The Freedom Rides forced white allies to show their hand; to show just how far they were willing to go before urging blacks to pull back or to adopt the gradualist approach of the likes of Nobel Prize–winning author, William Faulkner. Martin Luther King observed that writing in *Life* magazine in 1956, Faulkner "urged the NAACP to 'stop now for a moment.' That is to say, he encouraged Negroes to accept injustice, exploitation and indignity for a while longer."[64] King was rightly troubled and angered by this advice, believing that from a moral standpoint any oppressed group had a greater right to resist oppression than oppressors had to oppress them. In any event, black youths of the sit-in and Freedom Ride era were having none of this Faulknerian advice. Consequently, their efforts forced white liberals and moderates to reveal that while many of them were supportive of civil rights for blacks in theory, they had no more sense of urgency about this actually occurring than diehard racists. Nor were they interested in blacks obtaining full civil rights and equality. Indeed, after the Riders were attacked in Montgomery, attorney general Robert Kennedy urged King, James Farmer, and other civil rights leaders to stop the Freedom Ride until tempers cooled down and the administration could try to come up with a solution. Even liberal and moderate federal authorities clearly had no sense of urgency that blacks receive civil rights.

Although it was actually the students' decision and insistence on continuing the Freedom Ride that had forced the federal government

---

64. Martin Luther King Jr., "Our Struggle," in *A Testament of Hope*, 80.

to intervene in the first place, neither Diane Nash nor other student leaders were invited to participate in conversations with the attorney general to determine the viability of continuing the Rides. This gave the appearance of King and the elders acting as if they had been the cause of the Freedom Ride continuing. The media and the Kennedy administration seemed to be in agreement with this perception, which only served to widen the rift between King and some of the student activists. Robert Kennedy claimed to be shaken by the violence, but during this period it was known that he and President John F. Kennedy were actually more concerned about the nation's international image than the violence being done to the Freedom Riders. They knew that by this time people all over the world knew about the fate of the Freedom Riders. Robert Kennedy even wondered out loud whether the Freedom Ride had already made its point after the violence outside Anniston, and thus did not need to proceed to Jackson, Mississippi, and on to its final destination in New Orleans. King reportedly was inclined to agree with Kennedy, which is rather interesting, considering his reaction to Faulkner's call for a cooling-off period in 1956. When Diane Nash got wind of how King was leaning, she made her position and that of her youthful peers unequivocally clear when she said that "[w]e can't stop it now, right after we've been clobbered,"[65] a stance that would be echoed by Freedom Riders James Zwerg and John Lewis who both later sustained brutal beatings at the Montgomery bus terminal. The Rides would not be stopped by violence. That was the motto of the youthful activists; no amount of violence would stop their forward march to freedom. The Freedom Ride would, and did, continue on to Jackson.

---

65. Quoted in Olson, *Freedom's Daughters*, 188.

Freedom Ride scholar Raymond Arsenault is convinced that one of the lasting contributions of the Freedom Riders was the creation of "a new context for social activism. . . ."[66] The Freedom Riders did not usher in King's beloved community, but "they, more than any other activists of their day, foreshadowed the grassroots 'rights revolution' that would transform American citizenship over the next four decades." Arsenault went on to say:

> The rising movement for women's rights, military withdrawal from Southeast Asia, environmental reform, gay and lesbian rights, and the rights of the disabled all built upon the foundation of legitimacy and success established by Freedom Riders and other nonviolent activists in the early 1960s. By demonstrating the power of personal commitment and sacrifice in a new and dramatic way, the Freedom Riders countered traditional assumptions of institutional authority and top-down politics, pushing American democracy to what the journalist Malcolm Gladwell has called a "tipping point," and beyond.[67]

The Freedom Rides also inspired freedom movements in South Afrika, Australia, and other parts of the world. This was a kind of internationalization of the Freedom Rides. The impact of the Rides in the United States had significant consequences as well. "The most important and lasting consequence—the one that confirmed the Rides' status as a pivotal moment in American history—was a revolutionary change in the character of citizen politics. In the course of six months, the nation's first mobile nonviolent army expanded the realm of the possible in American political and social insurgency, redefining the limits of dissent and setting the stage for the escalating demands and rising expectations of the mid- and late 1960s."[68]

One of the most frequently overlooked lessons of the sit-in movement and the Freedom Rides is that they were led and

---

66. Arsenault, *Freedom Riders*, 512.
67. Ibid.
68. Ibid., 511–12.

courageously carried out by black youths. The late activist-historian Howard Zinn, reflecting on youth contributions to the movement, put it very well indeed when he said that "for the first time in our history, a major social movement, shaking the nation to its bone, is being led by youngsters."[69] It was no small matter that these "youngsters" were black. They had come of age almost unexpectedly, discovering virtually on their own, that they, like all other human beings, were made for freedom, and that something so precious as their freedom could not be left solely in the hands of others. Rather, they recognized that they were moral agents, and had to use what freedom they had in order to achieve their full freedom as autonomous beings created in God's image.

Martin Luther King's and SCLC's first major *planned* campaign utilizing children and youths in nonviolent demonstrations would occur approximately three years after the sit-ins started. At the time, Birmingham, Alabama was one of the most dangerous, racist, and segregated cities in the nation. For the first time in a King-led demonstration, we see black children and young people rescuing an enervated campaign against segregation. Indeed, we even see the children leading the way. The next chapter examines the role and contributions of black children and youth in the Birmingham campaign under the guidance of King and SCLC.

---

69. Quoted in ibid., 88. From Howard Zinn, *SNCC: The New Abolitionists* (Boston: Beacon, 1965), 34–35.

3

Birmingham and the Children's Crusade

Because he believed Birmingham, Alabama to be "a symbol of segregation for the entire South," Martin Luther King was adamant that if they could crack that city they could crack the South,[1] a point, we will see, that could also be made about the Mississippi Delta. The churches and homes of so many blacks in Birmingham, Alabama were bombed by white racists by the early 1960s that the city was given the nickname "Bombingham,"[2] the bombing capital of the United States. One black neighborhood was bombed so frequently that it was known as "Dynamite Hill."[3] Racism in Birmingham was often blatant and lethal. Incredibly, there was even a law against black and white children playing together.[4] Police Commissioner

---

1. Quoted in Sanford Wexler, *An Eyewitness History of the Civil Rights Movement* (New York: Checkmark Books, 1999), 172.
2. See Glenn T. Eskew's informative chapter, "Bombingham," in his *But for Birmingham: The Local and National Movements in the Civil Rights Struggle* (Chapel Hill/London: University of North Carolina Press, 1997), ch. 2.
3. Eskew, *But for Birmingham*, 68.
4. Charles E. Cobb Jr., *On the Road to Freedom: A Guided Tour of the Civil Rights Trail* (Chapel Hill: Algonquin Books, 2008), 249.

Theophilus Eugene "Bull" Connor, aptly described as "a lightning rod of racist wrong,"[5] brought all of the city's resources to bear in efforts to uphold the state's segregation code. For Connor, there could be no exception to this—a stance, ironically, that would later prove to be most beneficial to Martin Luther King and SCLC. Moreover, it was the Birmingham campaign that moved civil rights to the top of President John F. Kennedy's political agenda,[6] catapulted King to the forefront of the national civil rights leadership,[7] and helped to get the Civil Rights Bill of 1964 passed—a bill that King would later describe as weaker than the one passed in 1875, and neither was fully enforced.[8]

However, none of this should be taken to mean that King at any point became "the movement." King never thought of himself that way; never believed that he was the *only* major contributor and leader of the civil rights movement. In Montgomery, he said on a number of occasions that one person did not start the struggle and one person could not stop it.[9] King was always aware that there were many players in the movement—nationally and locally—who were making substantial contributions, and without whom the movement would stall out permanently. In this regard, he was unselfish; gracious; realistic. The problems adversely affecting his people were too great, complex, and varied. No one person or institution could do all that needed to be done. No one understood this better than Martin Luther King.

---

5. Ibid., 251.
6. Jonathan Rosenberg and Zachary Karabell, *Kennedy, Johnson, and the Quest for Justice: The Civil Rights Tapes* (New York/London: W. W. Norton, 2003), 105, 113.
7. Ibid., 94–95.
8. Martin Luther King Jr., "Transforming a Neighborhood into a Brotherhood," Speech to National Association of Radio Announcers in Atlanta, August 11, 1967, King Library and Archives, 9–10.
9. Clayborne Carson et al., eds., *The Papers of Martin Luther King, Jr.* (Berkeley: University of California Press, 2005, 1997), 5:342, 3:114.

The Rev. Fred Shuttlesworth, a member of the executive board of SCLC and pastor of Bethel Baptist Church in Birmingham, had organized and led civil rights demonstrations during the 1950s and concurrent with the Montgomery bus boycott. Shuttlesworth was able to garner only minimal participation and support from Birmingham's black citizens when he protested racial discrimination and led demonstrations, but he remained fearless and undaunted. It was through his persistence, determination, and persuasiveness that King and SCLC decided to use Birmingham as a test case for nonviolence. Two of the four major goals were the desegregation of lunch counters and other public facilities, and hiring blacks on a nondiscriminatory basis. Could a sustained nonviolent direct-action campaign break the back of racial discrimination? By all accounts the experiment with nonviolence had gone wrong on many levels in the shortlived Albany, Georgia campaign in 1961. After Albany, King was desperate to prove that the problem was not nonviolence, but inadequate planning, insufficient information about the local area, and attempting to do too much, rather than focus on one or two major objectives.

Fred Shuttlesworth, along with several other pastors—Nelson H. Smith Jr., G. E. Pruitt, T. L. Lane, Edward Gardner, Herman Stone, C. H. George, and Lucinda B. Robey (a layperson)[10]—founded the Alabama Christian Movement for Human Rights (ACMHR) after the NAACP was banned by Alabama state authorities in 1956, about six months after the bus boycott began in Montgomery. The goal of the ACMHR was to press for the desegregation of all city facilities, by breaking and challenging segregation ordinances through a combination of legal test cases in court and direct-action protest marches. The response of white segregationists was, not surprisingly,

---

10. Andrew M. Manis, *A Fire You Can't Put Out: The Civil Rights Life of Birmingham's Reverend Fred Shuttlesworth* (Tuscaloosa: University of Alabama Press, 1999), 95.

brutally violent. Shuttlesworth was severely beaten several times, his house was bombed on Christmas day in 1956, and his church was bombed multiple times. After the Christmas-day bombing he led fifty marchers downtown the very next day, where they boarded city buses to test the Supreme Court's ruling in the Montgomery bus boycott case that segregation on city buses throughout the state was a violation of the Fourteenth Amendment. Shuttlesworth and more than twenty others were later arrested. Bull Connor and his white-supremacist henchmen were implicated in the church bombings, but not surprisingly, none of them were ever arrested and prosecuted.[11] When Shuttlesworth was agitating for school desegregation in Birmingham in 1959 (nearly five years after the landmark Supreme Court decision in *Brown v. Board of Education*) Bull Connor, in a newspaper story, urged upstanding blacks to ignore his efforts. Not surprisingly, he accused Shuttlesworth of communist leanings and of seeking selfish ends.[12] This was a frequent accusation by southern racists whenever blacks mounted protests against racial discrimination and injustice. Many Deep South whites did not believe that, like themselves, blacks possessed an inherent sense of wanting to be free and treated justly. Instead, such whites conveniently believed that blacks were satisfied with their station in society, and that whenever they began pressing for freedom it was because of communist affiliations and/or outside agitation. As far back as the Montgomery bus boycott, literary artist-activist Lillian Smith had written King to say just how "irrational" the white South was about so-called "outsiders" interfering in its handling of its affairs. She thus advised him to seek their advice—quietly—but not to invite the actual participation of outsiders.[13] Indeed, we will see that even

11. Ibid., 168–73.
12. Ibid., 226.
13. *The Papers* (1997), 3:170.

King and SCLC were accused of being outsiders by eight white Birmingham clergymen.

Many black youths in Birmingham, including Shuttlesworth's children, Patricia Anne, Ruby Fredericka, and Fred Lee Jr., were avid participants in the pre-SCLC civil rights campaign in that city. Shuttlesworth even sent his children to the famous Highlander Folk School in Monteagle, Tennessee under the leadership of Myles Horton[14] to give them the opportunity to interact with other black, white, Latina/o, and Native American youths, and also to learn the basic principles of nonviolence. To a large extent, the purpose was for participating youths to experience the humanity and dignity of young people of other races and to discover firsthand that in the most fundamental sense all people are more alike than unalike, as literary artist-activist Maya Angelou reminds us.[15] Years later, Fred Jr. expressed this very point when he reflected on the Highlander experience, saying: "Your whole purpose was to get to know each other . . . to sing songs that make you come out of yourself. Go out and play ball and be yourself. . . . What impressed me was that they [whites] was all just like me."[16] Young people of different racial-ethnic backgrounds had the opportunity to see that in the most basic sense they were all human beings who possessed absolute dignity. As such, they should be willing to protest any policies and practices that undermine their sense of humanity and worth, or that of other human beings.

Not long after the experience at Highlander, the senior Shuttlesworth began training a group of ACMHR youths in the

---

14. Myles Horton was a student of theological social ethicist, Reinhold Niebuhr. See Elisabeth (Niebuhr) Sifton, *The Serenity Prayer: Faith and Politics in Times of Peace and War* (New York: W. W. Norton, 2003), 142.
15. See Maya Angelou, *Wouldn't Take Nothing for My Journey Now* (New York: Random House, 1993), 124.
16. Quoted in Manis, *A Fire You Can't Put Out*, 240.

techniques of nonviolent direct action.[17] "This extension of the civil rights movement to children," according to Shuttlesworth's biographer, "would come to fruition in the later demonstrations of 1963."[18] Although this is a story that begs for further exploration and attention, the focus here is on the involvement of Birmingham's black youths in the movement *after* Shuttlesworth successfully lobbied King and SCLC to lead nonviolent demonstrations in that city.

Martin Luther King committed to going to Birmingham in January 1963. The Birmingham campaign was named Project C (Confrontation), and was launched on April 3, with Miles College students staging sit-ins at five department stores. Unlike the president of their school, Lucius Pitts, the students—inspired by the earlier sit-ins in Greensboro, North Carolina and many other parts of the country—were committed to direct action. Once Project C got under way there were regular marches to city hall, as well as meetings with black community leaders to continue the hard work of enlisting the support of black businessmen and pastors. This was difficult work, since many among the black business, religious, and civic leaders were of the conservative traditional leader class, and considered King and SCLC to be "outsiders" coming in to stir things up. This was one of few points on which many blacks in Birmingham were in mutual agreement with white racists. We saw previously that writer-activist Lillian Smith had written King to discourage him from inviting "outsiders" to actually participate in the Montgomery campaign, but to solicit advice and ideas only. During that same period, King received similar advice from Charles R. Lawrence, national chair of

---

17. *The Papers* (2005), 5:497. On the return trip to Birmingham the three Shuttlesworth teens were arrested and assaulted by police for refusing to move to the rear of an interstate bus in Gadsen, Alabama. In 1946 the Supreme Court ruled in *Morgan v. Virginia* that segregation on interstate buses was unconstitutional.
18. Manis, *A Fire You Can't Put Out*, 240.

the Fellowship of Reconciliation and a Morehouse man. Archibald James Carey Jr., pastor of Quinn Chapel AME Church in Chicago, gave him similar advice.[19] In any case, it was not only white residents of Birmingham who seemed to go mad over the idea of "outsiders" presuming to tell them how best to handle the race problem in their town. A certain class of blacks were similarly affected.

Early in the Birmingham campaign, a state circuit court judge issued a temporary injunction against demonstrations, which King and SCLC leaders decided to violate. But then, quite unexpectedly, Birmingham authorities informed SCLC's bail bondsman that his financial assets were not sufficient, which meant that those who continued to march and were arrested would have to remain in jail, since there would be no bail money. Because it was Good Friday, it was the worst possible timing since any pastor who got arrested would not likely be in his pulpit on Easter Sunday if he could not make bail. Meeting in the Gaston Hotel, King, SCLC associates, and some local black businessmen discussed the matter, and before long he noticed that an eerie sense of gloom pervaded the room. Most of the two dozen or so men and women present were at their wits' end;[20] they were overwhelmed by fear, and simply not knowing what to do. Finally, someone spoke up and said that King could not go to jail because they did not have the money to bail him out. It was reasoned that only King had the status and contacts to raise the large amount of money that was needed for bail. King's arrest, it was argued, would quite likely mean the loss of the battle of Birmingham.[21]

---

19. *The Papers*, 3:138, 140.
20. For many years it was reported that those meeting at the Gaston Motel that day were men. We now know that at least one woman, Dorothy F. Cotton, was present. Cotton has written of the incident in her recent memoir, clearly acknowledging her presence. See her book, *If Your Back's Not Bent: The Role of the Citizenship Education Program in the Civil Rights Movement* (New York: Atria, 2012), 211.
21. Martin Luther King Jr., *Why We Can't Wait* (New York: Harper & Row, 1964), 70.

In those moments of uncertainty, King and those present did not know what to do. However, what Martin Luther King did next was nothing short of an act of faith, and a testament to his fundamental belief that God was on the side of right and justice; that God was their most dependable companion in the struggle, and would—if they did their part—provide what they needed to continue the struggle for justice and civil rights. Already, King had been involved in civil rights ministry long enough and had endured enough hardship to know what his paternal grandmother, Delia King, knew about the God of the Hebrew prophets and Jesus Christ. King knew that the God of his faith was trustworthy and would make a way out of no way for those who are obedient to God's call, and who relentlessly do their part in the struggle for justice and liberation. So he went into an adjacent room, prayed, changed into his denims, and returned to say that he had decided to go to jail. He was going to march, thus violating the court-ordered injunction. He did not know what he should do, he said, but he knew he could go to jail with the people. He told Ralph Abernathy that he knew he wanted to be in his pulpit on Easter Sunday morning, but he wanted him to go to jail with him. Unhesitatingly, Abernathy agreed. Then, King and the others stood up, joined hands, and began chanting "We Shall Overcome," which by now had become the "battle hymn" of the civil rights movement. Andrew Young believes that King's decision to go to jail that day was "the beginning of his true leadership."[22] King and the others filed out of the motel room to the street. They marched only a few blocks before a motorcycle cop pulled up in front of them, causing them to stop in their tracks. A policeman then grabbed King by the trousers and roughly pushed him into a paddy wagon along with Abernathy, and the two were taken to jail, along with many others.[23]

---

22. Quoted in Juan Williams, *Eyes on the Prize: America's Civil Rights Years, 1954-1965* (New York: Viking, 1987), 186.

By making this faith act, which was also an act of commitment to his civil rights ministry, Martin Luther King was also saying for all to hear that he was willing to accept the penalty for disobeying civil law, even though he believed both the law and the penalty assessed for violating it to be unjust. King's reaction was consistent with his doctrine of civil disobedience that required a willing acceptance of punishment for violating even unjust laws. Moreover, he could not, in good faith, ask black residents of Birmingham to go to jail with no hope of bail, if he was not willing to do the same. One of the lessons he learned during the Montgomery struggle was that a good leader leads in all areas, and never asks the people to do what the leader is not prepared and willing to do. In addition, as a religious leader, King's decision in that hotel room was another instance of his fundamental faith and trust in God; that God would make a way out of no way.

Bernita Roberson recalled being about ten years old when she began asking her parents about segregation laws and practices in Birmingham. Even as a child, she knew that such laws and practices made her feel inferior to whites. When King decided to march with the knowledge that there was no bail money, Roberson was a fourteen-year-old student who chose to disobey her father, and instead, to march with King. Looking back, she said that her father made it crystal clear that she and her two brothers were not to participate in the march. He especially stressed this to her. "Generally I was a good child," Roberson later recalled. "Dr. King made the call for people to join him, and all these people said they'd go to jail with

---

23. Dorothy Cotton contends that King had only taken a few steps after leaving the motel when he was grabbed and arrested (see Cotton, *If Your Back's Not Bent*, 212). Andrew Young remembered differently, claiming that King had marched about a half mile before being roughly handled by police and arrested (see Young's statement in Williams, *Eyes on the Prize*, 186). Young's memory is the more accurate. I have seen photos of King being grabbed by the trousers, and by this time they were some distance from the motel (see Charles Johnson and Bob Adelman, *King: The Photography of Martin Luther King, Jr.* [New York: Viking Studio, 2000], 116–17).

him. . . . [A] friend of mine said, 'Let's go!' I felt like a spirit was telling me to get out there. So I went down and volunteered and said that the next morning I would be a part of it."[24]

Roberson and a number of other youths were arrested along with King. Once at the county jail, she and the other children were removed to the Juvenile holding area. Roberson recalled that King hugged each of the children and shook their hands as they walked by.[25] She and the other young people felt good about themselves because they believed they made a difference. The next day, eight white clergymen published an open letter to King in the *Birmingham News*, calling his demonstrations "unwise" and "untimely," and said that he and SCLC were little more than outside agitators. These criticisms prompted King to respond by writing what came to be his famous "Letter from Birmingham Jail," a literary and theological classic that responded to each concern of the white clergymen and presented sound theological and moral reasons for SCLC's decision to be in Birmingham to protest the racial injustice and violence there.

When the Movement Stalled

By the middle of April, after just a few days of demonstrating, the Birmingham campaign stalled. Looking back, King said that from the beginning of the campaign he believed that student involvement would be needed if they were to succeed.[26] It is not clear whether he was aware that Gandhi also experimented with using children as volunteers in India during preparation for civil disobedience campaigns. Gandhi's, however, was a more limited use of children.

---

24. Ellen Levine, *Freedom's Children: Young Civil Rights Activists Tell Their Own Stories* (New York: G. P. Putnam's Sons, 1993), 82.
25. Ibid., 83.
26. King, *Why We Can't Wait*, 101.

Their job was to help with a large mailing.[27] What is clear, however, is that if King in fact early considered using children and young people on a massive scale, he had not thought through just how best to utilize them before the lull occurred in the Birmingham campaign, and what seemed to be certain defeat if the leadership could not quickly find a workable solution. He therefore sent for his youthful, impassioned staff member, James Bevel, who at the time was working on voter registration in Jackson, Mississippi along with his wife, Diane Nash Bevel. SNCC youths, under the leadership of Bob Moses, had already broken ground in the very dangerous Mississippi Delta.

King met with the fiery Bevel and the rest of the SCLC staff to discuss the challenge they confronted. At that time, Bevel and Ike Reynolds introduced the novel and controversial idea of using massive numbers of schoolchildren in the demonstrations.[28] Bevel reasoned that the few committed black adults in Birmingham were already in jail and there were few left to carry on the mass demonstrations and to fill the jails. However, there was an unlimited number of children, said Bevel, including an already "well defined, strong community" of young people in the high schools. These youths had been in school together for as much as ten years, having started out together in elementary school. They were not fragmented as a community, as was the case of the general black adult population in Birmingham, nor did they possess the same spellbinding fear as adults. Furthermore, Bevel argued, black children in the Deep South were "at least partially free," unlike black adults. He recalled that black youths in Mississippi were unafraid, bold, and as aware as adults that racial segregation was at the root of many of their problems. More than most black adults, black youths were ready to

27. M. K. Gandhi, *An Autobiography or the Story of My Experiments with Truth*, trans. Mahadev Desai (Ahmedabad: Navajivan, 1927), 140.
28. Eskew, *But for Birmingham*, 261.

strike blows for their freedom, and to endure the consequences. Bevel and his wife had learned this during their voter registration work in Jackson.[29] Young people there were ready for change and frequently led the way in the voter registration projects. The Jackson, Mississippi experience taught the Bevels something about "the willingness of young people—children, really—to take a risk and go ahead of their parents; to in fact lead their parents and other adults in their community. Now faced with a stalled campaign in Birmingham, [Bevel] believed that the only way they were going to have a mass base would be to start organizing among the high school students. And if need be, after that junior high, and if need be, elementary school kids."[30] Experience had shown the Bevels that it was black youths, more than their parents and other adults, who were willing and courageous enough to take real risks for freedom. And, they would take such risks whether their parents and teachers supported them or gave permission for their involvement or not. They would take the initiative and trust their own burning desire for freedom. Bevel was convinced that they would in fact take the lead if the adults continued to hesitate. In addition, he knew instinctively that black youths were in a different place than the older generation of blacks. A new age was unfolding, and black youths were the chief subjects. They were not willing to endure what their parents did. This very stance was vividly illustrated in the actions of fifteen-year-old Birmingham resident Grosbeck Preer Parham in a courtroom exchange with Judge Talbot Ellis, who had just released him and more than five hundred other youthful demonstrators in the custody of their parents. When the judge, presuming to lecture the young man, said that "there is no freedom without restraint," Parham replied: "You can say that about freedom because you've got your

---

29. David Halberstam, *The Children* (New York: Random House, 1998), 438.
30. Ibid., 438–39.

freedom. The Constitution says we're all equal, but Negroes aren't equal." His mother chimed in, saying: "I don't approve of street violence either. But after a civil rights meeting we did try to get in touch with city officials and they wouldn't see us. And I know this, Judge—these younger people are not going to take what we took."[31] The boy's mother saw and understood clearly what the judge and the vast majority of white Birmingham residents did not: younger blacks would not subscribe to the accommodation model of Booker T. Washington. They did not think like their elders, especially those in the traditional black leadership class. For black youths like Parham, a new day was emerging.

After a passionate debate on the minimum age for youth involvement, King, quite apprehensively in the beginning, decided that they would use only high school students. In addition, he said that the minimum age should be fourteen, but Bevel strongly objected. His argument won the day when he reminded King and others in the room that the black Baptist Church had never raised a concern over the fact that many children join church and make a faith commitment at age five or six, and no adult member contests it. Bevel said that the silence of adult members implies their belief that children at this age are old enough to have a sense of knowing what they are doing in this regard. Therefore, Bevel insisted, they should be allowed to *live* their faith, even to the point of participating in the demonstrations. If the children were not too young to choose Christ, he argued, they were not too young to choose to live out their faith by bravely participating in demonstrations for their freedom from racism and segregation. Bevel pressed his argument further, wanting to know whether King or anybody else in the room wanted to deny the children the right to live their faith through crusading against

---

31. Quoted in Eskew, *But for Birmingham*, 290.

injustice. Involving elementary through high school students would give the campaign not only the massive numbers of demonstrators needed, but a strong infusion of adrenalin, energy, and enthusiasm. In addition, Bevel saw that since the young people were not employed, they were not, like their parents and other adults, susceptible to economic reprisals and loss of jobs.[32] He appealed to each of these points as he made the case for the use of children in massive numbers in the demonstrations. This could lead to the long sought after—but to that point—elusive national publicity as well as the involvement of the federal government, which they believed was needed to ensure a successful outcome of the Birmingham movement. In addition, continued mass demonstrations would likely spark negative reactions from Bull Connor, the Klan, and the White Citizens Council, something that King and SCLC were actually counting on. The violence of Connor, the Klan, and White Citizens Council henchmen would surely attract widespread national media attention, as well as that of the federal government, since the Kennedy administration was hypersensitive about the nation's image in the international community.

Bevel, who was skilled at reaching something important inside black youths while also stimulating them to want to be civil rights activists,[33] argued that the "children were going to have to spend their entire lives struggling against racism in some form or another. It already affected and damaged them, no matter how young they were . . . ; it was already a poison in their systems. It was time to stop the age-old custom in black homes of trying to shield black children from something for which there was, finally, no shield."[34] That argument won the day, although King only "reluctantly

---

32. Gene Roberts and Hank Klibanoff, *The Race Beat: The Press, the Civil Rights Struggle, and the Awakening of a Nation* (New York: Alfred A. Knopf, 2007), 366.
33. Eskew, *But for Birmingham*, 262.
34. Halberstam, *The Children*, 439.

agreed" to proceed as Bevel demanded.[35] Bevel had the strong support of Andrew Young, Dorothy Cotton, Wyatt Walker, Fred Shuttlesworth, Ike Reynolds, and King's brother, A. D. (Alfred Daniel). Walker and Shuttlesworth agreed that the children would get a better education in a week of incarceration than five months in school. Shuttlesworth went further, saying that "the best education [for black children] was being educated to destroy the system which kept them enslaved."[36]

Martin Luther King knew that circumstances in a given local context might require major changes in strategy. He would not depart from nonviolent resistance of course, but the given local context might require a different nonviolent strategy, a different means of direct action than what was initially planned, or what was used in other communities. King seemed to acknowledge this very point when he said that "the nonviolent resister must never be so lofty in his idealism that he doesn't come down to earth and consider certain practical problems of strategy and certain practical everyday problems that people confront. And this to me would be a matter of comparing the relative losses in the particular situation at the moment with the possible gains for the future."[37] Birmingham was a case in point. They were confronted with the possibility of definite defeat early in that campaign, and in order to turn things around they had to resort to the extreme measure of utilizing massive numbers of youths of all ages. By agreeing to do this, King was only being consistent with his awareness of the need to adjust the nonviolent direct-action approach to the context in which they found themselves.

Not entirely unexpected, King was roundly criticized for giving in to Bevel's idea of putting children on the front line of the struggle.

---

35. Ibid., 440.
36. Manis, *A Fire You Can't Put Out*, 366.
37. *The Papers*, 5:547.

Rhoda Lois Blumberg rightly observes that people (read *white* people) suddenly began criticizing King's decision to use children in the demonstrations—people who had never even expressed concern for the rights and well-being of blacks in general, and those of black children in particular.[38] Mayor Albert Boutwell and other members of the Birmingham white community claimed to be deeply troubled by the decision to use children in the demonstrations. "When people who are not residents of this city, and who will not have to live with fearful consequences, come to the point of using innocent children as their tools . . . ," the mayor moralized, "then the time has come for every responsible white and colored parent in this city to demand a halt."[39] Boutwell went on to say that he could not condone the use of children, as if to imply that he was truly concerned about the safety and well-being of black children. In any event, criticisms also came from Washington. Attorney General Kennedy pointed to the danger of children participating in the demonstrations. "An injured, maimed or dead child is a price that none of us can afford to pay," said Kennedy.[40] Kennedy himself was not yet on the right side of the freedom struggle, and as we have seen, was more concerned about the nation's image abroad, than guaranteeing the safety and civil rights of black children. Of course, one would not hear the same sentiments expressed by whites in Birmingham when the four girl children were murdered in the bombing of the Sixteenth Street Baptist Church, along with two black boys later in the day, on September 15, 1963.

The criticisms that concerned Martin Luther King most came from various factions in the Birmingham black community, as well as black leaders in other parts of the country. Several local black

---

38. See Rhoda Lois Blumberg, *Civil Rights: The 1960s Freedom Struggle*, revised edition (Boston: Twayne, 1991 [1984]), 118.
39. Quoted in Eskew, *But for Birmingham*, 266.
40. Quoted in ibid., 266.

businessmen and professionals, including A. G. Gaston (owner of the Gaston Motel), Arthur Shores (an attorney who actually began legal challenges to segregation in Birmingham as early as the 1930s), and J. L. Wares went ballistic. "Gaston was horrified that King would 'use' young people. Injured children (or worse) would reflect as badly on the adults who had put them in danger as it would on the assailants."[41] Black Muslim leader Malcolm X declared that "[r]eal men don't put their children on the firing line."[42] As far back as 1956, Thurgood Marshall had reacted negatively to a comment that King made at a June 26 press conference that it might become necessary to boycott segregated schools to force compliance with the landmark *Brown* decision in 1954. Marshall's reaction was: "I don't approve of using children to do men's work."[43] King responded to such criticisms, saying that, by demonstrating, the young people "gained a 'sense of their own stake in freedom and justice.'"[44] Young people had as much right, if not more, as black adults to resist the wrongs and injustices being done to them. In any event, King knew that he would take a very hard hit from people in the black community regarding the decision to involve massive numbers of children and youths in the Birmingham struggle. In Montgomery, and during the sit-ins and Freedom Rides, he had learned (and this was reaffirmed for him by Bevel's argument) that the struggle for freedom and civil rights was as much about black youths as their parents and other adults. Why should they not be a part of the solution? To King's credit, he persevered, although this did not mean that it was an easy decision to include children on the frontline.

---

41. Diane McWhorter, *Carry Me Home* (New York: Simon & Schuster, 2001), 363.
42. Quoted in Wexler, *An Eyewitness History*, 165.
43. *The Papers*, 3:307 n. 26.
44. Quoted in Wexler, *An Eyewitness History*, 165.

Once the issue of youth involvement was resolved and the children hit the streets of Birmingham, *Newsweek* named it the *children's crusade*, which was launched on May 2. The code name was D-Day. When some of the first waves of hundreds of children were arrested and transported to the county jail, King talked with them outside the fenced area. This had the effect of easing their anxiety and uncertainty. Looking back to when she was seventeen years old, Judy Tarver recalled that she and the other children who joined up with Miles College students and were arrested, felt much better when King talked with and comforted them before they were transported to the juvenile detention center, and then on to the fairgrounds when the center was filled.[45]

Interestingly, when King later spoke favorably about having included massive numbers of children and youths as demonstrators, he only implied the influence of Bevel. "But most of all we were inspired with a desire to give to our young a true sense of their own stake in freedom and justice," he said. "We believed they would have the courage to respond to our call."[46] King reported that when an eight-year-old marcher was asked by an amused police officer what she wanted, she eyeballed him and said: "F'eedom."[47] It did not matter that she could not pronounce the word. Even at her tender age she had a sense of what it meant. King believed that the child who is raised well and has the higher values instilled in her understands—like many of the children who participated in the demonstrations—that the struggle for freedom is as much about them as anybody else. Consequently, he agreed that "they are not too young to participate,"[48] and one should ignore critics who make

---

45. Levine, *Freedom's Children*, 80, 81.
46. King, *Why We Can't Wait*, 102.
47. Ibid., 103.
48. King, "What a Mother Should Tell Her Child," Mother's Day sermon at Ebenezer Baptist Church in Atlanta, May 12, 1963, King Library and Archives, 10.

such charges. King recalled talking with Attorney General Kennedy, who said that the children were too young to participate in the demonstrations and might get hurt. King responded that black children get hurt every single day by the cruel discriminatory practices of racist whites. Elsewhere he said: "The minute they're born until the day they die, they're hurt in a much more damaging way. They're hurt spiritually. They're hurt and killed psychologically."[49] Ralph Abernathy told the *Baltimore Afro-American*: "Don't think these smallest ones don't know what they want. They do. They know they can't go to Kiddieland and ride the ponies like the white kids, and they know they can't appear on the afternoon TV shows like the white kids."[50] Indeed, one demonstrator, a young boy, was but four years old. His mother held his hand as she led one wave of young marchers, declaring: "This baby is mine and he's in it too!"[51] King did not disapprove of the role that such parents played in raising their children to contribute to the struggle in this way, and he most assuredly approved of the parents' witness and leadership. In fact, in his Mother's Day sermon at Ebenezer on May 12, 1963, he admonished parents to tell their young children that demonstrations such as those in Birmingham were a good fight, a fight to save the soul of this nation, and thus they should strongly encourage their children to get involved.[52]

Singing for Freedom

Not unlike the adults and older youths, the children sang as they marched. By noon, on May 6, thousands of young people packed

---

49. Ibid.
50. Quoted in Wexler, *An Eyewitness History*, 172.
51. Quoted in McWhorter, *Carry Me Home*, 371.
52. King, "What a Mother Should Tell Her Child," 11.

the Sixteenth Street Baptist. When the march began, they flooded out into the streets singing: "Don't mind walking, 'cause I want my freedom now." In an orderly fashion, they marched and sang about wanting nothing but freedom, as they were arrested by waiting policemen.[53] From the time of the Montgomery bus boycott, singing was a major part of movement strategy and practice, and its importance seemed to grow with each new campaign throughout the South.

Made popular by singing Baptist and Methodist hymns and "Negro Spirituals" at prayer meetings during the Montgomery campaign, the singing of these "freedom songs" went to a whole new level with SNCC youths during the Albany, Georgia campaign in 1961, as well as the Freedom Rides of that period. SNCC activists did not hesitate to change the lyrics of some of the songs and even gave some of them new tunes and a livelier rhythm and beat. In this regard, they went beyond traditional church music. Arguably, one of the greatest lessons of the Albany movement for black youths was that "they became more aware of the cultural dimensions of the black struggle, quickly recognizing the value of freedom songs to convey the ideas of the southern movement and to sustain morale."[54] So significant was singing during the Albany campaign that Albany student leader Bernice Johnson Reagon, who would later found the popular singing group, Sweet Honey in the Rock, characterized it as "a singing movement." Reagon and several other students were expelled from Albany State College for participating in civil rights demonstrations. She maintained that, somehow when they sang, their burdens were lifted, or at least were made lighter, and differences between them were minimized.[55] Singing, no less than praying, held

---

53. Eskew, *But for Birmingham*, 275.
54. Clayborne Carson, Tenisha Armstrong, et al., *The Martin Luther King, Jr. Encyclopedia* (Westport, CT: Greenwood, 2008), 314.
55. Carson, Armstrong, et al., *The Martin Luther King, Jr. Encyclopedia*, 314–15.

the demonstrators together in difficult and very dangerous times. Reagon reflected: "When I opened my mouth and began to sing ["We Shall Overcome"], there was a force and power within myself I had never heard before. Somehow this music . . . released a kind of power and required a level of concentrated energy I did not know I had."[56] Reagon's was an experience shared by many SNCC youths and black residents of Albany, and would increasingly have the same effect in subsequent campaigns throughout the movement. In the next chapter we will see that the white college volunteers who participated in Freedom Summer in the Mississippi Delta were also positively affected by, and fed off of the freedom songs, which helped them endure the daily dangers they faced.

Communal singing "created an important feeling of connected, of camaraderie."[57] Moreover, in some strange kind of way, one was often changed in the singing and hearing of these powerful songs. One could not hear them and "not be touched and stirred by them, finding new places inside yourself that propelled you into a new consciousness, places from which you would feel and act in new ways."[58] One was changed, challenged, and encouraged by singing the freedom songs. "After singing we were different," Dorothy Cotton reflected. "We felt different; we lost any residual fear; we were motivated and determined. There came a knowing that we would go on and continue 'to see what the end would be.'"[59]

In her memoir, *If Your Back's Not Bent* (2012), Dorothy Cotton pointed to a perfect illustration of what Reagon said about the transforming power and effect of the freedom songs. Cotton recalled an incident that occurred in Savannah, Georgia when a small group

---

56. Quoted in Clayborne Carson, *In Struggle: SNCC and the Black Awakening of the 1960s* (Cambridge, MA: Harvard University Press, 1995 [1981]), 59.
57. Cotton, *If Your Back's Not Bent*, 151.
58. Ibid.
59. Ibid., 154.

of them were singing during a demonstration. Unknown to them at the time, Henry Brownlee, an employee in a small factory nearby, heard the singing while he was working. Later, Brownlee told Cotton and others that when he heard them singing, "I woke up this morning with my mind stayed on freedom . . . hallelu, hallelu, hallelujah!," he just could not seem to hold himself back.[60] "I just got caught up in what y'all were doing," said Brownlee. "Somehow, it got to me. When I jumped that fence, it wasn't long before I knew I wasn't ever going back in that plant."[61] Singing did not affect everybody quite as dramatically as this, but it clearly had such an effect on some. Brownlee became very devoted to the civil rights cause, lending support anywhere in the movement that needed it. The songs that were sung were often those of ancestral blacks, although the words were often changed to adapt to the setting. Often it was a case of old songs taking on new meaning. "Legions of people were moved by communal singing, in new ways that often surprised them," said Cotton. "Like Brownlee, they became moved to assert themselves politically and socially."[62] The freedom songs energized movement participants when they were tired and weary. The songs also "affirmed and reconfirmed" the people's commitment to stay the course until freedom came.

As a boy, Martin Luther King himself had quite a singing voice and loved singing in church, often accompanied by his mother on the piano. Indeed, King wrote about the significant role that singing played in the mass prayer meetings in Montgomery. By the time of the Birmingham movement, he characterized freedom songs as "the soul of the movement" and "as old as the history of the Negro in America. They are adaptations of the songs the slaves sang—the

---

60. Ibid., 147.
61. Quoted in ibid., 147.
62. Cotton, *If Your Back's Not Bent*, 148.

sorrow songs, the shouts for joy, the battle hymns and the anthems of our movement."[63] During a press conference in Birmingham on November 4, 1967, after being released from jail for charges regarding his involvement in the Birmingham campaign in 1963, King referred to these as "the songs of Zion . . . , the great freedom songs that have moved us so meaningfully over the last few years."[64] He told the people that through his jail cell windows he could hear them singing these songs, and he thanked them for singing. Like their enslaved forebears, Movement people sang freedom songs because they were victims of injustice, and the songs lifted their spirits, inspired a sense of hope and determination for freedom. Indeed, just as singing helped enslaved blacks to retain a sense of sanity and wholeness of soul under the most extreme conditions,[65] so too did it help to uplift and inspire those involved in the civil rights movement.

It is of interest to note that some of the songs that older children in Birmingham sang might just as well been directed toward their black elders as white racists—songs such as "Which Side Are You On?" and "Will You Join Us or Will You 'Tom' for the Big, Bad 'Bull.'"[66] The children were angry and disappointed that many black adults were so apathetic and fearful. They knew almost instinctively that their future depended on their own willingness and determination to resist racial discrimination and the social evils associated with it; that they could not adopt the position of many black adults. Singing emboldened them, no less than adults. As we have seen, the freedom songs performed multiple functions. Leith Mullings and the

---

63. King, *Why We Can't Wait*, 57–58.
64. Transcript of Press Conference in Birmingham, Alabama, November 4, 1967, King Center Library and Archives, 3.
65. Solomon Iyobosa Omo-Osagie II, "'Their Souls Made Them Whole': Negro Spirituals and Lessons in Healing and Atonement," *The Western Journal of Black Studies*, 31, no. 2 (Summer 2007): 35.
66. McWhorter, *Carry Me Home*, 367.

late Manning Marable remind us of four roles: "[T]hey promoted solidarity, increased faith, expressed sorrow, and strengthened the wills of movement activists."[67]

Radio and the Children's Crusade

Looking back in 1967, Martin Luther King paid tribute to the prominent role that radio played in the Birmingham Children's Crusade. Addressing the National Association of Radio Announcers in Atlanta on August 11, 1967, King expressed his appreciation for "the role which the radio announcer plays in the life of our people. For better or worse," he said, "you are opinion makers in the community and it is important that you remain aware of the power which is potential in your vocation."[68] He went on to say that the masses of people who were victims of economic injustice depend heavily on radio announcers to help them understand what's going on around them in society. Television, he said, appeals more to the needs of the middle class. In his address, King made explicit reference to the important contribution of "Tall Paul" White during the Children's Crusade.[69] For King, it was a case of being committed and responsible enough to use one's vocation in ways that best serve those counted among the least of these. King recognized that this is no less important in ministry than in other vocations. In every vocation the question must be: What can I do to uplift and make the most of persons, especially those who are among the massive numbers of the left-outs? In this regard, adults in every vocation are charged with remembering (in the words of literary artist Alice

---

67. Manning Marable and Leith Mullings, eds., *Let Nobody Turn Us Around: Voices of Resistance, Reform, and Renewal* (Lanham, MD: Rowman & Littlefield, 2000), 396.
68. King, "Transforming a Neighborhood," Address to the National Association of Radio Announcers in Atlanta, August 11, 1967, King Center Library and Archives, 2.
69. Ibid., 3.

Walker) that "the world is not good enough; we must make it better,"[70] particularly for the voiceless and powerless. What a novel idea: to use one's vocation, whatever it might be, to make life for the least of these better than it is.

When hundreds of black children flooded into the streets of Birmingham on D-Day, they caught the white power structure completely off guard. In a way, the sheer numbers of children surpassed even King's greatest expectations, in addition to greatly strengthening his resolve to push forward. At the mass prayer meeting that night at Sixth Avenue Baptist Church, where there was standing room only, King lavished praise on the children, saying: "I have been inspired and moved today. I have never seen anything like it."[71] Interestingly, King himself had not issued the order for D-Day to commence that afternoon. It will be recalled that he had been subjected to strong criticism about the decision to use children. Some contend that when the time came to release the children from the Sixteenth Street Baptist Church into the streets of Birmingham, King remained in his motel suite in a state of indecisiveness. Whether it was true or not that King was unable to decide, critics contend that James Bevel and Wyatt Walker gave the order to commence D-Day.[72]

Bevel and others who worked with the children and youths had to have a way to communicate with them about the date, time, and location of the workshops on D-Day. It was important, however, that this information be kept secret until the date in question. Part of the strategy was to surprise the police and other authorities, as well as school officials. Since most of the students would be in school, Bevel and his co-workers needed to be able to communicate with

---

70. Alice Walker, "A Talk: Convocation 1972," in her *In Search of Our Mothers' Gardens: Womanist Prose* (New York: Harcourt Brace Jovanovich, 1983), 37.
71. Quoted in Eskew, *But for Birmingham*, 265.
72. Eskew, *But for Birmingham*, 264. See also 385 n. 11.

them, preferably through coded language that only the kids would understand. In this way, school officials, Bull Connor, and other public officials in the downtown area would not know precisely what was happening until it was already taking place. While today, the method of choice for communicating with students would likely be texting, since most youths carry iPhones, in 1963 it was the radio.

James Bevel managed to recruit two young local black disc jockeys who appealed to black youths: Shelley "the Playboy" Stewart and "Tall Paul" Dudley White. These had the assignment of communicating in code to young people where and when they were to congregate in preparation for the demonstrations on D-Day. Prior to that day, Stewart and White gladly accepted Bevel's request to go on radio to announce a luncheon at the Gaston Motel "for some of their friends—beauty queens and football stars they had gotten to know at school dances. Twenty or thirty high school big shots and church youth leaders showed up for a strategy meeting with Bevel." Organizers' thinking was that if they could recruit athletes and beauty queens who were generally looked up to as leaders by other students they would be the best source for recruiting their classmates for the demonstrations. The assignment of these leaders was "to start a 'whisper campaign' on upcoming workshops and youth rallies. To 'make them feel like they were doing something half-sneaky, half-devilish' [which played right into the hands of the youths], Bevel passed out small palm cards to conceal from the adults."[73]

The students were given leaflets instructing them to leave school on Thursday, May 2, to commence D-Day demonstrations at noon. They were to leave with or without their parents' or teachers' permission.

---

73. McWhorter, *Carry Me Home*, 361.

Alexander Brown, also a Shuttlesworth-influenced recruiter, remembered school officials' locking the doors of the schools in an attempt to dissuade their students from volunteering. Such efforts met with dismal failure as many students climbed out of windows to volunteer for the demonstrations. Disc jockey "Tall Paul" White used codes to tell students where to go to volunteer. Abraham Woods remembered: "You could see the students coming from every direction from high schools and some elementary schools to go to take part in the demonstrations."[74]

Right at noon, "Tall Paul" White, of WENN radio station, began announcing the coded instructions: "Kids, there's gonna be a party at the park. . . . Bring your toothbrushes because lunches will be served."[75] Soon afterward, throngs of black youths were seen converging on the Sixteenth Street Baptist Church. When they were released into the streets by Bevel and Walker, their sheer numbers stunned Bull Connor and police and fire officials. Hundreds and hundreds of students converged on the streets headed in different directions to the downtown area.

Children Exert Their Power

Without question, the massive drove of students, ranging from third grade to college, caught Birmingham authorities completely off guard. It was a masterstroke of strategy. Wave after wave of students left the Sixteenth Street Baptist Church and other church locations to march to designated areas in the downtown district. The students quickly filled all available paddy wagons. Bull Connor had to use police cars and, quite ironically, even school buses to transport the still growing numbers of youths to jail or makeshift juvenile detention centers. When there was no jail space, the children were transported

---

74. Quoted in Manis, *A Fire You Can't Put Out*, 368.
75. Quoted in ibid., 369.

to the state fairgrounds as a temporary prison, "the same fairgrounds amusement park," Judy Tarver recalled, that "I couldn't go to as a kid because they didn't allow black people in there."[76] The phenomenon of massive arrests of children caused King to recall Gandhi's idea about filling up the jails.[77] Addressing a large audience, King said: "This is the first time in the history of our struggle that we have been able literally to fill the jails. In a real sense this is the fulfillment of a dream because I've always felt if we could fill the jails in our witness for freedom it would be a magnificent expression of the determination of the Negroes and a marvelous way to lay the whole issue before the conscience of the local and national community."[78] This is precisely what happened because of the massive number of students being arrested. Indeed, David Halberstam contends that it was estimated that by the time the Children's Crusade ended, approximately ten thousand children had been jailed in Birmingham.[79] King said at a mass prayer meeting: "Never in the history of this nation have so many people been arrested for the cause of freedom and human dignity."[80] In some instances third-graders were in jail for as long as a full week. Audrey Faye Hendricks was one of these youthful "Freedom Fighters" or "Freedom Riders" (a badge of honor), as they called themselves.[81] Knowing that many parents were worried about the safety of their children, King sought both to comfort and encourage them at one of the mass meetings:

---

76. Levine, *Freedom's Children*, 81.
77. Gandhi was actually reacting to the tactic of nonviolent protesters during the South Afrika campaign to arrive at the prison in large numbers such that they would be overfilled. Gandhi said: "The community had resolved to fill up the jail after our arrests." See Gandhi, *Satyagraha in South Africa*, in *The Selected Works of Mahatma Gandhi*, ed. Shriman Harayan (Ahmedabad: Navajivan, 1968), 3:206–7.
78. King, "On the Significance of Birmingham," May 7, 1963, King Library and Archives, 1.
79. Halberstam, *The Children*, 441.
80. Clayborne Carson, ed., *The Autobiography of Martin Luther King, Jr.* (New York: Warner Books, 1998), 210.
81. Levine, *Freedom's Children*, 78–80.

Don't worry about your children, they're gonna be all right. Don't hold them back if they want to go to jail. For they are doing a job not only for themselves but for all of America and for all mankind. Somewhere we read, "A little child shall lead them." Remember there was another little child just twelve years old and he got involved in a discussion back in Jerusalem. . . . He said, "I must be about my father's business." These young people are about their father's business. And they are carving a tunnel of hope through the great mountain of despair. . . .[82]

Dogs, Fire Hoses, and Arousing the Conscience of the Nation

The first time that Bull Connor sicced police attack dogs on the peaceful demonstrators occurred on Palm Sunday, April 7 (about a month before the Children's Crusade). Connor had actually overreacted to a small group of demonstrators that had not shown signs of getting larger. Nor was the group in any way disorderly or a threat to public safety. The use of the attack dogs made national news and led a jubilant Wyatt Walker and Dorothy Cotton to declare ecstatically: "We've got a movement. We had some police brutality. They brought the dogs. They brought out the dogs. We've got a movement!"[83] Not all of the leaders were elated about this. Looking back, SNCC student activist James Forman claims to have been furious over the behavior and comments of Walker and Cotton. "It was a disgusting moment to me," said Forman, "for it seemed very cold, cruel, and calculating to be happy about police brutality coming down on innocent people, bystanders, no matter what purpose it served."[84] Right or wrong, what Walker and Cotton said was important, because by turning the dogs and high-powered water hoses on defenseless, nonviolent children, black Birmingham was in

---

82. Carson, ed., *The Autobiography of Martin Luther King, Jr.*, 211.
83. Quoted in Roberts and Klibanoff, *The Race Beat*, 314.
84. James Forman, *The Making of Black Revolutionaries* (New York: Macmillan, 1972), 312.

effect forced to unite behind King in what seemed an instant. As white attorney David Vann reflected, "[I]n the twinkling of an eye the whole black community instantaneously consolidated . . . behind Dr. King."[85]

In any case, Bull Connor had not learned from, or taken the advice of Sheriff Laurie Pritchett, who refused to use violence and rough tactics against the demonstrators in the Albany, Georgia campaign two years previous. He believed (rightly) that harming those people would be playing into the hands of King and his cohorts. Pritchett's tactic, like that of police in Jackson, Mississippi when the Freedom Riders arrived there, was "arrest-but-don't-harm."[86] This approach effectively neutralized any chance of drawing more than normal media attention and coverage. Not only did Pritchett not use violence against King and SCLC when they arrived in Albany, he—unlike the mistake made by Jackson, Mississippi police—did not rough up reporters. Pritchett had apparently studied King's methods, and had concluded that violence to demonstrators and reporters frequently led to massive outside media coverage. He therefore concluded that the best way to keep the media away and to minimize any chance that federal authorities might intervene was to ensure that there was no story to be reported. The best way to do this, Pritchett concluded, was to out-nonviolence King, and to even make it difficult for him to remain in jail, if arrested. In fact, there were reports of King's bail being paid by some mystery person (long suspected to be Pritchett).

Although Pritchett, like Bull Connor, was known for his short temper, as a strategist, he was by far the wiser of the two men. Indeed, it was common knowledge that Connor hated blacks as well as the outside press. This, in fact, was one of Fred Shuttlesworth's strongest

---

85. Quoted in Williams, *Eyes on the Prize*, 190.
86. Roberts and Klibanoff, *The Race Beat*, 257.

selling points to King as to why the next civil rights campaign (after Albany) should be in Birmingham. Shuttlesworth knew Bull Connor well, and knew that he would not be able to restrain himself if the movement came to his turf. He was convinced that Connor could almost assuredly be counted on to make missteps early and often, and, as some reporters held, "with force and about as much meanness as the American people could stand, or more."[87] Shuttlesworth reasoned that such miscalculations on the part of Bull Connor would surely bring the media to Birmingham in massive numbers and would also get the attention of the Kennedy administration. Indeed, King himself had seen how reporters spared nothing to get to those places where there was mob and/or police violence against nonviolent demonstrators. He saw this happen in the case of Autherine Lucy in 1952 when she tried to enroll at the University of Alabama. In addition, he had seen this very phenomenon at work during the Freedom Rides—how unprovoked mass violence by white racists against the nonviolent Riders had drawn massive media and national attention. King therefore knew almost instinctively that SCLC's strategy in post-Albany campaigns had to include a central place for media involvement—nationally and internationally. King believed that large-scale media presence would give them the national and international publicity and attention that would also contribute to sustaining the movement and driving its civil rights agenda. It would also put the blatant racism in Birmingham on public display for the entire nation and the world to see. Gene Roberts and Hank Klibanoff provide an apt characterization of what was needed in the next and subsequent civil rights campaigns: "They needed a drama, even a melodrama, featuring a sympathetic protagonist, a terrifying antagonist, and a simple theme. They needed an elevated stage, something that would allow the whole world to see without standing

---

87. Ibid., 269.

on its tiptoes, without even leaving its easy chair. They needed the press, the national press, to give the confrontation a high profile, so the world could bear witness."[88]

This emphasis on the importance of the press and the need for publicity in the matter of race was emphasized as far back as 1944 when social scientist Gunnar Myrdal observed how ignorant both whites of the North and South were regarding the plight of blacks and the effects of racial discrimination.

> The Northerners want to hear as little as possible about the Negroes, both in the South and in the North, and they have, of course, good reason for that. The result is an astonishing ignorance about the Negro on the part of the white public in the North. White Southerners, too, are ignorant of many phases of the Negro's life, but their ignorance has not such a simple and unemotional character as that in the North. There are many educated Northerners who are well informed about foreign problems but almost absolutely ignorant about Negro conditions both in their own city and in the nation as a whole.[89]

Very much on the right track in his observations about whites' ignorance of blacks and conditions adversely affecting them, Myrdal exhibited liberal naïveté and sentimentality when he went on to say that if they only knew the facts, most whites would willingly give blacks a fair deal. This was a common error among white liberals, both religious and secular. There was nothing in the history of white-black relations that justified the claim that increased knowledge of the black condition was all that was needed to elicit fair treatment and justice from well-meaning white people. However, Myrdal was without question on solid ground in his contention that media publicity was of the highest strategic value to blacks. Indeed, by

---

88. Ibid., 268.
89. Gunnar Myrdal, *An American Dilemma: The Negro Problem and Modern Democracy*, with the assistance of Richard Sterner and Arnold Rose (New York: Harper & Brothers, 1944), 48. See also 600.

the time of the Birmingham campaign, King himself was quite convinced of the significance of the press and the role it could play in assisting SCLC's efforts to arouse the conscience of the nation. King knew that this could happen only if the American public had media access to the demonstrations and the violent behavior of racist opponents. They could have such access through daily newspapers and televised news media. This would effectively remove the possibility of selective ignorance, since it is believed that from a moral standpoint, at least, one can be morally obligated only if she is aware of this or that problem. Ignorance may preclude one from moral responsibility. Today it is still tragically the case, however, that many simply do not want to know, and thus feel no moral compulsion regarding certain problems adversely affecting the lives of various groups. Such people resign themselves to the view that if they are ignorant of the existence of racism in a given community, for example, they cannot be held morally responsible. The presence of the media at civil rights campaigns generally reduced the tendency toward selective ignorance.

Although Martin Luther King and his staff did not know how, or whether, there would be strong media coverage in Birmingham, they were delighted when, early in that campaign, the media was out in large numbers, and once the Children's Crusade commenced, media presence swelled greatly. Furthermore, as we saw earlier, King grew increasingly aware of the Kennedy administration's sensitivity to the nation's image in the international community, and particularly among the Russians. He knew that it would be difficult to convince Russia and other nations of the virtue of democracy when images of police brutality against nonviolent demonstrators for freedom—including children—were flashed around the world in newspapers and on television. King also knew that if the President did not come to their aid out of moral considerations, he would be forced to do so for political reasons."

Previously, when Bull Connor ordered his men to hit peaceful demonstrators with cannon-like bursts of water from high-powered fire hoses and to sic dogs on them (on Palm Sunday) the event was captured on still cameras. But when Connor ordered his men to use the same tactics on the marching children on day two of D-Day, it was not only captured on still cameras, but on national television. The cannon blasts of water initially struck children ages thirteen to sixteen who covered their heads and faces with their hands and arms and then held on to each other in a kneeling position. Glenn Eskew tells what happened next. "As the firemen trained the stream on the lead youth, his shirt peeled away. A second group—mostly teenage girls—came into sight. The firemen turned hoses on them, the water lifting several off the ground and over a parked car. One girl received cuts around her eyes and one woman a bloody nose when struck by the blast. For the next two hours the fire hoses repulsed nonviolent protesters and angry black bystanders."[90]

Some of the policemen and firemen knew that what they were doing was morally unacceptable, or at least questionable. On the first day of D-Day, a fellow captain said to captain Glenn Evans: "Ten or fifteen years from now, we will look back on this and we will say, 'How stupid can you be?'"[91] Not unexpectedly, Evans responded by saying that he was only following orders and was being influenced by the white community to maintain and defend the status quo. He was obviously trying to justify his horrific immoral behavior by shifting the moral blame from himself to external factors over which he presumably had no control.[92] Since Martin Luther King accepted the

90. Eskew, *But for Birmingham*, 268.
91. Quoted in ibid., 268.
92. Interestingly, this same man, Captain Glenn V. Evans, later recalled wondering after he had seen Fred Shuttlesworth injured several days later when slammed into the brick siding of the

Christian, personalist, and existentialist view that persons are persons precisely because they are fundamentally free, he would have advised Evans that to deny moral culpability for his own choices is to act in "bad faith";[93] that as beings created in freedom, to be free, one can rarely make the case that he was compelled to choose a certain way and could not have chosen any other way. One can always choose differently. He simply has to be willing to face the consequences. He does not have to obey the command of a superior to sic a police attack dog on innocent children. He might lose his job by refusing to obey such a command from a superior, but he can still make the choice to disobey the command.

Black spectators did not like what they saw happening to black children and began hurling bricks and bottles at the firemen and policemen. Police attack dogs were unleashed not only on the crowd, but on the nonviolent children and youths. Dogs sank their sharp teeth into Milton Payne, Henry Lee Shambry, and others. This brutal attack on innocent children who were demonstrating for the right to be treated like human beings was not received well by many around the country who saw the horrific televised images. "Birmingham became, to the rest of the nation, not so much a city but an image, and a devastating one at that, where white cops could use maximum

---

Sixteenth Street Baptist Church and then rushed to the hospital: "What does this accomplish? What do we *hope* to do here by doing these kinds of things?" (quoted in Eskew, *But for Birmingham*, 282). Clearly, some of the firemen and policemen had a sense of the inhumanity and immorality of what they were doing, despite being under orders. And yet this does not let them off the moral hook. For even if it meant losing face in the white community or losing their jobs, it was still within their power to decide against subjecting blacks to blasts from high-powered fire hoses and the sharp fangs of police attack dogs.

93. Since one of the existentialist philosophers that King studied was Jean-Paul Sartre, he was quite likely aware of Sartre's view that it is not possible for human beings not to choose; that they are, in fact, "condemned to be free" (see Sartre, "Existentialism," in his *Existentialism and Human Emotions* [New York: Philosophical Library, 1957], 23). It was also Sartre's view that when one does not own up to her choices and actions she acts in bad faith (see his *Being and Nothingness*, ed. Hazel E. Barnes [New York: Philosophical Library, 1956], Book One, chapter 2, "Bad Faith").

force on children trying to exercise constitutional rights."[94] A *New York Times* editorial on May 5, 1963 expressed what many around the country felt about the violence toward the children and other nonviolent demonstrators.

> No American schooled in respect for human dignity can read without shame of the barbarities committed by Alabama police authorities against Negroes and white demonstrators for civil rights. The use of police dogs and high-pressure water hoses to subdue schoolchildren in Birmingham is a national disgrace. The herding of hundreds of teenagers and many not yet in their teens into jails and detention homes for demanding their birthright of freedom makes a mockery of legal process.[95]

Well-meaning white people all over the country were outraged by such blatant violence against children. They were indignant about this public display of barbarism, but unfortunately this did not mean that they were supportive of and willing to fight for blacks' freedom from *all* repression. Nor were they willing to fight for the full freedom and equality of blacks in this country. Indeed, historian Lerone Bennett Jr. said it best. "[Bull] Connor blundered into the hands of Negro demonstrators by using tactics (fire hoses and police dogs) that went beyond the 'polite repression' America had become accustomed to."[96] It was alright to mistreat blacks, to violate their personhood in any number of ways, but it had to be done within respectable limits. Well-meaning whites were outraged by the blatant violence against blacks, but at the same time, most were not concerned about the conditions that led to such treatment, a point that King made on more than one occasion.

---

94. Halberstam, *The Children*, 441.
95. Quoted in Wexler, *An Eyewitness History*, 172.
96. Lerone Bennett Jr., *Confrontation: Black and White* (Chicago: Johnson, 1965), 280.

Negroes were outraged by inequality; their ultimate goal was freedom. Most of the white majority were outraged by brutality; their goal was improvement, not freedom nor equality. When Negroes could use public facilities, register and vote in some areas of the South, find token educational advancement, again in token form find new areas of employment, it brought to the whites a sense of completion.[97]

Concerned about the nation's image in the international community because of the police brutality against nonviolent protesting children, Attorney General Kennedy sent Burke Marshall to Birmingham, not to order Bull Connor and other white officials to stop committing violence against the nonviolent demonstrators, but to urge King and SCLC to cease the demonstrations so that negotiations could commence. The white establishment, including the Kennedys, believed it was unacceptable to try to negotiate civil rights while under pressure of street demonstrations, boycotts, and such. But just here, it is important to say that much like the Freedom Rides, the Birmingham campaign continued to unmask naïve liberalism, religious and secular, as well as deeply entrenched racism among whites. The tactics of movement leaders in Birmingham forced white politicians, business, and religious leaders to show their true hand, which also revealed just how deep or shallow was their commitment to civil rights. In addition, and also reminiscent of what the Freedom Rides accomplished, the tactics in Birmingham forced Washington politicians to get involved—thanks to Bull Connor who fell victim to SCLC's strategy, which counted on him to react violently against the nonviolent demonstrators. The Kennedy administration was embarrassed by this, *primarily* because the world was looking on. At this time, President Kennedy did not yet see blacks' struggle as a moral struggle that concerned the entire nation. However—and to his

---

97. Martin Luther King Jr., "Impasse in Race Relations," in his *The Trumpet of Conscience* (New York: Harper & Row, 1967), 5–6.

credit—Kennedy, in a nationally televised speech on June 11, 1963, made it clear that he finally got the point of it all. In what was his most significant civil rights speech, the President said:

> The fires of frustration and discord are burning in every city, North and South. Where legal remedies are not at hand, redress is sought in the streets in demonstrations, parades and protests, which create tensions and threaten violence—and threaten lives.
>
> We face, therefore a moral crisis as a country and as a people. . . .
>
> I am therefore asking the Congress to enact legislation giving all Americans rights to be served in facilities which are open to the public—hotels, restaurants, theaters, retail stores and similar establishments. This seems to me to be an elementary right. . . .
>
> This is one country. It has become one country because all of us and all the people who came here had an equal chance to develop their talents.
>
> We cannot say to 10 percent of the population that "you can't have that right. Your children can't have the chance to develop whatever talents they have, that the only way that they're going to get their rights is to go in the streets and demonstrate."
>
> I think we owe them and we owe ourselves a better country than that.[98]

For too long, far too many otherwise well-meaning white people were more concerned about the nation's international image, than the safety, civil rights, and equality of black people. The Birmingham campaign, quite like the Freedom Rides, revealed the unwillingness of white leaders to accept any blame for racism and racial discrimination in their city, as well as their propensity to even blame blacks (such as King and other so-called "outsiders") for the disturbance and unrest in Birmingham.[99]

---

98. Quoted in Wexler, *An Eyewitness History*, 175.
99. See Eskew, *But for Birmingham*, 283, 295.

The abuse of black children as seen on national television and in newspapers throughout the country and around the world backfired on Bull Connor and Birmingham authorities and forced their hand in the negotiation process with King and SCLC. This led them to work out an "acceptable" agreement. However, the agreement fell short of what they initially demanded in their "Four Points for Progress" presented to Birmingham business leaders:[100] 1) The need to desegregate lunch counters, restrooms, fitting rooms, and drinking fountains; 2) The hiring of blacks on a nondiscriminatory basis; 3) Dropping all charges against demonstrators; and 4) Creating a biracial committee to work out a timetable for the eradication of all other discriminatory practices in the city.

Fred Shuttlesworth happened to be hospitalized when the "acceptable agreement" was reached, and thus was highly agitated and angered about it, preferring instead to continue the demonstrations for a few more days in order to pressure the white leadership to give more than the present "agreement" allowed. His anger was exacerbated by the fact that although they agreed to desegregation and to hiring blacks, there was no timetable for when either of these would occur. Nor was there specific agreement about the number of blacks to be hired. Too much, it seemed to Shuttlesworth, was being left to the goodwill of the white businessmen and city leaders. It was actually the representatives of the traditional black leadership class who agreed to end the demonstrations solely on the basis of the "vague" verbal promises of the white negotiators.[101] This idea (of placing a moratorium on the demonstrations during the negotiations) was actually proposed by the Kennedy administration. All that was needed was King's

---

100. Manis, *A Fire You Can't Put Out*, 375, 380.
101. Eskew, *But for Birmingham*, 285. The representatives of the traditional black leadership class on the negotiating team included Lucius Pitts, Arthur Shores, and John J. Drew.

approval. Based on his considerable experience as a longtime resident of Birmingham, Shuttlesworth saw no evidence or reason to suggest that the white negotiators should be trusted solely on the basis of a verbal promise. Shuttlesworth was angered all the more because the "acceptable agreement" was reached without consulting with him and his organization, the ACMHR. SCLC protocol required that decisions would not be made without consulting the organization or leaders that extended the invitation to stage demonstrations in a given local community.[102]

There is no evidence that Martin Luther King *intended* to proceed with negotiations without consulting with Shuttlesworth, nor that he meant that the demonstrations were to be called off permanently (especially if it appeared that the white leaders were not negotiating and making concessions in good faith). Under the circumstances, it seems that Andrew Manis, Shuttlesworth's biographer, has given a reasonable explanation of what most likely happened.

> As in many important historical events, certain accidental factors also help explain the incident. Of course his injury and resulting absence from the negotiations could not be helped, nor could King's failure to seek Shuttlesworth's approval for ending the protests. Unfolding events caused Shuttlesworth's absence, and under pressure King simply forgot to confer with him. In addition, King made an unfortunate and unintended choice of words at the Drews' home when he told Shuttlesworth of his decision. Instead of indicating that he had agreed to a one-day moratorium, King told him, "Fred, we got to *call off* the demonstrations." Shuttlesworth understood this to mean the protests were being ended for good, not a temporary suspension.[103]

Shuttlesworth had misunderstood. King's choice of words was unfortunate indeed, but he had not intended to convey the idea

---

102. See the informative discussion in Adam Fairclough, *To Redeem the Soul of America: The Southern Christian Leadership Conference and Martin Luther King, Jr.* (Athens: University of Georgia Press, 2001 [1987]), 128–30.
103. Manis, *A Fire You Can't Put Out*, 384.

that the demonstrations would be discontinued even if the white leaders were found not to be negotiating in good faith, or if they reneged on the agreement. It must be remembered that King was not naïve about human nature and powerful groups (such as white businessmen and politicians in Birmingham). He knew even better than Shuttlesworth that they dare not uncritically trust those who held the reins of power. As a student of Reinhold Niebuhr, and an Afrikan American who had grown up in the Deep South with his eyes and ears wide open in race relations, King most assuredly agreed with James Madison's declaration, quoted approvingly by Niebuhr: "The truth is, that all men having power ought to be distrusted."[104] And yet, it was also the case that some believed that King's mode of operation in civil rights campaigns was to accept less than what he and SCLC initially asked for. Indeed, one reason that Shuttlesworth was so upset was because when the Birmingham campaign began, King had said that they would not compromise on their four demands. In the end, King, by accepting what was essentially the white businessmen's verbal promise, actually received less than initially sought, because the "agreement" was based on an oral rather than a written agreement. There was, then, less chance that the agreement would be upheld. Of course, there was no guarantee that the businessmen would uphold the agreement even had it been signed by all concerned.

Although King had characterized the Birmingham struggle as "the most significant victory for justice we've ever seen in the deep South,"[105] most did not believe this to be the case. Moreover, although King referred to the white businessmen negotiators as "men of goodwill," one wonders why he did not name any of them when

---

104. Quoted in Reinhold Niebuhr, *Moral Man and Immoral Society* (New York: Macmillan, 1932), 164.
105. Quoted in Jim Bishop, *The Days of Martin Luther King, Jr.* (New York: G. P. Putnam's Sons, 1971), 310.

asked by the press. Except for Sidney Smyer, the other businessmen had asked that their names be kept private.[106] At any rate, most believed that the agreement was not all that King made it out to be, nor was it binding, since no city official had participated in the negotiations and the settlement. This was all done by local businessmen. Thus, King's statement about the agreement being the most significant victory for justice ever seen in the Deep South and that it was negotiated by men of goodwill was disputed by many, not least early King biographer Jim Bishop who responded: "Either Dr. King was lying to himself, or he was lying to the world."[107]

Be that as it may, it is significant that Martin Luther King praised black youths of Birmingham as "some of the most valued foot soldiers" in that campaign.[108] They were courageous and had little fear of facing down attack dogs and high-powered water hoses, or going to jail for their freedom. Despite all of his initial worry about the safety of the children and youths, King said on reflection that they seemed to know what was at stake, and this included even those who were thought to be too young to actually march. Recalling one such instance King said: "Once when we sent out a call for volunteers, six tiny youngsters responded. Andrew Young told them that they were not old enough to go to jail but that they could go to the library. 'You won't get arrested there,' he said, 'but you might learn something.'"[109] In addition, by involving the children, King and other leaders effectively aroused the moral conscience of the nation. People all over the country and the world were sympathetically affected by the involvement of the children and young people. In addition, the young people's involvement and the violence done to them was the unexpected catalyst that got many of their parents and

---

106. Eskew, *But for Birmingham*, 295.
107. Bishop, *The Days of Martin Luther King, Jr.*, 310.
108. King, *Why We Can't Wait*, 29.
109. Ibid., 103.

teachers involved in the demonstrations. In this, and other ways, the children themselves had led the way, and thus left their own legacy for young people who would come after them, a point that will be taken up in the final chapter of this book.

In any event, Martin Luther King recalled that when an elderly black woman during the Montgomery bus boycott was asked why she chose to walk rather than accept a ride from a legitimate Montgomery Improvement Association driver, she responded that she was walking not for herself, but for her children, and grandchildren. But in Birmingham, King observed, the children and grandchildren were marching for themselves, their parents and grandparents, and for those who would come after them.[110] And yet, he also realistically recognized that much work still needed to be done in Birmingham. That they came to an "acceptable" agreement with white businessmen did not mean, for example, that all public facilities would automatically be desegregated, or that businesses would move quickly to hire even a token number of blacks. They were not, and did not.

There was no doubt in King's mind that the black children of Birmingham—while not writing history—were *making* history, and he applauded them for it.[111] They had been brave and unrelenting, and even willing to defy parents and school officials in order to participate in the mass demonstrations. They quickly saw that going to jail for freedom and what one believed to be right was not something to be feared, but a badge of honor. They believed that they were somebody if they had been to jail in the fight for freedom. Black children of Birmingham had been the true heroes and sheroes.[112]

---

110. Carson, ed., *The Autobiography of Martin Luther King, Jr.*, 208.
111. Ibid., 210.

As implied throughout, for all his praise and support of student activists, conflicts emerged between King and his youthful colleagues in the movement. We saw evidence of this when Diane Nash and other Nashville student activists invited him to join the Freedom Ride, but he declined. We also know that tensions arose in the Albany campaign when SNCC activists complained that they had arrived on the scene long before King and SCLC and had done the hard groundbreaking work, only to have them come in and receive most of the news coverage and the lion's share of monetary donations. Tension between King and SNCC youths also arose in Birmingham. When James Forman and Len Holt visited an outdoor compound where children and young people were under arrest for participating in the demonstrations, they found them to be huddling under jackets and shirts trying to stay out of the rain. Forman's first response was to go to one of the mass prayer meetings that night to report what they had seen. His hope was that parents would take blankets and other necessities to their children, but Rev. Charles Billups advised against it. Instead, Billups suggested that they find out what King (who was at a different mass prayer meeting) would say. When they located King, Forman explained what he had seen and suggested that the parents be encouraged to take blankets to their children. King disagreed, and argued that if they told the parents, there was good reason to believe that other parents would not allow their children to march the next day. According to Forman, King said he would call Burke Marshall of the Justice Department to discuss the matter with him. "In one last effort," said Forman, "I tried to point out to him that constant calls to the Justice Department lessened the militancy of the people."[113] King made the call to Marshall anyway.

---

112. The term "shero" was coined by Maya Angelou. See "Maya Angelou: Resolving the Past, Embracing the Future," an interview with Esther Hill, 1981, in *Conversations with Maya Angelou*, ed. Jeffrey M. Elliot (Jackson/London: University Press of Mississippi, 1989), 112.
113. Forman, *The Making of Black Revolutionaries*, 313.

Part of what the youthful Forman believed he was hearing from his elders was that the young people's ideas and suggestions were not nearly as valuable as those of adult leaders. They also felt that their elders were too dependent on Washington. Forman was no doubt remembering the leadership of student activists in the sit-ins, Freedom Rides, Albany, and voter registration campaigns in Mississippi. When he later advised King and Shuttlesworth that students would be able to make their way to the downtown area of Birmingham again if they were broken up into smaller groups and sent simultaneously in different directions rather than in one big mass as the elders preferred, he was once again ignored. The result was that the mass of students were trapped by the police and firemen and violence broke out when spectators came to the rescue of the children. It is not surprising that Forman was among the staunchest of King's critics when he accepted the compromised agreement with Birmingham's white businessmen. "People had become too militant for the government's liking and Dr. King's image," Forman wrote in his memoir. "I felt that the masses of young people who were the backbone of the protest in Birmingham and throughout the South had been cheated once more. The mighty leader had proven to have heavy feet of clay."[114]

White Youth in the Birmingham Campaign

One cannot help but wonder about the role of white youths in the Birmingham movement. This is one of the significant untold stories in the annals of civil rights history. Suffice it to say that there is overwhelming evidence of sympathetic white youths in Birmingham and other places in the Deep South during the civil rights struggle.

114. Ibid., 315.

God *always* has witnesses, even within groups that oppress others. Indeed, there was even indication of this when the children of Fred Shuttlesworth were arrested in Gadsden, Alabama where, on their return trip from Highlander Folk School, they refused to give their bus seats to white patrons. After Shuttlesworth successfully bailed the children out of jail, he reported receiving a number of letters from white youths wanting to get involved in the struggle. One fifteen-year-old white girl, who had never had a conversation with a black person wrote, "Since you and your group have begun this noble work, I feel there is hope that I may yet have the chance to associate with and really get to know people of different races, creeds, nationalities, etc. . . . I feel much more that it isn't so useless to be for equal rights down here. . . . Maybe if all of us can have the courage you and others have, we will get somewhere soon."[115] Shuttlesworth noted that there were similar letters from others who identified themselves as white youths. He was encouraged by this, and said: "These contacts from the white youth of Birmingham prove again that there is no solid white South—even in Birmingham."[116] At a mass prayer meeting in Birmingham, Shuttlesworth introduced to the congregation three white students from Birmingham Southern College who sought involvement in the struggle. "King announced that two of the three were the children of preachers. When Shuttlesworth put his arms around the two female students, most of the audience bolted to its feet to cheer this astonishing public display of cross-racial, cross-sexual friendship. Police observers were correspondingly galled and disgusted."[117] The next day, police officers who had been in attendance at the mass prayer meeting reported the incident to Birmingham Southern officials, and received

---

115. Quoted in Manis, *A Fire You Can't Put Out*, 245.
116. Quoted in ibid.
117. Taylor Branch, *Parting the Waters: America in the King Years 1954-63* (New York: Simon & Schuster, 1988), 749.

the promise of swift disciplinary action against the two female students.

What is most important is that the students' appearance at the mass prayer meeting was indication that not all whites were ignorant in their racial views, even if officials at educational institutions were. Moreover, it will be recalled that in the discussion on the involvement of black youths in the Montgomery bus boycott, we saw that Joseph Lacey, who was thirteen when the boycott began, reflected that he believed there were white youths who also boycotted the buses as a sign of support for blacks and their cause. In addition, after seeing the images of the police and fire officials turning attack dogs and high-powered fire hoses on defenseless demonstrators in Birmingham, more than a dozen and a half Jewish rabbis boarded a plane in New York City and flew south to give their support. Although enthusiastically welcomed by blacks, the rabbis were shunned and criticized by local Jewish leaders. Glenn Eskew has written about this.

> Nineteen rabbis joined the revolution in a "testimony in behalf of the human rights and dignity" of African Americans by boarding a plane and heading to Birmingham. They equated silence on segregation with the atrocities of the Nazi Holocaust. Local Jewry failed to make the same connection. Angered by the unannounced visit of the national leaders of the conservative Rabbinical Assembly, local Jewish leaders such as William P. Engel and Abe Berkowitz pleaded with the New Yorkers to leave. Although they failed to persuade their coreligionists, they did succeed in keeping news of the visit out of the press.[118]

Needless to say, movement people were ecstatic, and welcomed the rabbis with love and open arms. They transported them from the airport, registered them at the Gaston Motel, and invited them to

---

118. Eskew, *But for Birmingham*, 283.

the mass prayer meeting at the Sixth Avenue Baptist Church, where more than two thousand people packed in.[119]

White Resistance after the Agreement

British King scholar, Adam Fairclough, summarized what happened after the signing of the Birmingham agreement.

> No sooner had the truce been signed than the merchants attempted to backtrack. On May 15, announcing his own version of the terms, [Sidney] Smyer held that stores were to desegregate not ninety days hence, but ninety days after the new city government took office. He also implied that the hiring of a single black clerk would satisfy the employment agreement. . . . It remained unclear . . . to what extent the Senior Citizens Committee actually supported the pact. . . . The deadline for the hiring of Negro sales clerks came and went. None had been employed by October.
>
> . . . The merchants had interpreted the agreement as narrowly as possible. The biracial committee did not meet until October. Negro policemen remained an unfulfilled promise. Above all, as King complained, "a bleakness of spirit militated against wholehearted progress." Typical of this bleak spirit was the reply of James O. Haley, president of the Birmingham Bar Association, to Jerome Cooper's application for membership. "We might be liberal in our attitude," Haley responded, "but I do not believe that Birmingham lawyers and their wives are willing at this time to associate socially with Negro attorneys and their wives." The admission of Negroes, he added, would merely aggravate racial tensions.[120]

This was not all. White resistance and racial violence continued in Birmingham and other Deep South cities long after the agreement. King said that even after the negotiated agreement "and grudging compliance with some of the settlement terms,"[121] white racists

---

119. Ibid., 283, 290, 291.
120. Fairclough, *To Redeem the Soul of America*, 132–33.
121. King, *Why We Can't Wait*, 122.

bombed the home of A. D. King and his wife. In Jackson, Mississippi, NAACP field secretary Medgar Evers was assassinated by Byron de la Beckwith. Another civil rights worker, William Moore, a white postman from Baltimore, was also murdered in Mississippi during this period. Moore was murdered as he "walked from Chattanooga to Mississippi wearing two signboards, END SEGREGATION IN AMERICA and EQUAL RIGHTS FOR ALL MEN."[122] He had been warned by racist whites that he would not live to complete his journey. Tragically, barely two weeks after the March on Washington for jobs and freedom later that year on August 28, the Sixteenth Street Baptist Church in Birmingham, having played a central role in the movement efforts, was bombed on what King described as "one horror-filled September morning. . . ."[123] Four black girls, one eleven, and the others fourteen, were murdered that morning. Addie Mae Collins, Denise McNair, Cynthia Wesley, and Carole Robertson had been in Sunday school. Mary Gadson told Ellen Levine that one of her girlfriends was in class with them. "When the bomb went off, the head of one of the girls passed straight in front of her."[124] In addition, a black child was killed by Birmingham police that day, and another was murdered by racist white youths solely because he was riding his bicycle. King lamented the fact that local white leadership expressed no remorse for the murders of the six black youths on that "horror-filled" day in September.[125]

Three of the funerals of the murdered girls were held at a single service, in which King eulogized Addie Mae Collins, Cynthia Wesley, and Denise McNair as "the martyred heroines of a holy crusade for freedom and human dignity."[126] King hoped that "this

---

122. Branch, *Parting the Waters*, 748.
123. King, *Why We Can't Wait*, 122.
124. Levine, *Freedom's Children*, 90–91.
125. King, *Why We Can't Wait*, 122.

tragic event may cause the white South to come to terms with its conscience."[127] It did not. Fred Shuttlesworth spoke on King's behalf at Carole Robertson's funeral the previous day, extolling her as an innocent victim who was also "a soldier killed in a great battle for justice."[128]

For Martin Luther King, the murder of these innocent children was the first major sign that the dream he had spoken of at the March on Washington was turning into "a nightmare."[129] By this, King in no way meant that prior to the church bombing blacks—indeed the nation—were not already living a nightmare, particularly in the areas of race and economic injustice. All over the country there was indisputable evidence of a white backlash against the meager gains made during the civil rights struggle to that point.[130] Unemployment and underemployment rates among blacks were utterly astounding. The poor, of all races, were becoming poorer. Racism was rampant, not only in the country at large, but in the U.S. Congress and throughout the judicial system. Indeed, King later spoke of racism running amok in Congress.[131] All of this was at best nightmarish. The bombing murders of the four girl children merely accentuated the already-existing nightmare, and reminded King that despite what was a high point for him and many others when he told America and

---

126. Martin Luther King Jr., "Eulogy for the Martyred Children," in *A Testament of Hope: The Essential Writings of Martin Luther King, Jr.*, ed. James M. Washington (New York: Harper & Row, 1986), 221.
127. Martin Luther King Jr., "Eulogy for the Young Victims of the Sixteenth Street Baptist Bombing," in *A Call to Conscience*, ed. Clayborne Carson and Kris Shepard (New York: Warner Books, 2001), 97.
128. Manis, *A Fire You Can't Put Out*, 405.
129. King, "A Christmas Sermon on Peace," in *A Testament of Hope*, 257.
130. See King, "Impasse in Race Relations," in his *The Trumpet of Conscience*, 6–10; and Martin Luther King Jr., *Where Do We Go from Here: Chaos or Community?* (Boston: Beacon, 1967), ch. 3, "Racism and the White Backlash," and 117–18.
131. King, "The State of the Movement," November 28, 1967, at Staff Retreat of SCLC at Penn Center, Frogmore, South Carolina, King Library and Archives, 4.

the world about his dream, the reality was that black, brown, and red people and the poor in general were in fact living a nightmare.[132]

By the end of the Birmingham campaign, Martin Luther King still hoped that that city would "one day become a model in southern race relations." In November of 1967 King spoke of how Birmingham had changed since 1963, but then noted that there was still much work to be done in that city.[133] Indeed, at this writing, King's hope for Birmingham and other cities in the nation has not yet materialized. And yet, we should remember that the Birmingham campaign contributed much to the passing of the Civil Rights Bill of 1964, just as the voting rights work in Mississippi, Selma, and other places in the Deep South was a catalyst in the passage of the Voting Rights Bill of 1965. Nowhere were the courage, commitment, and determination of student activists, particularly those affiliated with SNCC, more evident than in the Mississippi Delta. The powerful saga of that struggle and the contributions of black and white youths is the subject of the next chapter.

---

132. At the 50th anniversary celebration of the March on Washington for Jobs and Freedom and the "I Have a Dream" Speech at Christian Theological Seminary in Indianapolis, Indiana on April 12, 2013, I was the lead-off lecturer, followed by Allan Boesak, Walter Brueggemann, and Frank Thomas. During the question-answer period following my address ("When the King of Love Dreamed in Public"), Professor Brueggemann reacted strongly to my statement that King saw the murders of the four children as evidence that his dream had turned to a nightmare. Brueggemann remarked that it seemed strange to say that the dream was degenerating into a nightmare when blacks were already in the nightmare. I agreed then and now with his comment, with the caveat that inasmuch as I was reporting King's view, I could not alter what he himself said. However, I also said that whenever referencing King's view again, I would also state what I believe he actually meant when he referred to his dream degenerating into a nightmare.
133. See transcript of Press Conference in Birmingham, November 4, 1967, King Center Library and Archives, 4.

4

Mississippi

Made to Disappear

As vicious and violent as Deep South cities such as Birmingham, Alabama—the bombing capital of the United States of America—was toward blacks during the civil rights struggle, it is not an exaggeration to say that places in Mississippi such as McComb, Philadelphia, and the entire Delta region were in an entirely different category. Other Deep South cities such as Birmingham and Selma were without question dangerous places for black people, but arguably no state in the nation was more dangerous for blacks than Mississippi, especially counties in the southwestern part of the state, for example, Pike, Amite, and Walthall. This region of Mississippi seethed with hatred and disdain for black humanity, and there seemed to be no limits or restraints on white violence against blacks. This, in part, is what prompted historian Howard Zinn to say that Mississippi is not just a closed society like much of the South, but a locked society, for which the key must be found.[1]

Reflecting on what it meant to be a black Mississippian, Myrlie Evers, widow of slain civil rights activist Medgar Evers, spoke for all blacks in the state when she said: "To be born black and to live in Mississippi was to say that your life wasn't worth much."[2] This said it all. White Mississippians considered blacks to be nonpersons, and thus not worthy of being treated even with the respect one might give a dog, assuming that dogs have rights and are in any way due respect by human beings. This helps to explain why it was seldom sufficient in the minds of white racists to murder blacks who in any way stood up as human beings and demanded respect. Frequently, racist whites in the state felt they had first to savagely beat, disfigure, and break every bone in a black victim's body. A young fourteen-year-old black boy from Chicago was a case in point.

Emmett Louis Till had been indescribably brutally beaten to the point that he was not recognizable, and then murdered near Money, Mississippi on August 24, 1955. His body was wrapped in barbed wire, attached to a heavy metal weight, and dumped like a piece of garbage in the Tallahatchie River by men who considered themselves to be good, born-again Christian people. These men, Roy Bryant and J. W. Milam, saw no inconsistency between their profession of the Christian faith and what they did to young Till, a human being created in God's image. Since Till's mother, Mamie Bradley, insisted on an open-casket funeral so that all the world could see what white racists had done to her child, the photo of the completely unrecognizable face (published in *Jet* magazine) was a clear reminder to blacks, particularly to black males, that Mississippi was the most dangerous place in the nation for them.

---

1. Elizabeth Martínez, ed., *Letters from Mississippi: Reports from Civil Rights Volunteers & Poetry of the 1964 Freedom Summer* (Brookline, MA: Zephyr, 2007), 75.
2. Quoted in Juan Williams, *Eyes on the Prize: America's Civil Rights Years, 1954-1965* (New York: Viking, 1987), 222.

Although the state of Mississippi had a black population of 45 percent, the highest in the nation at the time, it also held first place in a number of less-than-admirable ways during the civil rights movement. It was the poorest state in the nation; led the nation in brutal beatings, lynchings, and disappearances of blacks; during the decade of the 1950s more blacks migrated from the state than any other (approximately 315,000); 75 percent of its college graduates, virtually all white, left the state. In addition, Mississippi had fewer medical professionals, for instance, doctors, nurses, and lawyers "per capita than any other state in the nation. In 1959, the NAACP counted only one black dentist, five black lawyers, and sixty black doctors in the entire state."[3] Population wise, blacks held a clear majority in many counties and could have easily controlled things politically through the vote. Barely 5 percent of the state's black citizens were in fact registered to vote. The chief criterion for accessing the ballot box was one that blacks did not have—white skin.

It was virtually impossible for blacks to obtain a good job in Mississippi. The state and its constitution placed little emphasis on education in general, and for blacks in particular. In fact, Mississippi law did not require that blacks attend elementary and secondary schools. This was linked to the requirement for voting. That is, one had to read *or* interpret a select passage from the state's constitution to the satisfaction of white-supremacist registrars. This was obviously a problem for most blacks in the state, since so many were uneducated and unable to read. Of course, when more blacks began learning how to read, the constitution was changed, requiring that one had to be able to read *and* interpret a select passage. Most blacks could not read or interpret the constitution any more than many of their white counterparts, because they were kept out of the educational

---

3. Williams, *Eyes on the Prize*, 208.

system. And when they did attend school, they received a second-rate education at best. Indeed, state officials did not even put a premium on bookstores and public libraries, which says something not only about the black population, but about those who were in law enforcement, government, business, and such. There was, across the board, a high level of illiteracy in the state. Ignorance ruled, and it was so deeply entrenched among many whites that they had no sense of just how ignorant they were as they sought to rule over blacks. Just as many blacks could not read and interpret select passages from the state constitution, many whites could not either. But they were, after all, white.

It should come as no surprise that most white Mississippians did not try in the least to hide their preference for life in a segregated state, with virtually no social, welfare, and legal responsibility toward blacks. The social, educational, legal, and political systems in the state existed primarily for the protection and well-being of whites. Those systems also existed in order to make life miserable for blacks.

Politicians, judges, prosecutors, and law enforcement officials were blatant racists and staunch advocates of states' rights. They loathed what they perceived as outside interference, including the federal government. There was utter resentment of the presence of the NAACP, SNCC, CORE, and SCLC, as well as local civil rights groups in the state. More often than not, law enforcement officials and the courts were in collusion with their white-supremacist neighbors and relatives who committed brutal acts of violence against civil rights activists. "There was no protection from the local racists at all, for those who were supposed to protect you, the state and local police, were agents of the forces of resistance, and in the most infamous lynching soon to come, the murder of three civil rights workers in Neshoba County in 1964, the sheriff and deputy sheriff had been the murderers."[4] This was not different than in other counties in Mississippi, for example, Franklin. "The Klan ruled the county and feared no one, including the law. The Klan was the law. The Klan even threatened to kill FBI agents.... [T]hey held Franklin County, black and white, under what lawmen would call a virtual reign of terror."[5] Moreover, Klansmen who terrorized and murdered blacks were frequently considered to be "serious churchgoers," if only in the sense of regularly showing up, participating in the liturgy, offertory, and so on. "Serious" in this sense generally had nothing to do with a commitment to the highest principles of Christianity. In far too many instances the enemy for black residents and the student activists in Mississippi was the local authorities in virtually every area, including the religious establishment. As we will see, it is no wonder that most black Mississippians rejected nonviolence in favor of self-defense, and thus owned guns. Many were not afraid to use those guns in defense of self, family, and friends.

Youthful Freedom Riders Bound for Mississippi

Bernard Lafayette was one of the original student activists in Nashville, Tennessee who came under the influence and nonviolence training of James Lawson. When Lafayette, James Bevel, John Lewis (now longtime U.S. Congressman), C. T. Vivian, and Lawson boarded a bus in Montgomery, Alabama in 1961 for the Freedom Ride to Jackson, Mississippi, the image that came to Lafayette's mind about black people in that state was of them hanging from trees with ropes around their necks[6]—what Billie Holiday called in her 1939 recording, "Strange Fruit,"[7] that is, innocent black bodies hanging

---

4. David Halberstam, *The Children* (New York: Random House, 1998), 389.
5. Harry N. Maclean, *The Past Is Never Dead: The Trial of James Ford Seale and Mississippi's Struggle for Redemption* (New York: Basic-Civitas, 2009), 39.
6. Halberstam, *The Children*, 334.

from trees. Indeed, in his reflections on black power and his urging that black power advocates not imitate the worst in white values and practices, Martin Luther King reminded his people that blacks had not indiscriminately lynched and murdered white people, and had not "hung white men on trees bearing strange fruit."[8] So this idea of strange fruit, of black bodies hanging from trees in Deep South towns, was emblazoned in the psyche of southern blacks.

Without question, Mississippi, particularly the Delta and Southwest region of the state, was anything but black people friendly. It was, rather, a most intimidating, life-threatening place for those with black skin, no matter what part of the country they were from, and no matter what was their social status. In some ways, Mississippi was just as intimidating and life-threatening to well-meaning white activists (including students) from the North as well as the South. White-supremacist segregationists could be—and frequently were—just as violent and murderous toward white activists as their black counterparts. In fact, because they were considered "nigger lovers" they were generally beaten more severely than blacks. For example, Rabbi Arthur Joseph Lelyveld sustained a savage beating in Hattiesburg during Freedom Summer. Lelyveld had accompanied a small interracial group of youthful civil rights activists, who had been handing out leaflets. They were attacked by two white men with tire irons. The students remembered what they learned in the nonviolent workshops about taking nonviolent self-defensive positions of crouching and covering their heads if attacked. Unfortunately, the rabbi either forgot what was learned, or had not undergone the training before accompanying the youths. Since he remained

---

7. Manning Marable and Leith Mullings, *Freedom: A Photographic History of the African American Struggle*, ed. Sophie Spencer-Wood (New York: Phaidon, 2002), 173.
8. Clayborne Carson, ed., *The Autobiography of Martin Luther King, Jr.* (New York: Warner Books, 1998), 331.

standing during the attack, his head was exposed, and was an easy target for the repeated blows by the savage attackers.[9]

Blacks had no civil and political rights in Mississippi, nor could they count on the police and the judicial system for protection and justice, for these were often complicit in terrorist acts against blacks, and whites who supported the civil rights movement. This is surely a reason why many black Mississippians owned guns and rejected nonviolence; who were staunch believers—like Hartman Turnbow—that blacks had to learn to speak the language that whites speak to them. If whites are nonviolent with blacks, blacks should be nonviolent with whites. But if whites are violent with blacks, blacks should be violent with their attackers.[10]

Julian Bond, one of the founders of SNCC, recalled that they once had a big debate in SNCC about carrying guns. Although most of the original SNCC activists (affiliated with the Nashville Student Movement) were against weapons of any kind, volunteers who were Mississippi residents insisted on the need to carry guns. Indeed, Bond reflected: "Almost everybody with whom we stayed in Mississippi had guns, as a matter of course . . ."[11] A white college volunteer in the Mississippi Summer Project in 1964 wrote to his parents that virtually every farmer in the Mississippi Delta, regardless of race, owned at least one gun. One of four volunteers staying with black farmer Robert Miles and his family, this same student told his parents that Miles owned seven guns, and kept them all loaded.[12] Moreover, like Hartman Turnbow, Miles and other blacks were not hesitant to use their guns in self-defense or defense of loved ones and

---

9. Michael B. Friedland, *Lift Up Your Voice Like a Trumpet: White Clergy and the Civil Rights and Antiwar Movements, 1954-1973* (Chapel Hill/London: University of North Carolina Press, 1998), 106.
10. Howell Raines, *My Soul Is Rested: Movement Days in the Deep South Remembered* (New York: G. P. Putnam's Sons, 1977), 263, 265, 266.
11. Quoted in ibid., 267.
12. Martínez, ed., *Letters from Mississippi*, 99.

friends. Muriel Tillinghast, COFO's project director in Greenville, recalled an incident in which a black resident made it clear to the local sheriff that if he did not do his job, they would retaliate in kind against the Klan. "[A]fter whites began shooting at the home of Silas McGhee in apparent retaliation for the family's civil rights activities, 'Mrs. McGhee called the sheriff and told him . . . she knew exactly who was out there shooting at her and that the sheriff should come and tell these here boys to go home, because they were going to be picking up bodies the next time that she called.'"[13] Even NAACP field secretary Medgar Evers carried a pistol in his car and kept guns at the ready in his home. According to Ruby Hurley (the NAACP's regional director in Birmingham), Evers "used to sit on it, under his pillow."[14] Hurley tried—in vain—to convince him that it did no good to carry the gun, since the segregationists were cowards and would very likely ambush him, if anything. Myrlie Evers told interviewers that "we had guns in every room of our house. I slept with a small revolver next to me on the nightstand. He slept with a rifle next to him. We had one in the hall, we had one in the front room."[15] Medgar Evers made it palpably clear that he would use the guns in defense of himself, his family, and his friends. Like those mentioned before, Evers was a black Mississippian for whom the nonviolence of Martin Luther King and many of the student activists simply did not make sense. Everything in his experience of living in Mississippi told him that he should be both willing and able to defend himself and loved ones from attackers of all hues, but most especially racist whites. The state of Alabama was a frightening place for blacks, but when it

---

13. Clayborne Carson, *In Struggle: SNCC and the Black Awakening of the 1960s* (Cambridge/London: Harvard University Press, 1995 [1981]), 122.
14. Quoted in Raines, *My Soul Is Rested*, 271.
15. Quoted in Henry Hampton and Steve Fayer (with Sarah Flynn), *Voices of Freedom: An Oral History of the Civil Rights Movement from the 1950s Through the 1980s* (New York: Bantam, 1990), 152.

came to inflicting the worst forms of violence imaginable upon them, the Mississippi Delta region was without rival. Black Mississippians knew this, and thus opted for self-defense. We will see in the next chapter that this was also the stance of many local blacks in Selma, Alabama as well.

Bernard Lafayette recalled the eerie silence on the bus when they crossed the state line into the magnolia state of Mississippi. In that moment, he also remembered participating in a sit-in at a hamburger shop near Vanderbilt University in Nashville. He remembered that "a young white student had come over and smiled at him in a sinister way and had said, 'You wouldn't be doing this if you were in Mississippi.'"[16] So outraged was jazz singer Nina Simone at Jim Crow practices, violence against, and disappearances of blacks and other freedom fighters in Mississippi and other places in the Deep South, that she wrote and sang passionately the song, "Mississippi Goddamn" in 1964 as part of her own artistic protest. Here we had a coming together of art and social protest. The opening line of the song says it all: "Alabama's got me so upset, Tennessee made me lose my rest and Ev'rybody knows about Mississippi god-dam."[17]

John Lewis recalled what he felt as the bus carrying the Freedom Riders crossed into Mississippi. "I'd never been to Mississippi before," Lewis said. "All my life I had heard unbelievably horrible things about the place, stories of murders and lynchings, bodies dumped in rivers, brutality and hatred worse than anything I'd ever heard of growing up in Alabama or attending college in Tennessee."[18] Lewis had a sense that they were "leaving America, if Alabama could be

---

16. Halberstam, *The Children*, 334.
17. The complete words of this song are found in *Sing for Freedom: The Story of the Civil Rights Movement Through Its Songs*, ed. Guy and Candie Carawan (Bethlehem, PA: Sing Out Corporation, 1992), 193.
18. John Lewis, *Walking with the Wind: A Memoir of the Movement*, with Michael D'Orso (New York: Simon & Schuster, 1998), 169.

called America, and going into some foreign land. In Mississippi, he had decided, even before they crossed the state line, the great victory would be simply going there, staying alive, and leaving."[19] The anxiety of the passengers deepened as they neared Jackson. Upon arrival, they were arrested, sent to jail, and then to Parchman State Penitentiary, "a notoriously brutal place, where everything, it was said, was done at gun point."[20] Every black child in the state knew about Parchman. Bob Moses, in charge of SNCC's voter education-registration project in the Delta region, described what it was like to be doing civil rights work there: "When you're in Mississippi, the rest of America doesn't seem real. And when you're in the rest of America, Mississippi doesn't seem real."[21] No one who did civil rights work in Mississippi would disagree.

Martin Luther King and Mississippi

In late July of 1964, Martin Luther King went to Philadelphia, Mississippi at the invitation of Bob Moses and as part of the SCLC "People to People" tour in support of the Mississippi Freedom Democratic Party.[22] Although King had a strong contingent of FBI agents along for protection, this would not be the case when he returned to Philadelphia two years later on June 21, 1966, to lead a memorial service for the second anniversary of the murders of James Chaney, Michael Schwerner, and Andrew Goodman. This would be an experience that King would not soon forget.

---

19. Halberstam, *The Children*, 335.
20. Ibid., 345.
21. Quoted in Charles E. Cobb, *On the Road to Freedom: A Guided Tour of the Civil Rights Trail* (Chapel Hill, NC: Algonquin Books, 2008), 259.
22. Seth Cagin and Philip Dray, *We Are Not Afraid: The Story of Goodman, Schwerner, and Chaney, and the Civil Rights Campaign for Mississippi* (New York: Nation Books, 2006, first published by Scribner, 1988), 380.

Upon arrival in Philadelphia, King led a procession of approximately three hundred people down the hill from Mt. Nebo Church to the courthouse where he planned to address the crowd. King stopped momentarily to pray at the jail where Goodman, Chaney, and Schwerner were incarcerated before being released and murdered by law enforcement officers and the Klan. As they continued toward the courthouse, a mob bearing clubs, ax handles, sticks, and hoes blocked each end of the narrow street and eventually attacked many people in the procession. Although the police were present, they made no attempt to stop the attackers. Upon reaching the courthouse, King confronted Deputy Cecil Price, who was one of the murderers. When Price would not allow him to ascend the courthouse steps, King turned to face the crowd and began speaking. Another crowd of mobsters, along with Price, stood behind King. Aware that Price was one of the murderers, King told the crowd:

> "In this county Andrew Goodman, James Chaney, and Mickey Schwerner were brutally murdered. I believe the murderers are somewhere around me at this moment."
>
> "You damn right," King heard Price say, "they're right behind you."
>
> "They ought to search their hearts," King continued. "I want them to know that we are not afraid. If they kill three of us they will have to kill us all. I am not afraid of any man, whether he is in Mississippi or Michigan, Birmingham or Boston. I am not afraid...."[23]

Seth Cagin and Philip Dray report that later that day, King described that experience "as one of the most frightening of his life. As he walked back to Independence Quarters, he told a reporter, 'This is a terrible town, the worst I've seen. There is a complete reign of terror here.'"[24] Under the circumstances, King had every reason to be afraid.

---

23. Quoted in ibid., 382.
24. Cagin and Dray, *We Are Not Afraid*, 382.

What was more important is that he did not allow the fear to stop or cause him to curtail his speech. King understood that fear is part of the human condition; that periodically, one might well be afraid, but this should not deter him from doing what he set out to do. One must manage the fear, and press onward to the goal.

Indeed, as far back as September 1959 Martin Luther King himself acknowledged the difficulty and danger of standing up for justice in Mississippi. In an address to a public meeting of the Southern Christian Ministers Conference of Mississippi on September 23, he said to those gathered: "As we all know, it is not easy to take a stand in Mississippi, for the possibilities of economic reprisals and bodily harm are much greater here than in other sections."[25] King referenced the murder of Reverend George Lee and the shooting of Gus Courts in separate incidents, because they registered blacks to vote in Belzoni, Mississippi. He also called attention to the brutal murders of Emmett Till, and the abduction from jail and brutal lynching of Mack Charles Parker in Money and Poplarville[26] respectively.

Martin Luther King was appalled that J. W. Milam and Roy Bryant were found not guilty for the murder of young Emmett Till. Although these men professed to be Christians, to King theirs was at best an emotional and superficial religion devoid of morality and a sense of appreciation for the ethical teachings of Jesus, which would seem to beg the question of whether they were in fact Christian. King saw these two men as examples of the "countless millions of people who worship Christ emotionally but not morally. . . . The white men who lynch Negroes worship Christ," he said in a Dexter Avenue Baptist Church sermon about a month after Till's murder. "That jury in Mississippi, which a few days ago in the Emmett Till

---

25. Clayborne Carson et al., eds., *The Papers of Martin Luther King, Jr.* (Berkeley: University of California Press, 2005), 5:282.
26. Ibid., 5:286, 287.

case, freed two white men from what might be considered one of the most brutal and inhuman [*sic*] crimes of the twentieth century, worships Christ. . . . The trouble with these people, however, is that they worship Christ emotionally and not morally. They cast his ethical and moral insights behind the gushing smoke of emotional adoration and ceremonial piety."[27] Referring to this same theme in the sermon outline, "Faith in Man" on February 26, 1956, he wrote: "We have looked to Missippii [*sic*] and seen supposedly Christian and civilized men brutally murdering the precious life of a little child."[28] In addition, King referenced the Till murder in a letter to Mississippi Governor James P. Coleman on April 24, 1956.[29] Approximately one year later, in the sermon, "Questions That Easter Answers," preached at Dexter, he again referred to the murder of young Till, asking God why blacks are treated so inhumanely in this country: "*Why* is it simply because some of your children ask to be treated as first-class human beings they are *trampled* over, their homes are bombed, their *children* are pushed from their classrooms, and sometimes little children are thrown in the deep waters of Mississippi?"[30] King was clearly deeply troubled by the brutal murder of young Emmett Till.

Most blacks and liberal whites rightly suspected that the members of the Klan and the White Citizens Council were thoroughly embedded in the political, legal, judicial, and educational system of that region. This explains, in part, how the state of Mississippi was able to become so proficient at making blacks disappear from jails, their homes, or right off the street. Those charged with protecting all citizens and ensuring freedom and justice for all were complicit in the

---

27. Ibid. (2007), 6:232.
28. Ibid., 6:253.
29. Ibid. (1997), 3:221.
30. Ibid., 6:289.

violence committed against black citizens and efforts to deny them justice and freedoms guaranteed by the Constitution.

Indeed, every black and white person who did civil rights work in Mississippi knew how quickly and easily they could be made to disappear. Roy DeBerry grew up in Holly Springs, Mississippi. He was in high school in 1963. Reminiscing many years later, he recalled that anybody who had been a part of the movement for any period of time "knew that *when you disappear in Mississippi, you're dead.*"[31] This is why SNCC activists in Mississippi had a rule that workers were *never* to violate under any circumstances. No one was to ride alone, whether in cars or on buses.[32] The obvious reason was that if one was alone and was abducted by the Klan or some other hate group, there would be no witnesses. But we will see that sometimes no witness was left, even if there were several activists traveling together. Any person in the United States who had eyes to see and ears to hear knew without question that Mississippi was for blacks nothing short of "the land of intimidation."

Generally, in virtually any place in the South, Martin Luther King's presence caused blacks to feel a sense of enthusiasm and expectation; a sense that change was on the horizon. Meeting places were frequently jammed to capacity and overflowing. The one exception, however, was a workshop on nonviolence given in Mississippi. Two years before the Freedom Ride from Montgomery to Jackson, James Lawson had been in Jackson with King doing a workshop on nonviolence. Lawson recalled that the meeting place for the workshop was only half filled, and those present were noticeably uneasy about being there. "A King audience was usually a confident one and more often than not an exuberant one, but not in this case."[33]

---

31. Ellen Levine, *Freedom's Children: Young Civil Rights Activists Tell Their Own Stories* (New York: G. P. Putnam's Sons, 1993), 113 (my emphasis).
32. Halberstam, *The Children*, 406.
33. Ibid., 338.

The atmosphere was thick with anxiety, as attendees quite likely thought they were under surveillance and that their names may be released to the authorities, who, generally, were white supremacists. The point is that Mississippi was known, even by movement people, to be the state they would have to crack if the movement in general was to have a chance to succeed. In the previous chapter, we saw that King held a similar view about Birmingham, but there is no reason to think that he would have been in disagreement with the stance regarding Mississippi. Student activists discovered very early that to do movement work in Mississippi, especially in the Delta region, meant being willing to risk lives, those of the youthful SNCC and CORE activists, as well as the local residents, for example, Herbert Lee, who courageously got involved.

Previously we saw that, not long after SNCC was founded, competing factions developed within the organization. One group was more religiously oriented and favored the direct-action approach of sit-ins, Freedom Rides, and such. The other was more politically inclined and favored the political approach, for instance, voter education-registration projects. At the advice of Ella Baker, SNCC leaders decided that both were relevant, and thus there was no need to focus only on one. They could divide up and do both. I return to this important point subsequently, but for now, suffice it to say that in 1961 the young people in SNCC led the way in the Mississippi Delta campaign, as they did (virtually simultaneously) in Albany, Georgia.

Bob Moses was among the first of the SNCC activists to go into Mississippi to begin the difficult and dangerous work of voter education and registration. The previous year he had gone to Mississippi to recruit youth activists for a SNCC conference in Atlanta. Moses had been stuffing envelopes for SCLC at the time. When SNCC needed someone to go to Mississippi to recruit, he eagerly volunteered, using his own money to purchase his bus ticket.

Upon arrival, he met Amzie Moore, president of the Cleveland, Mississippi chapter of the NAACP. Moore convinced him that what was needed was a group of fearless, determined SNCC recruits to come to Cleveland to develop a voter education and registration campaign. Moses promised Moore that he would take his recommendation to SNCC leadership in Atlanta, and that whether the Atlanta office agreed to send a team or not, he himself would return to Cleveland the following summer.[34] There was almost immediate mutual appreciation and respect between the two men.

> Moore saw in Moses the quiet courage black Mississippi needed to "uncover what is covered." And to Moses, the stout, stocky Moore suggested the old spiritual, "a tree beside the water" that would not be moved. Amzie Moore wasn't interested in sit-ins, Moses learned. Sharecroppers earning $500 a year could not afford to eat at lunch counters. Voting, Moore said, was the key to change in Mississippi. Blacks outnumbered whites two to one in the Delta, but only 3 percent could vote. Since World War II, even the smallest registration campaigns had sparked shattering violence.[35]

As he would find in the case of numerous other blacks in the Delta, Moses noticed that Moore kept a loaded rifle at his side. Moore drove Moses around the Delta introducing him and letting him get a feel for the culture and rhythm of things. He also had him speak at a number of black churches to get a sense of how he handled himself, and how the people reacted to him. Moses told the people: "There's something coming. . . . Get ready. It's inevitably coming your way whether you like it or not. It sent me to tell you that."[36]

---

34. Vincent Harding, Robin D. G. Kelley, and Earl Lewis, "We Changed the World: 1945-1970," in *A History of African Americans from 1880*, ed. Robin D. G. Kelley and Earl Lewis (New York: Oxford University Press, 2005), 222.
35. Bruce Watson, *Freedom Summer: The Savage Season That Made Mississippi Burn and Made America a Democracy* (New York: Viking, 2010), 27.
36. Quoted in ibid.

There had been significant breakthroughs in voter registration in every southern state, except Mississippi. In fact, after Moses had done voter registration work for some months in the Delta region, he wrote a report to the Voter Education Project (a funding source for their work) saying: "We are powerless to register people in significant numbers anywhere in the state and will remain so until the power of the Citizens Councils over state politics is broken, the Department of Justice secures for Negroes across the board the right to register, or immediate registration to vote. Very likely, all three will be necessary before a breakthrough can be obtained."[37] To say that Moses' conclusion was prophetic would be an understatement. Moses could see early on the systemic nature of the problems preventing blacks from registering to vote in the Delta. As long as the decision as to whether blacks could register was in the hands of white supremacists, and as long as the federal government refused to intervene to guarantee their constitutional right to vote, no matter how much money was thrown at voter registration projects, there would be no significant breakthroughs in terms of numbers of blacks registered to vote. The experience of Moses and his SNCC colleagues convinced him of this fact.

Competing but Interrelated Factions within SNCC

When SNCC was founded during Easter weekend of 1960 at the conference at Shaw University, a number of the youthful leaders had long been involved in the Nashville Student Movement, and had been trained in the theory and techniques of Gandhian nonviolence by James Lawson. Most were Southerners, and were deeply religious in outlook. In addition, they were committed to the idea that

---

37. Sanford Wexler, *An Eyewitness History of the Civil Rights Movement* (New York: Checkmark Books, 1999), 197.

nonviolent direct-action campaigns, such as sit-ins, were the best means to freedom and civil rights. Before long, Northern black youths began going south to join SNCC and other youth organizations.

Frequently, black Northerners were more politically astute and driven and had less appreciation for religion, church, and nonviolence than their Southern counterparts. Not surprisingly, before long, tension began to develop as a division started to emerge between (roughly) the original Nashville group, and the Northerners who joined later. The former saw it as a theologico-political struggle, while the latter saw it as a strictly political struggle. What essentially emerged, especially after a SNCC leadership conference at the Highlander Folk School in Tennessee in August 1961, were both a religious or theologically driven faction, *and* a politically driven contingent. The big difference between the two had to do with issues of strategy. One preferred direct action, while the other felt that voter registration in the South was most needed. Fortunately, Ella Baker was able to help them see that because SNCC's aim was to do its part in the civil rights and freedom struggle for blacks, there was room for both factions. One would focus on direct-action campaigns such as sit-ins, and the other could do voter education and registration work. As noted earlier, what SNCC activists would discover, especially while engaged in voter education and registration projects in Mississippi, was that doing voter registration work in that state was nothing short of direct action.[38] Moreover, the dangerous work in Mississippi would prove that politicians such as the Kennedys, who sought to steer SNCC activists away from direct-action campaigns, especially Freedom Rides, and toward activities (naïvely believed to be) less prone to arousing violence, such as voter

---

38. Halberstam, *The Children*, 390.

registration, had been wrong; that voter registration in the very backwards, uncivilized state of Mississippi produced as much, if not more, violence than direct-action campaigns.

Roughly, we may say that Diane Nash (one of the original Nashville student leaders) was the leader of the religious and direct-action faction of SNCC, although we will see that this did not preclude voter registration work. Bob Moses was the leader of the voter registration group. Almost simultaneously, in July 1961, the Moses group began beachhead work in McComb (the Delta region), and members of the Nash contingent began similar work in Jackson, after James Bevel and Bernard Lafayette did a stint in Parchman prison because of their involvement in the Freedom Ride.[39]

Freedom Ride to Jackson and Recruitment of Youth Activists

When James Bevel completed his sentence at Mississippi's infamous Parchman prison after being arrested for the Freedom Ride to Jackson, he decided that he would remain in the state. After all, he was a Mississippi native. He would remain in Jackson to recruit young blacks, believing even then, that high school recruits were better than college ones. They were more teachable and had less to lose. Although Bevel hoped that he would not have to go to the ranks of junior high school youths, it was not out of the question. In chapter 3, we saw that he and Diane Nash learned a great deal from this experience with black youths and their sense of commitment to the struggle. Bernard Lafayette, who had been in Parchman with Bevel, decided that he could not allow him to take such a risk by himself, and thus decided to remain in Jackson to work with him.

---

39. Ibid., 404.

The work of Bevel, Lafayette, and Diane Nash in Jackson in youth organizing and voter registration, not unlike the work of Moses, Dave Dennis, Bob Zellner, Chuck McDew, Charles Jones, and many others in the Delta, was thought by some to be the next step in the larger strategy that was driving the Freedom Rides.[40] It was a twofold strategy. The first step was to continue the work of opening the eyes of the federal government to the deeply entrenched injustices and inequities to which blacks were subjected in Deep South states like Mississippi, Georgia, and Alabama. Throughout the period of the sit-ins and the Freedom Rides, as well as the Birmingham struggle, federal authorities did not seem to get that the authorities in places like Mississippi were committed absolutely to white supremacy and race discrimination. Indeed, they were just as committed to using every resource of the state to enforce racial exclusion. Federal authorities were naïve, to put it very mildly. They seemed to think that the problem was just a very few racists in places like Mississippi, while the vast majority of white Mississippians were presumably good people who were committed to treating everybody fairly. The work of SNCC activists would quickly prove this to be the lie it was, and to show instead that more often than not, the Klan and White Citizens Councils, legislators, law enforcement officers, judges, and such, were one and the same. A Klan attack on blacks was a police attack on them, so embedded was the Klan in the local police departments. SNCC's presence and actions revealed that there was no way such people would do justice where blacks were concerned; that the only way this would happen would be through strong federal intervention.

The second part of SNCC's strategy in Mississippi was to break through the fear of local blacks, who had known nothing but intimidation and acts of terrorism from white Mississippians. The

---

40. Ibid., 389.

SNCC youths knew that only when local blacks get beyond their fear, would they demand their rights as American citizens. Only then would they understand that their particular town, for example, McComb, was not a separate island unto itself, but a part of the United States of America, and therefore was expected to behave in a civilized manner toward *all* of its residents.

James Bevel was street smart and a youth at heart. This made it easier for him to relate to young people. At the beginning of their work, he and Lafayette knew that there was no better way to recruit young people than to work the streets of black residential areas, particularly in places where young people typically hang out, such as street corners, playgrounds, and parks where they played basketball. They also went door to door in black neighborhoods, which allowed them to meet and get to know parents as well, many who were not terribly enthusiastic about their recruitment efforts. Lafayette saw immediately that Bevel had a knack for getting through to young people. He could speak their language and could hold his own in conversation and argument with them. He would even go so far as to instigate a fight with one or more youths, before finally beginning to talk with them about the real fight that they all had before them. It seemed to Lafayette that Bevel was committed to using any means necessary to recruit young people for the struggle. Another technique that was always useful for the two men was to introduce themselves as Freedom Riders. Because of the huge amount of publicity and criticism directed toward the Freedom Riders in the press and other media, everybody in Jackson knew about them. The fact that the media was critical of the Freedom Riders made them heroes and sheroes to black youths. In many instances, this made it easier to break the ice with younger blacks.

Working in tandem, Bevel and Lafayette were able to draw in many black youths. They insisted to the youths that because of the seriousness of what lay before them, *commitment* was a key ingredient. One way they could show their commitment at the outset was by agreeing to show up for a very early-morning meeting at six a.m. If they could not be there by that time, they were not to come. If they were there, this would be evidence that they were serious and willing to do what was asked of them. Lafayette spoke with the parents of each youth that volunteered. Needless to say, if the youths participated in protests, they also had to be willing to go to jail, and many did.

Although they initially focused on recruiting high school youths, it was not long before Bevel began recruiting even younger students. Lafayette believed (as King initially did in Birmingham when Bevel argued for using massive numbers of children) that recruiting younger students was problematic. They were just too young, he reasoned. Furthermore, Lafayette did not want to be the one to explain to parents that they had recruited fourteen-year-olds and younger to participate in the protests. When Bevel insisted on continuing this practice, both he and Lafayette were arrested and jailed for two weeks for contributing to the delinquency of minors. Their sentences and fines were suspended, but their work in Jackson was for all intents and purposes ended.

Moses in the Mississippi Delta

When Bob Moses returned to Cleveland, Mississippi to do voter registration work with Amzie Moore, he discovered that Cleveland was not set up to do such work. Consequently, he was invited to target nearby McComb to try to implement the project there. As Bevel, Nash, Lafayette, and others tried to establish a foothold in Jackson, Moses and his group of SNCC activists tried to do the same in the dangerous Delta region. "McComb and the surrounding region were, even by the cruel standards of Mississippi, considered uniquely mean and dangerous."[41] Indeed, Moses was baptized early when, a few weeks after his arrival in July, he tried to register several local blacks in the town of Liberty on August 29. The venture failed, and he was severely beaten by Billy Jack Caston, who happened to be the cousin of the racist sheriff and the son-in-law of the racist local state representative, E. H. Hurst. Hurst murdered Herbert Lee—black resident and supporter of the SNCC activists—in cold blood. When witness and local black resident, Louis Allen, mustered the courage to testify, he too was killed. Allen had told the FBI that he would testify against Hurst if he could get federal protection, but none was given. He eventually decided that it was in his best interest to leave Mississippi for Milwaukee. Tragically, just hours before he was to leave the state he was gunned down. Herbert Lee and Louis Allen were the first casualties of the Delta campaign.[42] The murders of the two men were underreported in major newspapers. "The killing of Herbert Lee had been reported in just one major newspaper; the murder of Louis Allen was found only on back pages."[43] The murders were a devastating blow to Moses and the SNCC activists. Moreover, Moses had to endure the angry outrage of Lee's widow. At Lee's funeral, his wife had shouted at Moses, "You killed my husband! You killed my husband!"[44] This was a tremendous weight on the shoulders of one so young.

The immediate lesson learned was that blacks stood no chance of obtaining voting rights and justice as long as white supremacists were in charge of voter registration, the police force, the courts, and the state legislature. Without federal intervention there was no chance for a successful voter registration campaign. There was no other way,

---

41. Ibid., 401.
42. Quoted in Hampton and Fayer, *Voices of Freedom*, 143.
43. Watson, *Freedom Summer*, 93.
44. Halberstam, *The Children*, 309.

since racist murderers were also the relatives of racist legislators, law enforcement officials, court officials, and jurors.

In fairly quick order, Moses developed a reputation among the locals that helped to give him legendary status. Wherever he worked in the Delta, he exhibited a penchant for being patient with, and listening to poor blacks, that made them feel like what they said really mattered. He not only listened to the locals, but heard them. Furthermore, he did not pretend that he was in any way better than them, and had no desire to tell them what to do. "He was not only educating himself, but letting them know they were worth listening to. Within the Movement, as Julian Bond noted, he was gaining a reputation as a saint. . . ."[45] Some even considered him "the reluctant 'Jesus of the movement.'"[46] The stance of Bob Moses was quite different from many Northern blacks who came down, who exhibited "a barely concealed contempt and condescension" toward black Southerners.[47] Moses met them where they were; accepted them for who they were; and respected them for what they were willing to contribute toward fighting for their voting rights and freedom.

The fact that Moses and other SNCC activists met with violence early in their voter registration work in the Delta is yet another reminder of just how clueless the Kennedy administration was about what was really happening in Deep South states. More concerned about the nation's image on the international level than the safety and civil rights of blacks in the South, the Kennedys sought to steer SNCC and other youth activists away from direct-action campaigns to what they believed would be civil rights efforts that would not lead to racist violence against the activists. They believed, quite naïvely,

---

45. Ibid., 403.
46. Watson, *Freedom Summer*, 101.
47. Halberstam, *The Children*, 403.

that voter registration projects were the perfect solution. To this end, Robert Kennedy sought ways to secure funds for such projects. In April 1962 the Voter Education Project (VEP) began as an outgrowth of Kennedy's efforts to get private tax-exempt support for voter registration in the South. His real aim, of course, was to move SNCC and other youth activists to more nonconfrontational methods. Kennedy was proven wrong, since Moses and his project met with severe violence not long after he arrived in the Delta.

When Bob Moses and other SNCC activists implemented the voter education-registration project in McComb, they knew from the beginning that because of the sheer racist meanness of many whites in the Mississippi Delta, they and local activists could, indeed would very likely be, subjected to violent acts, and even death. They obviously had no desire that such things happen, but they understood—where others did not—the reality and likelihood of their occurrence. "As Moses had known all along, the idea that a voting project would provoke less violence than a Freedom Ride was totally out of touch with the reality of white Mississippi."[48] The only ones who believed such nonsense were out of touch, insensitive, and naïve white liberals and politicians in Washington. Such tragic acts of violence occurred early, beginning with the murder of local farmer and activist Herbert Lee.

Although not planned by Moses and SNCC, high school students staged sit-ins at the local Woolworth's lunch counter, the first direct action against segregation of that type in McComb history. The two youths in this case, Curtis Hayes and Hollis Watkins, were arrested and sentenced to thirty days in jail. A few weeks later, fifteen-year-old Brenda Travis, and five older high school students staged a sit-in in the "white" area of the bus terminal, for which they were

---

48. Quoted in Hampton and Fayer, *Voices of Freedom*, 150.

arrested. Travis was also expelled from school. When black students marched on city hall to protest the arrest, jailing, and expelling of Travis and others, they too were arrested. Moreover, when Herbert Lee was murdered, Moses and SNCC activists Charles McDew and Bob Zellner, and more than a hundred black high school students marched through the streets of McComb. They stopped to pray on the steps of city hall, at which time Zellner was viciously attacked by several racist thugs. Moses and McDew tried to shield him from the attacks as best they could. Zellner recalled hearing the awful thud sound of blackjacks hitting the heads of Moses and McDew. When the two men were incapacitated by the blows, the mob was able to continue beating Zellner. He had observed that although the police were present, they did nothing to stop the attackers. He noticed, instead, that their body language seemed to encourage the mob to especially beat him. Zellner recounted the incident for Hampton and Fayer.

> They said, "Bring him here, we'll kill him." They were screaming just absolutely like animals. I was holding this Bible and they started dragging me out in the street, and I realized that if they got me in the street, no matter what the cops did, nothing was gonna stop that mob from killing me. So I put the Bible down and grabbed ahold of the railing that went down the City Hall steps. I resisted. I don't know if I would have done that if I'd had a lot of nonviolent workshops. But I hadn't had very many nonviolent workshops. I remember thinking to myself, God helps those who help themselves. So I helped myself to the railing....[49]

The three SNCC activists were placed under arrest, along with 119 students. This was the pattern in Deep South states. The nonviolent demonstrators, not the thugs and hoodlums who savagely attacked them, were arrested by law enforcement officers. The three SNCC

---

49. Quoted in ibid., 146.

workers and nine local activists were later fined and sentenced to four months in jail. Once released on bond, Moses and SNCC activist Chuck McDew started what they called a Nonviolent High School for students who were expelled from the public high school. Several weeks later, they were arrested for contributing to the delinquency of minors and sentenced to four months in jail. After this incident, Moses' time in McComb was shortlived, inasmuch as the voter registration project there came to an end on December 1, 1961.

C. C. Bryant, leader of the local NAACP in McComb, had begun calling for SNCC to leave. Bryant and other local traditional leaders said that they had not expected sit-ins, demonstrations, murder, mayhem, and the arrests of their children.[50] Essentially, Bryant and local black leaders were the victims of the same naïve thinking as Bobby Kennedy. They thought that voter registration projects would not produce the level of violence that was often associated with direct-action campaigns such as Freedom Rides and sit-ins. Before long, it was evident that in places like Mississippi *anything* that blacks did to obtain their civil rights and freedom, including voter registration projects, was perceived by white Mississippians as direct action. Therefore, whatever steps blacks took only intensified the white violence that already existed.

Fortunately, as the student movement progressed further into the decade of the sixties and gained more support of black parents, local leaders like C. C. Bryant changed their minds about the protest tactics of the youthful activists in SNCC and other civil rights groups. For his part, Bryant later declared the sentiment of many older blacks at a mass meeting: "*Where the students lead we will follow.*"[51] This same sentiment would be expressed by many older black residents during the Freedom Summer Project in 1964. "Ralph Featherstone,

---

50. Williams, *Eyes on the Prize*, 213.
51. Quoted in Cobb, *On the Road to Freedom*, 287 (my emphasis).

director of the McComb freedom school [during Freedom Summer], asserted that 'old people are looking to the young people and the [young people's] courage is rubbing off.'"[52] In any event, SNCC's first attempt at voter registration was rejected, and there were even calls for its leaders to leave McComb. But looking back, it is clear that not all was lost. Indeed, in 1962, SNCC joined with SCLC, CORE, and the NAACP to form the Council of Federated Organizations (COFO), which received financial assistance from foundation funding that was arranged by the Kennedys for a Voter Education Project.

A number of important lessons were gained from the McComb voter education-registration project that proved useful to the movement going forward, especially with reference to what could be expected of black youths throughout the subsequent Mississippi campaigns, Birmingham, and Selma. Some of the important lessons learned from the initial efforts at voter registration in the Mississippi Delta include: 1) Local black leaders proved to be courageous and determined to pursue voter registration even in the face of violence and death; 2) Leaders such as Amzie Moore made it clear that they wanted the presence of SNCC activists such as Bob Moses because of their fearlessness and the fact that they "was for business, live or die";[53] 3) Black youths in high school and junior high school saw the struggle for civil rights and freedom as much their own as black adults', and were willing to do their part regardless of the potential cost; 4) There was growing evidence that although blacks retained a healthy sense of fear of white retaliation, increasing numbers refused to be paralyzed by fear; and 5) The early efforts of SNCC aided in exposing the depth and entrenchment of police violence and brutality against blacks.

---

52. Carson, *In Struggle*, 120.
53. Quoted in Raines, *My Soul Is Rested*, 236.

Freedom Summer and the COFO Kids

When COFO was formed, Aaron Henry was selected as chair, and Bob Moses (SNCC) and Dave Dennis (CORE) as co-directors. COFO's first major project was Operation Freedom Vote, which occurred in the fall of 1963. There was a mock election component of Freedom Vote. Whites were not allowing blacks to vote in the upcoming gubernatorial election, so they selected and voted for their own candidates in the mock election. Aaron Henry, a black pharmacist from Clarksdale, was the candidate for governor, and Reverend Edwin King, a white chaplain at the all-black Tougaloo College, was his running mate. In order to get out the vote, Bob Moses, the chief field organizer for the project, along with Allard Lowenstein, who proposed the idea of the mock election, invited sixty white students from Yale and Stanford Universities for two weeks of canvassing black neighborhoods to get the word out about the election. Some of the volunteers were beaten and arrested, but they persevered, and the election was a big success, with 93,000 people casting votes. The Freedom Party candidates, Aaron Henry and Edwin King, were the victors. If there had been doubts before, within any group on any level, as to whether blacks both wanted to vote and would do so if allowed to register, the Freedom Vote project erased them.[54]

COFO's next major voting rights project was to be launched the following summer of 1964. The organizers were mostly from SNCC and CORE. The leadership would vastly expand the idea of using white volunteers from primarily white colleges and universities, an idea that not all of the staff agreed with, especially black members from the South. The young activists laid out the problem and their intention in the "Prospectus for the Summer."

---

54. Williams, *Eyes on the Prize*, 228.

> It has become evident to the civil rights groups involved in the struggle for freedom in Mississippi that political and social justice cannot be won without the massive aid of the country as a whole, backed by the power and authority of the federal government. Almost no hope exists that the political leaders of Mississippi will steer even a moderate course in the near future; in fact, the contrary seems true: As the winds of change grow stronger, the threatened political elite of Mississippi become more intransigent and fanatical in their support of the status quo. . . . Negro efforts to win the right to vote cannot succeed against the extensive legal weapons and police powers of local and state officials without a nationwide mobilization of support.
>
> Therefore, a program is being planned for this summer which will involve the massive participation of Americans dedicated to the elimination of racial oppression.[55]

The primary focus was on voter education and registration.

Charles Cobb was one of the most vocal, staunchest opponents of the idea, arguing that to invite such a massive number of young white volunteers implied that SNCC and black Mississippians were not able to take care of their civil rights business. "You're conceding that you're not able to deal with the situation," he told Howell Raines. "I mean, the reason for the 1964 Summer Project was simply that we weren't able to cope with the violence in the state."[56] And yet, Cobb saw clearly why those who were against the idea could not prevail. Since their inception, SNCC, SCLC, NAACP, and CORE were organizations that stressed integration and desegregation. Moreover, all but SCLC had integrated memberships. Desegregation and integration were built-in components of these organizations. Consequently, Cobb rightly argued, ". . . you are victims of your own rhetoric, because at the same time [some of us were rejecting the

---

55. Quoted in Fred Powledge, *Free at Last?: The Civil Rights Movement and the People Who Made It* (New York: HarperPerennial, 1991), 562–63. From "Prospectus for the Summer," undated, mimeographed copy of an SNCC working paper in Powledge's private collection.
56. Quoted in Raines, *My Soul Is Rested*, 286n.

idea of a massive influx of white college student volunteers], we were arguing desegregation, integration . . . the necessity for a society in which black and white did not make a difference. So you couldn't argue that you were opposed to white people coming down."[57]

Another staffer who rejected the idea of bringing in a massive number of white college student volunteers was Hollis Watkins, a black Mississippian who joined SNCC in Pike County, Mississippi in 1961, and was the COFO director for Holmes County during the summer of 1964. His rationale was different than, but also related to, Cobb's.

> "I was against it," he explained, "basically because I felt that we had reached the point where we were making pretty good headway in getting local people from Mississippi involved and getting local people to take the initiative. And I felt that to bring in Northerners who had no knowledge of the South and who had no prior experience in dealing with people from the South, who could come in with a certain attitude, a certain mentality—that that would ultimately lead to squashing this initiative that the people in Mississippi had just begun to take. And I felt that once it was squashed, then it would leave those of us like myself who were from Mississippi, who would forever, for the most part, be here, with just that much heavier burden in trying to get people restarted all over again."[58]

Watkins claimed that his issue was not with bringing in "outsiders," but bringing in massive numbers which, in his view, would stifle the emerging grassroots leadership. Although there was clearly concern about the attitude that whites might bring, this was not entirely a concern with race. It will be recalled, for example, that some of the founding SNCC members, especially those from the South, were concerned about the attitude of superiority over black Southerners that was detected in some Northern blacks who joined SNCC's

---

57. Quoted in ibid., 287.
58. Powledge, *Free at Last?*, 579, 80.

efforts in the South. Some of this had to do more with regional, class, and cultural differences. But it was also surely the case that the race element was a factor regarding some whites. As it turned out, Watkins's prediction about the stifling of local leadership came true in some instances, but he was just as quick to acknowledge that some very good things came out of the Freedom Summer project, for example, the establishment of Freedom Schools.

The plan for Freedom Summer was first presented at a COFO staff meeting in Greenville, Mississippi, in the spring of 1964. The meeting was chaired by co-director Dave Dennis. Bob Moses was unable to attend. The staff voted against the idea. Lawrence Guyot recalled that when Moses returned the next day, he said: "Look, I'm not gonna be a part of anything all-black. We're gonna have the Summer Project. We need it."[59] Moses recalled that with some exceptions, local blacks wanted the students to return. Fannie Lou Hamer was one who had fond memories of the Yale and Stanford kids who helped with the mock election of Operation Freedom Vote. "Nobody never come out into the country and talked to real farmers and things . . . ," Hamer reflected. "And it was these kids what broke a lot of this down. They treated us like we were special and we loved 'em."[60] In any case, Moses was certain that there were bigger things happening in the country, such as the passage of the Civil Rights Bill. "Mississippi was reacting to that," said Moses, "and we were feeling the backlash . . . growing in Mississippi against gains [for blacks] that were made nationally but which were not having any immediate effect in Mississippi . . . burning churches, murder. . . . I felt in that context I had to step in . . . between the staff and the people we were working with. And so that's how the decision was made to actually invite the students down for the summer of '64."[61]

---

59. Quoted in Raines, *My Soul Is Rested*, 287.
60. Quoted in Watson, *Freedom Summer*, 13.

One might reasonably ask, Why white student volunteers? Why not send out the call for black student volunteers? Dave Dennis put it bluntly:

> We knew that if we had brought in a thousand blacks, the country would have watched them slaughtered without doing anything about it. Bring a thousand whites and the country is going to react to that in two ways. First of all is to protect. We made sure that we had the children, sons and daughters, of some very powerful people in this country over there, including Jerry Brown, who's now governor of California, for instance. . . . The idea was not only to begin to organize for the Democratic Convention, but also to get the country to begin to respond to what was going on there. They were not going to respond to a thousand blacks working in that area. They would respond to a thousand young white college students, and white college females who were down there.[62]

Since most of the white students were middle to upper middle class, attended some of the best universities, and were from homes with professional parents, their involvement meant that middle-class elements of the country would be forced to be concerned about the Mississippi project and the plight of poor blacks there. After all, their children would be working there. Bob Moses expressed this very point, saying: "These students bring the rest of the country with them. They're from good schools and their parents are influential. The interest of the country is awakened, and when that happens, the Government responds to that interest."[63] The federal government had not responded responsibly before now because blacks were the primary victims. Although a sad commentary on the nation, the bottom line was, the death of a black student would bring less national attention to Mississippi than the death of a white student. To

---

61. Williams, *Eyes on the Prize*, 229.
62. Quoted in Raines, *My Soul Is Rested*, 274.
63. Quoted in Carson, *In Struggle*, 112.

their credit, Moses, Dennis, and other COFO workers figured this out long before the Freedom Summer Project was conceived.

Because 1964 was a presidential election year, the Freedom Summer project would focus on both voter education and registration. During his recruitment efforts at Stanford University in February, Moses told the students that the project had four goals: 1) to expand black voter registration throughout the state; 2) to organize a legally constituted "Freedom Democratic Party" that would challenge the racist Mississippi Democratic Party; 3) to establish Freedom Schools to teach reading and math to black students for whom there was no state-mandated school attendance; and 4) to open community centers that would provide for a myriad of needs for the black poor, for example, medical, legal, recreational, and social welfare. Driving these goals was the idea to literally force a confrontation between racist, Klan-infested Mississippi authorities and the federal government. The aim was for the federal government to intervene and force local authorities to stop interfering with the voter education-registration project and blacks' right to vote. Moses had worked in the Delta long enough to know that white supremacists in the state would not voluntarily grant blacks civil and voting rights. They would have to be made to do so, and thus the decision of SNCC to implement the Freedom Summer Project as a means of forcing a confrontation between Mississippi authorities and the federal government. Moses "described SNCC's plan as an annealing process. Only when metal has been brought to a white heat, can it be shaped and molded," he said. "This is what we intend to do to the South and the country, bring them to white heat and then remold them."[64]

On Sunday afternoon, June 14, training for the first group of volunteers began on the campus of Western College for Women, in

---

64. Quoted in ibid., 98.

Oxford, Ohio. This was the official start-up of the Freedom Summer Project. Volunteers underwent a week of intensive orientation and training by SNCC field secretaries, native Mississippi civil rights workers such as Fannie Lou Hamer, and a few outside "experts." As noted before, some native Mississippians and COFO staffers expressed concern as to whether some of the white volunteers would be willing to submit to the supervision of blacks. And of course, as we have seen, some had earlier questioned the usefulness of the project. Whether they tried to conceal their view or not, it was transparent for some of the young volunteers during the orientation period. "A few days after arriving in Oxford, a white volunteer noted that the black staff members, especially those from Mississippi, were 'very much an in-group, because of what they have gone through together. They tend to be suspicious of us, because we are white, northern, urban, rich, inexperienced. We are somewhat in awe of them, and conscious of our own inferiority.'"[65]

At a number of points the training staff questioned the level of maturity and seriousness of some of the volunteers. This became evident on June 16 when the staff and volunteers were watching a televised report on the voter registration work in Mississippi. When college volunteers "began to laugh at the 'idiotic registrar' and the 'incredible double-talk of the rabid lawyer' who had prevented blacks from registering to vote," recalled student volunteer Bill Hodes,[66] some of the staffers arose from their seats and left the room in disgust. SNCC scholar Clayborne Carson tells what happened next. "Afterward, an older staff member declared, through tears, 'Maybe you won't laugh when you meet these guys and hear them talk, and know that they are doing it every day with or without the Feds.'"[67]

---

65. Carson, *In Struggle*, 112.
66. Ibid., 113.
67. Ibid.

The remark snapped the volunteers into the reality that what they were about to embark on was a matter of utmost seriousness.

The students had probably meant no harm, and some of the staffers likely overreacted. Indeed, more of the onus was on the staffers since they were the experienced ones. And yet, leaving the room, as a number of them did, also taught the volunteers something about the life-or-death seriousness of the project in which they were preparing to engage. When the two groups came back together, a staffer told of the beating and shooting of colleagues in Mississippi, and warned that "if they were not scared, they should 'get the hell out of here because we don't need any favors of people who don't know what they are doing here in the first place.'" Another staffer counterbalanced this by saying: "'We cried over you in the staff meeting, because we love you and are afraid for you.' He assured the volunteers that although staff members had walked out during their laughter, no one would walk out when they confronted white violence: 'When you get beaten up, I am going to be right behind you.'"[68] The two staffers related different, but important sentiments, which Carson helpfully described as "the complex interplay of resentment and compassion that was to affect their relationships with white volunteers throughout the summer."[69]

It was important that the volunteers understand before they left Ohio, that there was much to be afraid about in Mississippi; that fear itself in such a violent context was a necessary survival aid. All volunteers were warned that any one or more of them could be killed on any given day or night, and that they could not trust that the police would save them, since the police were often the Klan and the Klan the police. They were warned that many Mississippi policemen had barely a fifth-grade education, and so when stopped by them,

68. Ibid.
69. Ibid.

they were not to resist in any way, or try to give them a lesson in constitutional law.⁷⁰ In any case, they were not to allow fear to incapacitate them.

The volunteers were to use the fear of being in the Delta region as a means to helping them remain alert at all times, taking nothing for granted, and being slow to uncritically trust local whites. CORE worker Isaac Reynolds said it best: "If you had fear, then you had to maintain your sharps. Because it was dangerous. You had to be sharp at all times, because we were in a war. And we didn't have any guns, and the other side did. We didn't have the law with us. The other side did. In many places before things really would explode, we did not have the press with us. So we had to be alert at all times."⁷¹ One had to keep her guard up at all times. A healthy fear of the Mississippi Delta enabled one to retain such alertness and sharpness. Reynolds went on to speculate that Chaney, Schwerner, and Goodman were murdered because they got careless and dropped their guard.⁷² Being chased by police and Klansmen after they were released from jail at night, the three men should not, under any circumstances, have stopped their car, despite being summoned to do so by police. "That was the general belief throughout the South," said Reynolds, "that if you were out there on the highway, and particularly at night, then you don't stop for anybody. You stop when you get where you're going."⁷³ In Reynolds's view, Chaney, Schwerner, and Goodman made a deadly mistake by stopping.

70. Williams, *Eyes on the Prize*, 230.
71. Quoted in Powledge, *Free at Last?*, 571.
72. It is important to note that Chaney and Schwerner were CORE staff members. Goodman was a Freedom Summer volunteer who was selected by Schwerner and Chaney to work with them. SNCC's first worker to be killed was twenty-one-year-old Tuskegee resident and college student Sammy Younge Jr. (See John Neary, *Julian Bond Black Rebel* [New York: William Morrow, 1971], 89.) He was murdered on January 3, 1966, by a white gas station attendant for trying to use the restroom. (See James Forman, *Sammy Younge, Jr.: The First Black College Student to Die in the Black Liberation Movement* [New York: Grove, 1968].)
73. Quoted in Powledge, *Free at Last?*, 571.

The COFO trainers knew that the survival of the youthful volunteers depended heavily on their fear of Mississippi, and that they must carry that fear into the state with them. The trainers also drilled into them the fact that white Mississippians will view those affiliated with the Freedom Summer project as "niggers" and "nigger lovers," and will generally treat them more harshly,[74] something to which Bob Zellner and Jim Zwerg could testify. Indeed, staff trainers shared hate mail with the prospective volunteers that was sent to the campus of Western College for Women, just to give them an even clearer sense of how real was the danger before them in the Delta. "Phrases from one letter leaped out: 'Morally rotten outcasts of the White race. . . .' 'White Negroes' are the rottenest of the race-mixing criminals. . . . [I]t will be a long, hot, summer—but the 'heat' will be applied to the race-mixing TRASH by the <u>DECENT</u> people who do not believe in racial mongrelization through racial prostitution."[75]

It is to their credit that most of the volunteers made the conscientious decision to go to Mississippi even though they learned of the disappearance of Schwerner, Chaney, and Goodman *before* they left Ohio. The news scared most, and even caused some to feel petrified with fear, but the vast majority had made up their minds to go anyway, although a few would last only a week before deciding to return home.[76] Indeed, one student reflected that while standing before the students and talking about the three who had disappeared, Moses seemed to want all of the volunteers to pack up and go back home.[77]

Peter Orris was a Harvard freshman who volunteered for the Freedom Summer Project. He recalled how he and several other

---

74. Wexler, *An Eyewitness History of the Civil Rights Movement*, 208.
75. Quoted in Watson, *Freedom Summer*, 32.
76. Watson, *Freedom Summer*, 103.
77. Martínez, ed., *Letters from Mississippi*, 36.

volunteers had driven to Washington to plead for federal intervention in the project. When they returned to the campus of Western College for Women, they were shocked to find people in a deep state of grief and sadness. They joined a large circle of SNCC veterans and student volunteers holding hands and singing freedom songs. They were told that Goodman (who was one of the college volunteers, who had just left Ohio for Mississippi the previous day), Chaney, and Schwerner had disappeared. "Our reaction was horror," said Orris. "The sorrow that went through the camp [sic] was profound."[78]

After Rita Schwerner addressed the volunteers and made an emotional appeal to the students to use their influence and that of their parents to put pressure on the Justice Department and then left, Bob Moses decided that they needed to be straightforward with the students about what they believed had happened to the three civil rights activists. From the moment he was informed of the disappearances, Moses had believed they were dead. When told that they had first been arrested, and then released after nightfall, he knew that a cover-up was under way, and the three men would not be seen alive again.[79] "If, in fact, anyone is arrested and then taken out of the jail [as was the report about Chaney, Schwerner, and Goodman], then the chances that they are alive were just almost zero," Moses told the students. "We had to confront the students with that before they went down, because now the ball game had changed. We talked to them about the fact that as far as we could see, all three of them were dead. And that they had to make the decision now as to whether they really wanted to carry through on this and go down."[80] In fact, Moses and SNCC staffers had been brutally honest with the volunteers from

---

78. Quoted in Hampton and Fayer, *Voices of Freedom*, 189.
79. Watson, *Freedom Summer*, 101.
80. Quoted in Hampton and Fayer, *Voices of Freedom*, 190.

the beginning, making it palpably clear that they could be subjected to violence and death. It just so happened that one of the student volunteers' own (Goodman) was murdered the day after arriving in Mississippi and before they themselves actually left Ohio. One of Moses' final pieces of advice to the volunteers, some of whom were grief-stricken to the point of crying, was that if there was any hesitation at all about going to Mississippi, they should return home. "Because what has got to be done had to be done in a certain way," he said, "or otherwise it won't get done."[81]

Indeed, the presence of SNCC in Mississippi was the beginning of what would soon be large numbers of Northern white college students from various places in the country working with local black activists such as Fannie Lou Hamer of Ruleville, Mississippi, in a massive voter registration campaign. This was a significant occurrence, not least because it was further evidence of black youths' coming of age from a leadership standpoint. Many had given up middle-class materialist values, for example, careers and the hope of attaining wealth, and many (who King referred to as "constructive school dropouts"[82]) even dropped out of college to provide leadership in the struggle for freedom and equality. White students worked primarily in support roles, a fact that did not escape King's attention. Looking back, he said that black students "ceased imitating and began initiating. Leadership passed into the hands of Negroes, and their white allies began learning from them. This was a revolutionary and wholesome development for both."[83] King referred to the voter education and registration effort of the Freedom Summer youths as "one of the most creative attempts I had seen to radically change the

---

81. Watson, *Freedom Summer*, 102.
82. King, "Youth and Social Action," in his *The Trumpet of Conscience* (New York: Harper & Row, 1968), 46.
83. Ibid.

oppressive life of the Negro in that entire state and possibly the entire nation."[84]

"... the Way of Love and Constructive Goodness"

As noted above, before the young volunteers could make progress on the project, tragedy struck. At the beginning of the Freedom Summer Project, CORE field secretary Michael Schwerner, student volunteer Andrew Goodman (both Jews from the North), and CORE employee James Chaney, a black activist-organizer from Meridian, Mississippi, went to Longdale, Mississippi, to investigate and record witness accounts of the burning destruction of the Mount Zion Baptist Church. On Sunday morning, June 21, cognizant of SNCC's security handbook rule requiring that there always be more than one activist traveling in a car or on a bus in the state, most especially at night, the three activists left for Longdale, and disappeared.

Schwerner, Chaney, and Goodman visited the site of the burned church, and interviewed several witnesses. In the process, they learned what must have been most disturbing, namely that Klansmen had come into Longdale looking for Schwerner on the night the church was firebombed and burned to the ground. An execution order had been given by "soft spoken businessman,"[85] Sam Bowers, imperial wizard of the White Knights of the Klan, to kill Schwerner.[86] After the murders, Bowers was quoted as saying: "It was the first time that Christians had planned and carried out the execution of Jews."[87] Years later, Bowers was convicted (after four mistrials) of the murder of local farmer and activist Vernon Dahmer.[88]

---

84. Carson, ed., *The Autobiography of Martin Luther King, Jr.*, 249.
85. Watson, *Freedom Summer*, 278.
86. Cagin and Dray, *We Are Not Afraid*, 12.
87. Watson, *Freedom Summer*, 279.
88. Ibid., 292.

Schwerner had been working in Mississippi for six months, and knew that most whites resented the civil rights work he was engaged in. He had been warned of the consequences if he did not stop what he was doing and leave the state. Mount Zion Church was targeted because Schwerner had spoken there barely three weeks earlier, and had gained permission to use the church as a Freedom School, where voter education would take place. Schwerner and Chaney had convinced the members to participate in the project. On the night the church was burned, the Klan first threatened several members who were leaving the building after a meeting. They savagely beat and stomped Jim Cole as his praying wife looked on helplessly and horrified.

Chaney, Goodman, and Schwerner left Longdale in plenty of time to return to Meridian by the designated time of four p.m. If they—indeed any field workers—did not return by the previously agreed-on time, protocol required that an alarm be initiated by the communications person on duty. Ironically, Louise Hermey of Drew University, one of six college volunteers (along with Goodman), who made the trip from Oxford, Ohio the day before with Chaney and Schwerner, was the person on duty at the COFO office in Meridian that Sunday afternoon. Like Andrew Goodman, it was her first day as a student volunteer. If Hermey had any doubts at all as to the seriousness of what she had volunteered for, that all changed in an instant. She initiated the alarm by phoning COFO headquarters in Jackson to report that field workers due to check in at four o'clock had failed to do so. She was advised to wait an hour, in the event they were delayed by some unforeseen legitimate circumstance, such as car trouble. After an hour passed, she phoned again, and was instructed "to activate the search procedure. Hermey steeled herself to make inquiries at the local jails from the master phone list, and called places where the group might have turned up safely. Movement veteran Sam Block, who turned up instead, volunteered to check the city jail. About ten o'clock, Hermey called Mary King in the Atlanta SNCC office."[89] Mary King, a white SNCC activist, initiated the next phase of the alert.

As Schwerner, Goodman, and Chaney approached Philadelphia on their way to the main highway that led back to Meridian, they were stopped, ostensibly for speeding, by Klansman deputy sheriff Cecil Price. The three activists were placed under arrest and taken to jail, intentionally held until nightfall, and then released. They were then chased down by several carloads of Klansmen, among them Deputy Price. Bullets from a .38 caliber weapon were found in the bodies of the three men. The bodies were found buried in an earthen dam on a farm in Philadelphia, on August 4, after an extensive search led by the FBI and U.S. sailors. An independent coroner's report written by Dr. David Spain, an expert New York pathologist, revealed that the earlier autopsy report "had grossly understated Chaney's injuries," and that the wounds and bone condition revealed that he likely endured a savage beating, although it was not possible to determine whether the beating occurred before or after he was killed. In the report written to COFO, Spain said that "the jaw was shattered, the left shoulder and upper arm were reduced to a pulp; the right forearm was broken completely across at several points, and the skull bones were broken and pushed in toward the brain."[90] Although Spain's findings could not be disproved, it is also fair to say that no corroborating evidence of his findings has ever emerged either.

Edgar Ray Killen, Klansman and presumed "preacher" (ordained a Baptist minister![91]) was the one who summoned the lynch mob to murder Chaney, Schwerner, and Goodman. One of his fellow-

---

89. Taylor Branch, *Pillar of Fire: America in the King Years 1963-65* (New York: Simon & Schuster, 1998), 361.
90. Cagin and Dray, *We Are Not Afraid*, 406.
91. Ibid., 36.

Klansmen later confessed to FBI agents that it was Killen who assured his murderous partners: "We have a place to bury them, and a man to run the dozer to cover them up."[92] "Klansman" and "Christian preacher" are oxymoronic at best. In 1967, Killen was ultimately charged with three counts of manslaughter.[93]

While searching for the three youths, authorities made the gruesome discoveries of at least seven other blacks who were involved in the civil rights struggle (though not the Freedom Summer Project) and who had also disappeared long before Chaney, Goodman, and Schwerner.[94] Two of these were Henry Hezekiah Dee and Charles Eddie Moore. They were abducted on a rural highway in southwest Mississippi near Natchez on May 2, 1964, taken deep into the Homochitto National Forest, bound to a tree, and savagely beaten to death by James Ford Seale and other Klansmen. The bodies were tied to an engine block and dumped into the river.[95] The body of a black teen, never identified, was found in the Big Black River. The body had on a CORE T-shirt.[96]

There was anger and much speculation among many white and black SNCC activists who believed that had Schwerner and Goodman been black, like Chaney, there would not have been as

---

92. Watson, *Freedom Summer*, 272.
93. Ibid., 295.
94. See Raines, *My Soul Is Rested*, 278, 288; and Williams, *Eyes on the Prize*, 232.
95. Seale was convicted in 2007, and was serving three life sentences at the federal prison in Terre Haute, Indiana for the murders. He died there in 2011. Although Seale and Charles Marcus Edwards faced state murder charges in 1964 in the deaths of Dee and Moore, the charges were quickly dismissed, on the claim of insufficient evidence. This was consistent with the sustained practice of either dismissing cases involving whites' murders of blacks, or finding the guilty parties not guilty. And why would this not be the case, since law enforcement and the courts at all levels in Mississippi were massively infiltrated by the Klan and representatives of other white hate groups? One could not distinguish law enforcement and officers of the courts from the Klan, and vice versa. Moore was a student at Alcorn A & M. Dee was a twenty-one-year-old. Neither man had been a participant in the civil rights movement. Their half-bodies were discovered by navy frogmen as they searched for Goodman, Chaney, and Schwerner (John Dittmer, *Local People: The Struggle for Civil Rights in Mississippi* [Urbana/Chicago: University of Illinois Press, 1995], 251).
96. Dittmer, *Local People*, 251–52.

much national outrage, or as extensive a search for them.⁹⁷ SNCC activist John Lewis expressed this sentiment as well.⁹⁸ In addition, Schwerner's wife, Rita, articulated the same thing when she spoke of the close relationship between her husband and Chaney: "It's tragic that white northerners have to be caught up into the machinery of injustice and indifference in the South before the American people register concern. I personally suspect that if Mr. James Chaney, a native Mississippian, had been alone at the time of the disappearance, this case, like so many others, . . . would have gone completely unnoticed."⁹⁹ Jane Stembridge, a white SNCC leader and activist then serving in Greenwood, Mississippi, echoed the same conviction in a document she sent to Mary King at the SNCC office in Atlanta:

> America, if Jim Chaney had gone to Neshoba alone and disappeared somewhere out there, it would not have made very much difference. Because, America, Jim Chaney is black. Black men have disappeared for three hundred years across the length and width of this nation. You did not care. If you had cared, you would have done something about it . . .
>
> You have noticed Mississippi now, because two white men are missing along with Jim Chaney. Andy Goodman and Mickey Schwerner had to come down here before you heard of Jim Chaney. . . .¹⁰⁰

Many of those who were expressing outrage, fear, and demanding what was previously not available to local activists, namely, federal protection, were white parents, relatives, and friends of the hundreds of mostly white college students participating in Freedom Summer. For the first time, many well-meaning northern white people recognized that the racial violence in Mississippi not only threatened the safety and lives of black children, but their own children as

---

97. Halberstam, *The Children*, 479–80.
98. Carson, *In Struggle*, 115.
99. Quoted in Williams, *Eyes on the Prize*, 231.
100. Quoted in Wexler, *An Eyewitness History*, 209.

well.[101] These white parents clearly did not share Martin Luther King's conviction about the relational nature of *all* human beings, that what happens to any person anywhere in the world affects—directly or indirectly—persons everywhere, including God. Had whites held a similar conviction, they surely would have been morally and otherwise outraged and concerned enough to go to Mississippi and also to demand the involvement of their political representatives, regardless of the racial-ethnicity of the three murdered civil rights activists.

The parents of Schwerner and Chaney expressed the desire that their sons be buried side by side,[102] but this was a violation of Mississippi segregation laws, which applied in death as in life. Plans to inter the two bodies together in a black cemetery were dropped when the black mortician handling Chaney's funeral refused to touch the remains of Schwerner. "He told the Schwerners he feared Mississippi authorities would revoke his license—or worse—if he did. Several white Meridian undertakers were contacted, none of whom were willing to transport Mickey's body to a Negro cemetery."[103] Chaney was buried in a segregated cemetery in Meridian,[104] and Goodman and Schwerner were buried back in New York. So moved was Schwerner's mother (Anne Schwerner) by the friendship and hospitality shown her son by Chaney and his family that she told the *New York Times*:

> I want to say something about James Chaney. He was a Negro, a friend, and a brother to my boy Mickey. Mickey knew this was a bright, bright boy, and he opened a world of hope for [him]. They would go out in the field together . . . working together to help the people. Mickey and

---

101. See Cobb, *On the Road to Freedom*, 278–79.
102. Cagin and Dray, *We Are Not Afraid*, 406.
103. Ibid., 408.
104. Williams, *Eyes on the Prize*, 235.

Rita ate in the Chaney home, and when there was no food for anyone else, Mrs. Chaney somehow found some for them.

I've never met Mrs. Chaney, but . . . I wish . . . I could take her in my arms.[105]

Not surprisingly, the murders of the three youthful civil rights activists devastated their colleagues in COFO. Nowhere was this expressed more graphically and passionately than in Dave Dennis's eulogy of Chaney. Because Chaney's mother had asked him to eulogize her son at the after-burial memorial service at the First Union Baptist Church in Meridian, Dennis wanted to do a good job and to be as polite and respectful as he could. He had also been advised by the national CORE office to be mindful of his tone and what he said. He wanted to do that. He worked hard to discipline himself to do it. But then came the moment of truth. As he stood before the congregation, and looked out at the face of Chaney's little brother, Ben, he snapped. "[I couldn't] talk about things getting better, and how we should do it in an easy manner with nonviolence," he said. In part, Dennis told those in attendance:

> . . . as I stand here I not only blame the people who pulled the trigger or did the beating or dug the hole with the shovel. I blame the people in Washington, D.C., and on down in the state of Mississippi for what happened just as much as I blame those who pulled the trigger. . . .
>
> I don't grieve for James Chaney. He lived a fuller life than many of us will ever live. He's got his freedom, and we're still fighting for ours. I'm sick and tired of going to the funerals of black men who have been murdered by white men . . .
>
> I've got vengeance in my heart tonight, and I ask you to feel angry with me. I'm sick and tired, and I ask you to be sick and tired with me. The white men who murdered James Chaney are never going to be

---

105. Quoted in Wexler, *An Eyewitness History*, 209.

> punished. I ask you to be sick and tired of that. I'm tired of the people of this country allowing this thing to continue to happen . . .
>
> We've got to stand up. The best way we can remember James Chaney is to demand our rights. Don't just look at me and go back and tell folks you've been to a nice service. Your work is just beginning. If you go back home and sit down and take what these white men in Mississippi are doing to us . . . if you take it and don't do something about it . . . then God damn your souls![106]

Dennis cried through much of the eulogy. He had not planned such an outburst, and really did intend to be controlled as he gave his comments. One of the student volunteers who was present at the service reflected that "it was as if he was realizing his anger and feeling only as he spoke. As if the deepest emotion—the bitterness, then hatred—came as he expressed it, and could not have been planned or forethought . . ."[107] Asked to also be one of the speakers at Schwerner's funeral (James Farmer, John Lewis, and attorney William Kunstler were the other speakers), Dennis expressed his true feelings there as well. As he had said at Chaney's memorial service, he told those in attendance that the murders probably would have gone unnoticed had all three victims been black. "'They were not the first to be killed in Mississippi,' he reminded the members of the audience. 'I feel they are not going to be the last. Tomorrow it might be your son or daughter, or you yourself.'"[108] After the murders of Chaney, Goodman, and Schwerner, Dennis was less convinced than ever of the viability of nonviolence as a strategy, let alone as a way of life. Instead, he was convinced that as a strategy nonviolence was "a waste of good lives. You have to put some injury on your enemy to get respect,"[109] he said. Nevertheless, in his eulogy of Andy Goodman,

---

106. Quoted in Williams, *Eyes on the Prize*, 239, 240.
107. Martínez, ed., *Letters from Mississippi*, 219.
108. Quoted in Cagin and Dray, *We Are Not Afraid*, 412.
109. Quoted in Dittmer, *Local People*, 249.

Rabbi Arthur J. Lelyveld said of the three youths: "Theirs is the way of love and constructive service."[110] This was their legacy.

In any event, despite the efforts to run them out of Mississippi, only a very few of the Freedom Summer volunteers chose to leave the project after Chaney, Schwerner, and Goodman were disappeared. One of the student volunteers, in language not unlike that of Freedom Rider Jim Zwerg (from his hospital bed), told a reporter: "Their disappearance, although it might have been calculated to try to drive people out of the state, had just the opposite effect on me and everyone else. Whenever an incident like this happens . . . everyone reacts the same way. They become more and more determined to stay in this state and fight the evil system that people have to live under here."[111] This reaction was right in line with SNCC philosophy: "When beaten down, get right up again; when intimidated, carry on in the face of fear."[112]

A backstory that we do not often hear much about has to do with the second group of Freedom Summer volunteers being trained in Oxford, Ohio and how they reacted to the news of the disappearances and presumed murders. This group was comprised of the teachers for the Freedom Schools. Only a loving parent can imagine the horror and sense of terror experienced by their parents, especially since they now knew without a shadow of a doubt that the Klan and other white hate groups in Mississippi did not stop at making deadly threats, but carried them out with regularity and with a vengeance. These parents had all the evidence they needed that their children could be the next Chaney, Goodman, or Schwerner. So the volunteers had a tough time explaining to their parents why, in the face of the disappearance of the three civil rights workers,

---

110. Quoted in Cagin and Dray, *We Are Not Afraid*, 411.
111. Quoted in Williams, *Eyes on the Prize*, 231–32.
112. Ibid., 232.

they must go to Mississippi. Freedom Summer scholar Bruce Watson includes excerpts from a couple of the letters that students wrote their parents trying to explain why they must go forward instead of returning to the safety of their homes. A portion of one, written on June 27 follows.

> Dear Mom and Dad,
>
> This letter is hard to write because I would like so much to communicate how I feel and I don't know if I can. It is very hard to answer to your attitude that *if* I loved you I wouldn't do this—hard, because the thought is cruel. I can only hope you have the sensitivity to understand that I can both love you very much and desire to go to Mississippi . . .[113]

After the disappearance of Goodman, Schwerner, and Chaney the student volunteers knew that there could be more casualties, and they did not hesitate to tell their parents. They also told them that not even more deaths would deter them from their mission; that they were in it for the duration.[114]

In a draft of the statement regarding the murders of Chaney, Goodman, and Schwerner, Martin Luther King said that what happened to them "provide[s] final confirmation of the enormity of the outrage committed against them." The letter goes on to say: "The attack on these courageous and dedicated young men was also an attack on the elementary and constitutional rights of the Negro people; an attack on the very concept of a democratic society, and an attack on the human brotherhood taught by all the great religions of mankind."[115] King urged religious leaders of the many faith traditions in the United States, including those who adhered to no faith tradition, to hold memorial services or some other "special

---

113. Quoted in Watson, *Freedom Summer*, 100.
114. Martínez, ed., *Letters from Mississippi*, 37.
115. King, Draft of the statement regarding the murders of the three civil rights workers, drafted by Bayard Rustin, King Center Library and Archives, August 4, 1964, 1.

observance" for the young activists later in the week. King expressed the hope that the martyrdom of the young men would somehow contribute to eradicating prejudice, hatred, and fear in the nation, while also contributing to the impetus toward nonviolence as the sole way toward the freedom and equality of all.[116]

It is important to mention a lesser-known voter education-registration project that was inspired by the Freedom Summer Project, and was influenced by the energy generated by the voter registration-education campaign in Selma in 1965. A child of SCLC and done in conjunction with SNCC, this project, the Summer Community Organization and Political Education Project (SCOPE), was launched on June 15, 1965 when Martin Luther King addressed the volunteers in the orientation session in Atlanta. The project was under the supervision of Hosea Williams, director of SCLC's voter registration and political education initiative. There were approximately 1,200 volunteers, including SCLC staffers, local volunteers, and more than six hundred college students from across the nation. These worked on voter education and registration in six southern states. In many instances the work was as dangerous and life-threatening as the work in the Mississippi Delta during Freedom Summer a year earlier. One such instance was the work done in Wilcox County (Camden), Alabama, the boyhood home of renowned King scholar Lewis V. Baldwin, who, as a boy, participated in the mass prayer meetings.[117] SCOPE was to the voter

---

116. Watson, *Freedom Summer*, 183, 189.
117. I first learned about the SCOPE Project at the retirement celebration of Lewis Baldwin at Vanderbilt University, where he served with distinction on the faculty for thirty years. This event occurred November 7–9, 2013. More specifically, I learned of the SCOPE Project during a presentation at that ceremony by Maria Gitin, a veteran of that project who happened to be a white college student volunteer in Wilcox County. Gitin has authored a book of remembrances by some of the surviving local residents in Camden, titled *This Bright Light of Ours: Stories from the Voting Rights Fight* (Tuscaloosa: University of Alabama Press, 2014). Gitin shared a few of these stories on the last day of the Baldwin retirement celebration. Considering the ages of the storytellers in the book, I would say that this is bound to be a very significant work on the

education-registration project in Selma, what Freedom Summer was to the voter education project in the Mississippi Delta.

King, Mississippi, and Student Activists

As Martin Luther King was making plans to go to Mississippi to assist in the civil rights effort, he received word that a white-supremacist guerrilla group was plotting to assassinate him when he arrived. Typical of King, he rejected advice to cancel the trip. He staunchly believed that the work needed to go forward. And more, not unlike the Nashville student activists who insisted that the Freedom Rides must not be called off because of the violence done to riders outside Anniston, Alabama, King could not allow threats to his life to stop the forward work of the movement. "If I were constantly worried about death," he said, "I could not function."[118] He had been receiving daily threats against his life since the Montgomery campaign. Always aware of his call to ministry, and the fact that he was much in the national and international spotlight, King concluded that he simply had to come to terms with the possibility that his life could be taken at any moment. This did not mean that he never experienced fear, as he surely did when he returned to Philadelphia, Mississippi in 1966 in observance of the second anniversary of the murders of Chaney, Goodman, and Schwerner. It did mean, however, that because of the depth of his faith and commitment to God, he was able to manage the fear in ways that allowed him to keep pressing forward. He would not allow threats against his life to hinder his movements throughout the country. He knew well the potential cost of such a commitment.

---

movement as more and more members of that generation are transitioning from this world. Indeed, it occurs to me that the stories of the likes of Maria Gitin, that is, white college student volunteers in projects like SCOPE and Freedom Summer, also need to be told and preserved in book and other media forms.

118. Carson, ed., *The Autobiography of Martin Luther King, Jr.*, 250.

King arrived in Mississippi one month after the *disappearance* of the three young civil rights activists. What he referred to as the "hideous triple lynchings in Mississippi" was for King one of the shocking events of 1964 that shook the nation. The three activists had been "savagely murdered,"[119] King said. Tragically, and ironically, the murders occurred not long after the passage of the 1964 Civil Rights Bill. King had nothing but praise for the work of the COFO activists and the young white college volunteers who courageously descended on the state during Freedom Summer. While in the Delta region, he toured a number of the poorest areas, meeting and talking with impoverished blacks.

To their credit, black and white SNCC activists most assuredly and realistically retained a healthy sense of fear of Mississippi, and as we saw earlier, this helped to keep them sharp and alert, most of the time. It is no small matter that their commitment and their sense that the work for justice was morally right, would not allow them to miss the chance of bringing the movement to that most intimidating state. Nevertheless, before embarking on the journey to Mississippi, many already had a sense of the very real possibility that their involvement in the state could prove deadly for self, their colleagues, and local residents who were brave enough to work with them. Everybody involved in the voter registration campaign in Mississippi was vulnerable to terrorist attacks and death, at the hands of white supremacists.

Nevertheless, the young activists persevered, and King himself was inspired by their courage and determination in what he knew to be a very dangerous situation. The student volunteers set up Freedom Schools for the local children, "the first comprehensive educational program for a large number of black youngsters"[120] in

---

119. Ibid.
120. Carson, *In Struggle*, 119.

Mississippi. They discovered that they had to unlearn much of what they had learned at Harvard, Yale, Stanford, and other universities about teaching. It was quickly apparent that black kids in Mississippi learned differently. "The standard academic approach has not worked at all well . . . ," one volunteer wrote. "The kids we are dealing with are not trained to listen, and absorb information presented in an organized, 'logical,' manner. . . . They learn by talking, by conversation, by rambling around and beating the nearby bushes. And they learn by acting things out."[121]

Freedom School teachers introduced black children to the literary works of black artists such as James Baldwin, and taught them about Afrikan American contributions to building this nation. They were "offered courses in creative writing, drama, art, journalism and foreign languages."[122] Black children and youth had not been taught many of these things before. The experience awakened in many of them a sense of pride of race for the first time in their young lives. For many of those children who attended the Freedom Schools, it was their first real social interaction with whites who showed them respect and were willing to sacrifice their lives for the cause of their freedom. Thelma Eubanks reflected that the experience in the freedom school in McComb "made me know that everybody in the world wasn't like the [white] southerners."[123] In the white northerners, she experienced for the first time white people who were both humane and respectful in their treatment of blacks. Euvester Simpson had fond memories of making friends not only with black student activists, but white ones as well.[124] Larry Martin was an eleven-year-old in Meridian when he met Mickey Schwerner, his wife Rita, and Frank and Judy Wright. He had warm memories of

---

121. Martínez, ed., *Letters from Mississippi*, 115.
122. Carson, *In Struggle*, 120.
123. Levine, *Freedom's Children*, 94.
124. Ibid., 95.

how humanely they treated him and other black youths; how they taught them about the importance of adults registering and voting; how they got the children involved in movement work, and how some of the children were so devoted to helping, they would forego many of the regular childhood activities, such as playing games of various kinds, in order to help out. "We started passing out leaflets saying there was going to be a meeting," Martin recalled. "We'd walk for miles a day passing out pamphlets, trying to get people registered. We weren't out there shooting basketball or playing marbles. A lot of times I didn't even go swimming. I'd rather pass out leaflets, sit-in, or something."[125]

The reflections of Eubanks, Simpson, Martin, and other blacks who were teenagers and younger in the Mississippi Delta during Freedom Summer says much about the preparation that the college volunteers received during the orientation week at Western College for Women in Oxford, Ohio. In his session with the students, Bob Moses emphasized that they need not "come to Mississippi this summer to save the Mississippi Negro. . . . Only come if you understand, really understand, that his freedom and yours are one . . . ."[126] This sounds amazingly like Martin Luther King's staunch conviction about the interrelated structure of the universe; that all life is tied together in a single garment of destiny, such that what affects one, affects all, including God. The salvation and freedom of every person is inextricably connected to that of every other person. In a sense, then, Moses was telling those young white students to come to Mississippi, if, and only if, they understood and believed that their own salvation and freedom were as much at stake as that of their black sisters and brothers. We know from some of the letters that students wrote their parents that some did indeed make this

---

125. Ibid., 97.
126. Wexler, *An Eyewitness History*, 207.

connection. One student wrote that freedom is that which "none can have until everybody has it."[127] Another was just as passionate when explaining her sudden and forceful realization that black people in the Mississippi Delta were as much her people as any, and that their sorrow was hers as well.[128] She was bound inextricably to them, and they to her. From the testimonies and memories of Thelma Eubanks, Euvester Simpson, Larry Martin, and other black Mississippians, many of the white students got the point of Bob Moses' message.

The Mississippi Toll

Even before SNCC youths went into Mississippi, a number of its members—black and white—who participated in the Freedom Rides, had suffered brutal beatings. No one can forget the photographic images of the beatings sustained by John Lewis (who would also be beaten severely during the Selma, Alabama campaign in 1965) and Jim Zwerg at the Montgomery bus station. Lewis was beaten until he was bloodied, and then left unconscious in the street. Zwerg was also beaten unconscious, was hospitalized, and unable to continue the Freedom Ride to Jackson, Mississippi. But even when subjected to severe violence, the youths were absolutely defiant about the need for the rides to continue for freedom, justice, and equality. The badly beaten Zwerg told reporters that they would continue their journey one way or another; that they may be attacked again, and even bombed, but in the end they would prevail, because they were ready for anything.[129]

The SNCC and CORE youth had every reason to fear Mississippi and all that it stood for, and they did. They worked through well-

---

127. Martínez, ed., *Letters from Mississippi*, 38.
128. Ibid., 65.
129. Williams, *Eyes on the Prize*, 155.

managed fear every day. The constant harassment and arrests they endured, the beatings they incurred, the murders of colleagues and local residents that they had to live with, all took a major toll on them, as well as the college volunteers in the Freedom Summer Project. We saw what happened to the otherwise mild-mannered Dave Dennis, having lived through the murders of Medgar Evers, Herbert Lee, Michael Schwerner, James Chaney, Andy Goodman, and others. Dennis and others also suffered a great deal of guilt because of their decisions that put colleagues, local residents, and student volunteers in harm's way.

Bob Moses was devastated by the report that Goodman, Chaney, and Schwerner had not reported in. When Moses had slipped away from the rest of the group in Oxford, Ohio to reflect solemnly on the disturbing news, Victoria Gray had sought to console him, saying: "You are not responsible for this."[130] But Moses knew that to the extent that it was his decision to proceed with Freedom Summer, he was indeed responsible, and would have the impossible task of living with his decision and the consequences. He made it clear that he felt responsible for the deaths of Chaney, Goodman, and Schwerner, but also for Herbert Lee and Louis Allen.[131] It was the burden of leadership, really. Although devastated when Lee's widow accused him of being responsible for her husband's murder, Moses finally decided that the way he and others continued and carried on in the struggle was the best way to honor Lee, Allen, and others who had lost, and would lose, their lives in the struggle for civil rights and freedom. When John Blake interviewed Moses around 2003, he asked him whether he had been plagued by feelings of guilt. "I think more that the responsibility was making sure that I honor their demise with my life," Moses responded. "When Herbert Lee

---

130. Quoted in Branch, *Pillar of Fire*, 363.
131. Watson, *Freedom Summer*, 101.

was murdered in 1961, what we were able to say and eventually do was offer our commitment to continuing this struggle. So that kind of eases the responsibility, the feeling that maybe this is all kind of using somebody."[132] And yet, by the time Moses left Mississippi, having worked there in the trenches for nearly four years, he was "embittered, exhausted, but somehow still alive,"[133] and significant changes were on the horizon for Mississippi. What is important for our purpose is that virtually everybody who participated in the Mississippi campaign paid dearly for it.

Earlier we saw that Dave Dennis, who was known to be cool and calm under pressure, gave a powerful and uncharacteristically emotional eulogy at the memorial services for James Chaney and Michael Schwerner. The pressure and pain of the violence endured by the young freedom fighters, and the murders of so many who were close to him, caused him to just lose it once he began speaking. It does not take a psychiatrist to know that what Dennis and others experienced in Mississippi would have long-term consequences for their mental health. Some years later, after he was practicing law in New Orleans, Dennis told Howell Raines that the experience in Mississippi just wore him out, and he finally had to leave, for the sake of his own sanity. Interestingly, Dennis told of being in the law library at the University of Michigan (where he took his law degree), and by chance, recognized a young white woman who had been one of the student volunteers in the Delta region. He recalled that while in Mississippi, she had been subjected to a brutal incident with the Natchez police. They played Russian roulette with her. The experience shattered her psychologically. Dennis said that although he did not know it at the time, her work in the law library was actually part of her ongoing therapy at the hospital she entered

---

132. Quoted in John Blake, *Children of the Movement* (Chicago: Lawrence Hill Books, 2004), 43-44.
133. Watson, *Freedom Summer*, 27.

immediately after the horrific experience with the Natchez police. At the time of his conversation with Howell Raines in the mid-1970s, the young woman had been institutionalized for eleven years and counting.

This, and related experiences, was a heavy burden for Dennis and other CORE and SNCC activists, especially those in leadership who made the decisions to send activists to the various rural towns in the Delta to work at voter registration projects and to establish and teach in the Freedom Schools. In 1961, Dennis was CORE's field director for Mississippi, and when CORE, SNCC, SCLC, the NAACP, and local civil rights groups joined to form COFO, he was made co-director with Bob Moses. Although Allard Lowenstein had suggested the idea of inviting massive numbers of white college student volunteers to Freedom Summer, the decision to go forward with the project was shared by Dennis and Moses. They had wanted to proceed with the project, even though many of the COFO staffers rejected the idea for reasons previously noted. So, naturally the two men took it very hard when volunteers and others were subjected to violence and murder. It is hard to imagine how they felt when student volunteer Andy Goodman was murdered after having been in the Project for only one day.

Not unlike Moses, Dennis felt responsible for what happened to the three civil rights workers, not only when it happened, but long after he left the Project. "I mean, it's the price that I had to pay and the price that I still pay for that decision," he told Raines. He and other COFO activists thought about Mississippi the way black Mississippians did: it was like being in a war zone. One had constantly to be on guard, which made it virtually impossible to relax, for relaxing could cause one to make deadly mistakes. He confessed that they tried to have fun when they could, but they actually had very little fun.

What happened to Chaney, Schwerner, and Goodman shocked and scared all of the youthful activists. They knew something like this could happen; had been happening all along, and long before they went to Mississippi. As for himself, Dennis said that for weeks, his was a kind of "shock-fear" reaction to the murders. It freaked him out almost completely, so much so that one night he lost it, and told himself that he couldn't deal with what had happened. So in a moment of what can only be described as delirium, one night after the disappearances, he left the COFO office, jumped in his car, and drove to Philadelphia, Mississippi where the murders took place. Clearly out of his mind in those moments, Dennis said that he just drove around in Philadelphia, and after talking with people at the COFO offices, he drove back. It was a dangerous thing to do, and a violation of COFO policy (i.e., that no one was to travel alone in a car or on a bus, especially at night!), but he felt that he had to do it in order to be able to handle the disappearances. He had to live with the fact that he had assigned Schwerner to the Meridian and Philadelphia areas.

Student activists were not only emotionally and psychologically stressed out when they finally left Mississippi after Freedom Summer. Some had to leave because of physical maladies as well. Lawrence Guyot, SNCC field secretary, said that he left because of high blood pressure and heart trouble. He got to the point that he just could not take the pressure. When he saw an internist in Chicago in 1968, he asked about the wisdom of returning to Mississippi, and the doctor told him that "if you go back to Mississippi you have about two months to live."[134] That was enough. The almost nonstop pace of the student activists, under constant murderous circumstances, took a huge toll on most of them. Probably, more than one of them

---

134. Quoted in Raines, *My Soul Is Rested*, 290.

had an old, aged heart by the time they left Mississippi. This was surely the case of George Raymer, who was under thirty years of age when he died of a heart attack. According to Dave Dennis, doctors said that at his death Raymer had the heart of a seventy-two-year-old. Even before Freedom Summer, the Mississippi experience had been overwhelming for SNCC veterans. *After* Freedom Summer they were even more exhausted and beaten down than the college volunteers, many of whom experienced a mental-emotional disorder that mental health professionals did not know as much about in the early to mid-1960s—post-traumatic stress disorder (PTSD). I return to this momentarily, since the phenomenon affected vast numbers of the volunteers, as evidenced by their behavior at home and at their respective colleges.

We have seen that almost simultaneously SNCC activists began direct action and voter registration projects in Jackson and the Mississippi Delta region. The level of danger that these young people faced—especially in the Delta—defies description. The things that they encountered and witnessed firsthand in Mississippi surely must have angered all of heaven, not least God. It is hard to assess how most black Mississippians felt about the youthful college volunteers during the Freedom Summer project. We have seen that some were very supportive and even hopeful that their presence and work would make things better for blacks in substantive ways. Others remained skeptical at best, and some outright rejected the plan to invite them to Mississippi in the first place.

When the student volunteers arrived in Mississippi, they were generally serious about voter registration and other assignments given them. Many were mostly idealistic and naïve, thinking that all they had to do was let black residents know that they were there to encourage them to register to vote, and they would comply. They found out very quickly that it did not work that way; that blacks had been left out of the political process for so long, and had been systematically intimidated and terrorized for so long, that many of them had no reason to believe that even if they did register to vote, that in itself would make a difference. So they discovered when canvassing black neighborhoods that very many adults were hesitant, even resistant, which meant that the work went much more slowly than the young idealists initially thought. An important lesson they learned was that blacks had good reason to be doubtful, and that one Freedom Summer Project could not eradicate the damage caused by generations of systemic oppression and terrorism.

It is reasonable to conclude that virtually all of the college volunteers who participated in the Freedom Summer Project were influenced and traumatized in some way or other by the experience. Mario Savio was one of the twenty-three volunteers who worked with Hollis Watkins, COFO project director for Holmes County. Savio was a student at the University of California at Berkeley. According to Watkins, Savio told him that when he returned to school in the fall "he was going to give them hell."[135] It pleased Watkins that Savio kept his promise. In the fall of 1964 a University of California (Berkeley) student was arrested for handing out CORE leaflets. Before long the patrol car in which the student was detained was surrounded by massive numbers of students who were singing Freedom Songs, as student after student climbed on the roof of the car and spoke about free speech. Although Watkins remembered Savio's promise, he also remembered that he had not exhibited leadership ability during Freedom Summer. But it turned out that day that the most eloquent and passionate speaker was Mario Savio. Savio told of his experience of terror in Mississippi, of being "chased by angry whites in Jackson, hearing the bombs in McComb, talking in

---

135. Quoted in Powledge, *Free at Last?*, 581.

sharecropper shacks."[136] How could he forget Mississippi, he asked the crowd? Much influenced by the civil rights work with SNCC and the unsettling experience in the Delta, Savio founded and became the leader of the Free Speech Movement among students at the university. "Last summer I went to Mississippi to join the struggle there for civil rights," Savio told his campus peers. "This fall I am engaged in another phase of the same struggle, this time in Berkeley. . . . In Mississippi an autocratic and powerful minority rules, through organized violence, to suppress the vast, virtually powerless majority. In California, the privileged minority manipulates the university bureaucracy to suppress the students' political expression."[137] In December, Savio led students to engage in a sit-in that literally closed down the administration building on campus. The Berkeley movement sparked student protests all across the country, as they protested against the war in Vietnam, the draft, and patriarchy. Bruce Watson made the important and telling observation that "in the forefront of each [of the protests] were veterans of Freedom Summer: who had seen democracy denied, who had watched 'the law' subjugate an entire people, and who had come home angry and disillusioned."[138]

The youthful SNCC workers who went to Mississippi quickly gained a reputation among local blacks of going where others had not gone before, and would not choose to go. This is how Unita Blackwell, who attended a voter registration meeting at a church in Sunflower County, Mississippi, remembered Bob Moses, one of two SNCC activists who led the meeting. "SNCC went where nobody went. They [Moses and the other fellow] was about the nuttiest ones they was. Ended up in some of the most isolated places and drug

---

136. Watson, *Freedom Summer*, 266.
137. Quoted in Carson, *In Struggle*, 129.
138. Watson, *Freedom Summer*, 266.

people out of there to vote. Mrs. Fannie Lou Hamer said to me, 'Girl, these here young people know something, don't they?' And I said, 'Yeah, they sure do.'"[139] Hamer and Blackwell were not the only locals who applauded the efforts and contributions of the young college students. Another local black woman spoke at a Fourth of July celebration that summer and said: "These young white folks who are already free, they come here only to help us. They is proving to us that black and white can do it together, that it ain't true what we always thought, that all white folks is booger men, 'cause they sure is not."[140]

Without question, the Mississippi experience, especially the Freedom Summer Project, marked forever the lives, not only of SNCC activists and local residents, but the hundreds of college students as well. In the nation they had been taught was the greatest, richest, and most democratic in the world, they had witnessed atrocities done to black citizens, and were themselves often the victim of Klan violence. Many of them returned home—if it was possible to ever really return to home as they knew it after Freedom Summer—angry, disappointed in their country, resentful of authority, impatient with what they once thought were friends who were not racists, and so forth. They were forever changed, and it took a long time for some of them to come to terms with this. A case in point was Fran O'Brien, one of the Freedom School teachers in Vicksburg. After Freedom Summer she had returned to school.

> Back at her Oregon college, Fran O'Brien was restless and angry. The once demure teacher now argued with old friends who seemed to have become bigots. No one understood what Fran had been through, but no one failed to notice her testiness. "I didn't realize yet that it was because *I* was a different person, so my whole senior year was confusing," she remembered. Fran talked about the children of Mississippi but told no

---

139. Quoted in Hampton and Fayer, *Voices of Freedom*, 180.
140. Martínez, ed., *Letters from Mississippi*, 72.

one about being beaten by Klansmen. She did not even tell herself. And so the horror festered, leaving her alone, aloof, and strangest of all, dreaming of returning to Mississippi the following summer. A similar estrangement could be found at colleges around the country.[141]

O'Brien and numerous other volunteers found that in a sense they could never again return to the homes they left when they went to Mississippi. "Many volunteers had thought they were used to the stress, but when they returned home, they discovered that they would never return home. Not for the rest of their lives."[142]

The parents of the white volunteers noticed the change in their children when they returned. One white mother lamented the change that her child underwent. Many of the former volunteers sat in their rooms for long periods of time, in part dealing with their sense of guilt for having left suffering blacks in Mississippi. Everything changed for many of these once-patriotic, law-respecting, and law-abiding young people who were certain that they lived in a real democracy, and that elected officials cared about the well-being of all citizens. Then they went to Mississippi, and their eyes were opened to the real reality. Watson discovered that when sociologist Doug McAdam surveyed a quarter of the volunteers, he made some provocative discoveries. McAdam "found that Freedom Summer had moved two-thirds leftward and crippled respect for authority. In just ten weeks, 42 percent lowered their estimation of the president, 40 percent lost esteem for Congress, half for the Justice Department, and nearly three-quarters for the FBI."[143] These changes would lead to youths spearheading a challenge to the nation the likes of which it had not experienced.

---

141. Watson, *Freedom Summer*, 264. For an account of O'Brien's beating by the Klan, see 232–34.
142. Ibid., 263.
143. Ibid., 265.

McAdam also found that many of the ex-volunteers felt lonely, isolated, unmarried or divorced, and "increasingly restless. Many remained searchers, moving from job to job or relationship to relationship, looking for what one called 'the ultimate Mississippi.'"[144] We saw earlier in this chapter that some even suffered severe mental and psychological disorder. What happened to Dennis Sweeney is a worst-case scenario. Sweeney was recruited as a college volunteer by Allard Lowenstein, who spearheaded the Freedom Vote in 1963, and devised the Freedom Summer Project idea with Bob Moses. Having been subjected to a number of severe beatings and numerous arrests in McComb, Sweeney suffered a concussion that left him a paranoid schizophrenic. In March 1980 he took a pistol into Lowenstein's Manhattan office and emptied the gun into his former mentor's body, killing him. He was confined to a mental facility for twenty years.

It was all so very terrible in Mississippi, and yet, even in the midst of omnipresent danger and fear, there were also those memorable, cathartic moments when the college volunteers sat around in the shacks that were the homes of local activists, and talked the talk, while eating southern cooked fresh pinto beans; blacks and whites together, sitting around in an impoverished house communicating with each other like the human beings they were, and eating delicious pinto beans, and all the while, becoming more real to each other. Reflecting on her memory of Freedom Summer, local activist Unita Blackwell provides the story.

> Black and white had come from the North and from the West and even from some cities in the South. Students came and we wasn't a closed society anymore. They came to talk about that we had a right to register to vote, we had a right to stand up for our rights. That's a whole new era for us. I mean, hadn't anybody said that to us, in that open way. . . .

---

144. Ibid., 290.

There was interaction of blacks and whites. I remember cooking some pinto beans—that's all we had—and everybody just got around the pot, you know, and that was an experience just to see white people coming around the pot and getting a bowl and putting some stuff in and then sitting around talking, sitting on the floor, sitting anywhere. . . . We was sitting on the floor and they was talking and we was sitting there laughing, and I guess they became very real and very human, we each to one another.[145]

It is of interest to note that Blackwell, who had been a student of COFO's Muriel Tillinghast, would be elected Mississippi's first black female mayor in 1977, remaining in that office for two decades.[146] Another significant event happened in 1989 during the first reunion of volunteers who participated in Freedom Summer. Mississippi's attorney general issued a formal apology to the families of Chaney, Goodman, and Schwerner.[147] Such events give new meaning to a favorite statement that Martin Luther King liked to quote: "The arc of the moral universe is long, but it bends toward justice."[148] I may not live to see justice done, and you may not live to see it. But according to King, the universe itself is so constructed, and God's nature is such that justice will ultimately be done.

The SNCC activists knew beforehand that Mississippi was the meanest, "most antagonistic state," in the nation, one where whites had full protection of the law, and blacks had neither this nor the vote. Furthermore, blacks had neither civil nor political rights in that state. And yet, these young people knew also that the movement could not win in the South if they did not go to Mississippi; and they could not go to Mississippi if they were not willing to risk it all, even life—their own, as well as those of the local residents who had

---

145. Quoted in Hampton and Fayer, *Voices of Freedom*, 193.
146. Watson, *Freedom Summer*, 282.
147. Ibid., 283.
148. King, "The Current Crisis in Race Religions," in *A Testament of Hope: The Essential Writings of Martin Luther King, Jr.* ed. James M. Washington (New York: Harper & Row, 1986), 88.

the courage to get involved. The youthful activists of SNCC would also find Selma, Alabama to be a tough and dangerous challenge, but as they had done in Albany and the Mississippi Delta, they blazed the trail anyway. As in the dangerous Delta region, SNCC youth went in to Selma and established a beachhead, thus making it possible for Martin Luther King and SCLC to do their voter education and registration work there in 1965.

5

Selma

"What We Talk about Has Also to Do with the Children"

Selma, Alabama is the seat of Dallas County, located above the Alabama River. It was at one time a major cotton center and slave market. This all changed when, in 1848, a group of German immigrants arrived and turned toward iron making and manufacturing guns of all kinds. Second only to Richmond, Virginia, Selma became a major munitions supply center during the Civil War. Unfortunately, it also became a center of Klan and White Citizens Council activity, which did not bode well for its black residents.

During the civil rights movement, blacks comprised about 57 percent of the population of Dallas County, but were less than 1 percent of the registered voters. White Selma residents feared allowing blacks to register and vote. This was the case of most whites in the Black Belt region, just like the Mississippi Delta. Whites knew that if they allowed blacks to vote, they would not be able to retain their political advantage; for the black majority could easily vote whites out of public offices. Indeed, in some counties, for example, Wilcox and Lowndes, blacks were 78 percent and 81 percent of the population, respectively. However, no black person was registered in either of those counties.

Much like the Mississippi Delta region, blacks in Selma were kept out of the political process primarily through the use of terrorism. Just as in Mississippi, many blacks, especially in rural areas of the Deep South, owned guns and were not afraid to use them in defense of self, family, and friends. Local black leaders and militant farmers chose self-defense over the nonviolence approach of SCLC and early SNCC activists. As more and more black Northerners and Deep South blacks joined SNCC, tension arose between the adherents of nonviolence and those who rejected it. For example, when a SNCC activist in southwest Georgia was arrested for possession of three pistols, project director for that region, Roy Shields, had to respond to criticisms by SNCC leadership and others who were diehard proponents of nonviolence. When Shields was criticized for not doing more to prevent the carrying of weapons, Stokely Carmichael and other members of the Alabama staff "vigorously defended" him. "We are not King or SCLC," Carmichael exclaimed. "They don't do the kind of work we do nor do they live in the areas we live in. They don't ride the highways at night."[1] For King, Carmichael quite accurately said, nonviolence is a philosophy or way of life. Indeed, for increasing numbers of SNCC activists, nonviolence was at most a technique or strategy. "Carmichael recalled that the discussion ended when he asked those carrying weapons to place them on the table. Nearly all of the black organizers working in the Deep South were armed."[2] With them, their life experience in the Deep South, in their

---

1. Quoted in Clayborne Carson, *In Struggle: SNCC and the Black Awakening of the 1960s* (Cambridge, MA: Harvard University Press, 1995 [1981]), 164.

particular contexts, required that they own and carry guns and other weapons. They had not grown up on the equivalent of Sweet Auburn Avenue in Atlanta, as King had. As time went on, and especially with the continued influx of Northern youth with different values, cultural sensitivities, and religious affinities, fewer SNCC members were committed to nonviolence as anything more than a strategy.

Selma and surrounding counties were Alabama's equivalent of the Mississippi Delta region. The whites in Selma were mean and brutish in their treatment of blacks, and expected them to stay in their appointed place of submission, disenfranchisement, and disempowerment. Whites were vicious, and many blacks tended to be passive and fearful in Selma. SNCC activist Bernard Lafayette, who had insisted on being given his own project in order "to experiment with this thing the way *I* want to do it," was finally given the leadership of the Selma voter registration project to be launched in February 1963. Lafayette's friends strongly urged that he not accept the assignment. He rejected their advice, both because he wanted to do it, and because SNCC had received information that the United States Justice Department would be going to Selma to take a long hard look at its voter registration practices. The Justice Department had convincing evidence that Selma was the textbook example of fraudulently denying blacks the right to register and vote in the Black Belt region of the South. Lafayette was determined to accept the challenge because of his strong desire to see what really could be accomplished under his leadership. Fifteen thousand blacks were eligible to vote in Selma, but only a very small percentage of them were registered in Dallas County, the location of SNCC's headquarters.[3] The problem was real, and it was massive. Lafayette, it will be recalled, had done some organizing with James Bevel in

2. Ibid.
3. Ibid., 158.

Jackson, Mississippi after they spent time in Parchman prison for their involvement in the Freedom Rides. He felt himself up for what he knew would be a challenge in Selma.

Lafayette and his student activist wife, Colia, knew that if SNCC could gain a strong foothold in Selma, this would go a long way toward pressuring the federal government to work on a voting rights bill. He also knew that like the work in Mississippi, this would be very hard, very dangerous work. He found this to be the case when he went on a scouting mission to Selma in 1962. At that time, SNCC leadership concluded that blacks' state of repression in Selma was too entrenched, and consequently, it was not likely that much headway could be made in voter education and registration. Local blacks were subjected to a high level of terrorism. SNCC leaders sensed that outsiders would be subjected to the same.

After the scouting trip, even Lafayette concluded that whites in Selma seemed meaner and angrier than other racist white Alabamians. But this was not the only thing. Local blacks were nervous and suspicious of him, and most did all they could to avoid contact with him. Most blacks even avoided eye contact with Lafayette when they would pass him on the street. In addition, even local black ministers initially preached against him, telling their parishioners that he was an outside troublemaker who had come to make trouble for them, and that he would afterward make a fast exit from Selma, leaving them to deal with the fallout. Although Lafayette knew that one of SNCC's criticisms of King and SCLC was their perceived tendency to make a quick exit when they believed they had accomplished *their* goals (not necessarily the goals of the local community), he did not believe this was the way that SNCC operated. Rather, he knew that SNCC tended to remain in a local campaign for the long haul, remaining there and working with the local leadership long after King and SCLC were gone. Moreover,

Lafayette also knew that blacks had understandably good reasons to be suspicious of him and any other "outsider." Rather than discouraging him, however, this knowledge only helped him to press on through the initial suspicions and resistance.

When SNCC chairman, James Forman, offered him the Selma project after Lafayette refused to be denied, Lafayette went about his task with an abandon.[4] This was just one of the admirable qualities of the youthful activists of that era. They literally sought out opportunities to provide leadership in the struggle, and to contribute in whatever way they could, even in the most dangerous areas of the country. They were not incapacitated by fear; were not passive onlookers. To many SNCC activists, it was an opportunity to contribute in substantive ways toward the liberation of their own generation, as well as generations that would follow them. Many of them seemed to have a sense of contributing to both the future, and to history, in this regard. Lafayette, Bob Moses, Dave Dennis, Diane Nash, and many other SNCC youths knew beforehand that they were going into hell when they agreed to serve in Deep South towns; knew that they would, on a daily basis, be dealing with white racists who were no less brutal in their treatment of blacks than the Nazis were in their treatment of Jewish sisters and brothers, other non-Aryans, the disabled, and infirm. These young people saw it as an *opportunity* to do battle with such mean-spirited people, by showing them the power of relentless nonviolent direct action.

Bernard Lafayette had gotten good advice from veteran Montgomery bus boycott leader, Rufus Lewis, on how to cautiously proceed in Selma. "Go in as quietly as you can, Lewis had warned. Be low-key. Don't go in with a lot of fanfare, don't call a lot of attention to yourself. Above all, try not to provoke the white people

---

4. David Halberstam, *The Children* (New York: Random House, 1998), 411.

because the more you do that, the more they will turn the screws on the black people before you even get started. Find a black contact person whom you've been told about and who has the respect of the other people in the community."[5] We will see that Samuel Boynton was one such indigenous leader in Selma. His wife, Amelia Boynton, was another. In any case, with the advice given by Lewis, Lafayette courageously went about the business of getting to know the people, in the hope of earning their trust. Such efforts, he believed, would contribute much to community making, as well as establishing the foundation for a people's movement. By all accounts, the ultimate "success" in Selma and the Voting Rights Act of 1965 that was much influenced by that struggle, had much to do with the trailblazing work of Bernard Lafayette and his wife. Essentially, the two were able to establish a foothold for the ongoing voter registration work, whether done by SNCC or by King and SCLC.

Once Lafayette and his wife left Selma to return to college, SNCC's voter registration project continued under Worth Long, John Love, and then under the direction of Silas Norman in the spring of 1965. According to Julian Bond, prior to SCLC's arrival, SNCC had had five people in Selma "really softening the community up."[6] In addition to Long, Love, and Norman, Bond's reference was to the work of Lafayette and his wife, as well as the adult literacy work done in Selma in 1963 by SNCC field secretary Mary Varela.

In early 1965, Martin Luther King announced that SCLC would launch a major voter education campaign in Selma. Wilson Baker, Selma's Public Safety Director, claimed that King's briefcase was lost or misplaced in Anniston, Alabama in early October 1964, and that officials were able to get from it a copy of "what [King] called Project

---

5. Ibid., 419.
6. Quoted in Howell Raines, *My Soul Is Rested: Movement Days in the Deep South Remembered* (New York: G. P. Putnam's Sons, 1977), 214.

Alabama," which outlined plans for a voter registration campaign in Selma. Baker said he believed that "every law enforcement officer in the state had a copy of that thing."[7] He implied that this was somehow a boon for Selma and state officials. However, Andrew Young did not see it that way. Acknowledging the rumor that Baker somehow managed to get a copy of their plan for Selma, and even took copies to Burke Marshall in Washington to see what officials could do to stop the plan before it was actually implemented, Young conceded that it was quite probable that Alabama officials had copies of it. He went on to say that King and SCLC officials knew that frequently there would be John Birch Society and White Citizens Council members in the mass prayer meetings in Selma who would tape and film the meetings. "And we didn't put them out," said Young. "We knew who they were. We would take the microphones off from wherever they would hide them, under the pulpit, and put them right out on top. . . . It didn't disturb us that everybody knew our plans. We wanted them to know our plans."[8]

Many SNCC activists viewed Selma as "SNCC territory," and thus resented SCLC's plan to do a voter registration campaign there. The idea was met with ambivalence by SNCC members. "They knew that King's effort would aid their own voter registration work by attracting national publicity and perhaps prompting federal intervention against white Alabama authorities. With the exception of Mississippi, Alabama had the lowest proportion of blacks on the registration rolls. . . . Yet staff members feared that King's presence would undermine their longstanding efforts to develop black leadership."[9] From almost the beginning, the King-SNCC

---

7. Quoted in ibid., 197.
8. Quoted in Henry Hampton and Steve Fayer (with Sarah Flynn), *Voices of Freedom: An Oral History of the Civil Rights Movement from the 1950s through the 1980s* (New York: Bantam Books, 1990), 215–16.
9. Carson, *In Struggle*, 157–58.

relationship was a complex love-hate relationship. There was mutual admiration between them, and yet there was a difference in method and the way things should be done when attempting to work with the people, that caused each side considerable frustration. To complicate things even more, some of the SNCC youths did not trust King. This distrust dated back to the period of the Freedom Rides, when King did not accept the youths' invitation to join the Ride. We will see that other things would happen during the Selma campaign that would only deepen the frustration and the divide between King and SNCC youths.

Gestapo Sheriff

The Sheriff of Selma was Jim Clark. He was every bit as cruel as his counterpart in Birmingham, Bull Connor, and Albany's Laurie Pritchett. Clark had no desire to serve and protect black residents in Selma. Rather, he was notorious for showing up unannounced at meetings held by local blacks just to let them know that they were being watched, and that he expected them to remember their place. His point was to harass, intimidate, even terrorize black residents, thereby keeping them in a constant state of fear. Although most of the officers under Clark's command were at best poorly educated rednecks, his posse (a separate group) was, for the most part, much worse. Although there were presumably a few "decent" people in the posse (who made the conscious decision of going along with the vicious behavior of the majority), most were thugs and members of the Klan and other racist hate groups.

Wilson Baker, Selma's public safety director, observed that "Clark's excuse for having [the Klan] in his posse was that if he had the Klan there he could control them, but he couldn't. They could form his opinion, too, and they would get to him."[10] That Clark could not control the posse did not mean that he was any less vile and vicious than they when it came to the treatment of blacks. When SNCC and local activists held a Selma Freedom Day on October 7, 1963 to launch the voter registration workshops, the "official" harassment of SNCC activists and local blacks affiliated with the project began immediately. Clark and his henchmen arrested the organizers, while FBI agents and Justice Department lawyers stood by and did nothing. The organizers were charged with "unlawful assembly." Clark had pictures taken of all demonstrators who had lined up to register to vote, and threatened to show them to their employers. This was one of numerous tactics used to frighten blacks into staying away from voter registration stations. Clark was determined to do anything and everything to dehumanize blacks and to deny their civil and voting rights.

Martin Luther King believed that Jim Clark was one of the main roadblocks to blacks' civil and voting rights in Selma. King believed that Clark had a "Gestapo-like control" over the black population in Selma. There was, King said, "a carefully cultivated mystique behind the power and brutality" of men like Jim Clark. "The gun, the club, and the cattle prod produced the fear that was the main barrier to voting,"[11] said King. Andrew Young, then executive director of SCLC, characterized Clark as "a near madman." Clark expected there to be no resistance to any command he gave, especially to blacks seeking to register to vote at the courthouse. "It just infuriated him for anybody to defy his authority, even when they just wanted to vote," said Young. "If he said you couldn't vote, you were supposed to go away. And just to stand there enraged him."[12] Clark's response was to insult and beat those standing in line to register to vote.

10. Quoted in Raines, *My Soul Is Rested*, 200.
11. Clayborne Carson, ed., *The Autobiography of Martin Luther King, Jr.* (New York: Warner Books, 1998), 272.
12. Quoted in Hampton and Fayer, *Voices of Freedom*, 214.

However, we will see that, ironically, his mean-spirited, hateful attitude toward blacks, like that of Bull Connor's in Birmingham, backfired and became a huge disadvantage to the white-supremacist cause in Selma. It is almost comical that this would happen, considering that Clark was fully aware of Connor's experience with the demonstrators during the Birmingham campaign two years earlier. Wilson Baker answered in the affirmative when asked if Clark was aware that by not arresting and behaving violently toward the demonstrators, the city of Selma could avoid a huge media presence and the possibility of federal intervention, thus lessening the chance of a movement gaining momentum. Clark was very much aware of this, since he and city officials not only knew of what had happened in Birmingham, but had also studied what Laurie Pritchett did to defuse the King-led demonstrations in Albany. The fact that Clark lost control and subjected demonstrators to violence played right into the hands of SCLC's strategy. Consequently, early in the Selma movement, the demonstrators went back to the church "and voted [Clark] an honorary member of SNCC, SCLC, CORE, the N-Double-A-C-P," said Baker. "They voted him an honorary membership in that and openly stated that they could depend on him from now on to do anything foolish they wanted him to."[13] Clark was aware of what movement leadership thought of him, because his behavior was openly talked about in the mass meetings. Clark and Baker taped the meetings, and got recordings of what was said. And yet, so deeply ingrained was Clark's racism and bitterness toward blacks that he was still unable to control his behavior, although each time he heard the tapes he would swear that he would remain under control when the next encounter occurred. His racism had clearly eaten away at his moral fiber such that he had virtually no control

---

13. Quoted in Raines, *My Soul Is Rested*, 200.

over his treatment of blacks who demanded their right to register and vote.

Role Model of Courage

Bernard Lafayette and his wife found it slow going when they first arrived in Selma. As noted before, Lafayette understood the people's initial suspicion of him and SNCC; suspicion that was caused by deeply ingrained fear and a long history of intimidation by the Klan and other white hate groups. Even black ministers initially tended to dissuade their parishioners from working with the Lafayettes. The situation with the ministers changed significantly when longtime local businessman, civil rights and voting rights activist, Samuel Boynton, died. Lafayette and his wife thought it would be a good idea to honor Boynton through a memorial service. "The timing was right," said Lafayette. "If we'd tried to call people together for a mass meeting, it would've flopped because they were afraid. We would have had a struggle getting a church."[14] However, Boynton had done a great deal toward urging and helping blacks to get registered to vote. Because he himself had been registered for a long time, he served as a voucher for others seeking to register. It was required by law that a registered voter vouch for one seeking to register. Boynton had done this and many other things for the local black community. The Lafayettes reasoned that surely no local black minister would reject the request for a memorial service for such a man. The pastor of the Tabernacle Baptist Church offered the use of that church for the service. This did not mean that fear was no longer a factor in Selma by this time. It was. "The minister's deacons worried that the church would be bombed and its stained-glass windows broken. A

---

14. Fred Powledge, *Free at Last?: The Civil Rights Movement and the People Who Made It* (New York: HarperPerennial, 1991), 617.

Negro printer didn't want to print the leaflets for the mass meeting. Lafayette realized that he needed something else."[15] The people's fear was very real, and understandable. Many had suffered beatings and various forms of intimidation, or knew someone who had. Some knew of people who were literally run out of town by the forces of racism. Lafayette reasoned that what the people needed were models of courage. It just so happened that on the night of June 12, 1963, the night that Medgar Evers was murdered in Jackson, Mississippi, Lafayette was ambushed and beaten severely in Selma. He spent the night in the hospital, but when he was released, he successfully organized the people for a mass meeting. What happened to him, and what he did next, was a testimony to his courage and his determination to continue the work of the struggle. "I provided the role model for the people," he reflected; "the beating did not stop me from continuing my work."[16] The beating did not stop him; the fear did not stop him. Through his courage and fortitude, Lafayette showed the people that it was possible for them to press on through the fear and acts of terrorism. In any event, after he was beaten, and made the decision to continue with his work, Lafayette no longer had problems securing a place for mass meetings. Local blacks knew without question that he was devoted to their cause and would not allow beatings to stop him.

Local blacks who were previously too afraid to get involved with the voting rights campaign, were inspired to do so after Jim Clark and his underlings stormed into the memorial service for Boynton, who "not only laid the historical foundation for the Voting Rights Act, but also invited the first black lawyers into the black belt to pursue civil rights cases."[17] Waving a court order as he entered the

---

15. Ibid.
16. Quoted in ibid.
17. Quoted in Amelia Platts Boynton Robinson, *Bridge Across Jordan*, rev. ed. (Washington, DC: Schiller Institute, 1991), 112.

church, Clark claimed that he and his deputies had a right to be there to ensure that no laws were being broken. In addition, he took pictures of blacks entering the church. Clark's utter disregard and disrespect for blacks at that memorial service resulted in unintended but positive consequences for the developing voting rights campaign in Selma. Blacks saw Clark's action as little more than an attempt to further intimidate them. They were outraged by his breach of respect by showing up at the memorial service as he did. The unintended result was that blacks began to rally and to feel that they could overcome their own historic fear, and begin to unite in the struggle.

Local Activist Calls on SCLC

Martin Luther King and SCLC did not pick or choose Selma on their own. Local black leadership in Selma actually sought them out, according to Andrew Young. SNCC had worked to establish a beachhead and had launched the voter registration project with Freedom Day on October 8, 1963. With hundreds of blacks lined up outside the courthouse to register to vote, they stood in line all day, and only five people were registered. SNCC continued trying to work with local leadership to get more people registered, but the progress was too slow. This is when local leaders, led by Amelia Boynton (widow of Samuel Boynton), turned to King and SCLC for assistance. According to Andrew Young: "Mrs. Boynton came to the SCLC board meeting, just after Dr. King won the Nobel Prize (in December 1964), and she told us about this situation, and she asked us if we would come over there to work with her."[18] The local court had issued an injunction that not more than three people could walk down the street together in Selma, and there could be no public

---

18. Quoted in Hampton and Fayer, *Voices of Freedom*, 214.

meetings of more than three persons without permission from local authorities. King decided to announce SCLC's involvement in Selma on Emancipation Day in early January 1965. Because they would not be seeking the permission of white authorities, this would be a clear violation of the injunction, but it was also part of the strategy.

Not long after arriving in Selma, King led demonstrators to the courthouse to register to vote. When they arrived, he was confronted by Jimmy Robinson of the racist National States Rights Party. From the photo of the encounter,[19] Robinson was in clear disagreement with the demonstration, and seemed to be giving King and his followers an earful about it. Later that day, while King and his staff were testing the Civil Rights Bill of 1964 (which banned segregation in public facilities) by registering successfully at the Hotel Albert, Robinson attacked King from behind. The force of the blow to his head staggered King, as his head crashed down on the counter. Dorothy Cotton looked on as Ralph Abernathy and others got between King and his attacker, as other staff members restrained him. The police placed Robinson under arrest immediately. As he had done on similar occasions, for example, at a staff convention in Birmingham,[20] King did not want the assailant arrested, nor taken to jail. His understanding of the ethics of the Sermon on the Mount, as well as his awareness that his actions modeled those of Gandhi, assured King that his was the best approach; the approach that was

---

19. See Charles Johnson and Bob Adelman, *King: The Photobiography of Martin Luther King, Jr.* (New York: Viking, 2000), 169.
20. During the SCLC convention in Birmingham in 1963, King was standing on the stage speaking, when a white man in the audience walked up and punched the left side of his jaw, causing him to stagger backward and to spin halfway around. The audience was stunned by what they saw, but many believed, in the moment, that King and the man were engaging in socio-drama, which was a major component of nonviolent workshops. When the man proceeded to strike King again and again, a number of people surged toward the stage to restrain him. King would not allow anyone to harm the man, but chose to pray for him. The man was a member of the American Nazi Party. King also refused to press charges when the police arrived. The full story is recounted in Taylor Branch, *Parting the Waters: America in the King Years, 1954-63* (New York: Simon & Schuster, 1988), 653–54.

most consistent with agape and the idea of nonviolence as a way of life.

The Emancipation Day service was packed with people. King told those in attendance, "We are not asking, we are demanding, the ballot,"[21] and promised to get federal intervention by marching thousands to the courthouse to get registered. Surprisingly, no arrests were made that day. On January 18, King led approximately four hundred demonstrators to the Dallas County Courthouse to register to vote. Although King and the demonstrators were met by Sheriff Clark when they arrived, there was no police violence against them that day. At least on that occasion, Jim Clark showed amazing restraint.

Martin Luther King was convinced that if blacks in Selma had the vote "there would be no Jim Clarks, there would be no oppressive poverty directed against Negroes."[22] As important as the vote was, however, King was naïve in thinking (like many in his day and since) that this alone would get rid of the Jim Clarks, and the poverty that afflicted so many blacks; that because blacks could vote and did so in large numbers, things would change significantly for them materially. What King failed to consider in this instance was the integral relation between politics and economics in the U.S., and the fact that the wealthy actually dictate political policy and use their considerable power, influence, and other resources to ensure that it is carried out. Consequently, even if blacks and their allies succeed in electing a black President (as happened in 2008, with reelection in 2012, of Barack Hussein Obama), their material condition would not likely change substantially for the better (and has not at this writing!).

Significantly, as with the voter registration work in the Mississippi Delta led by Bob Moses, the work in Selma was also spearheaded

---

21. Quoted in Powledge, *Free at Last?*, 622.
22. Carson, ed., *The Autobiography of Martin Luther King, Jr.*, 275.

by SNCC youths, most of whom had been in college and dropped out to do movement work. Diane Nash Bevel and James Bevel arrived in Selma in late fall of 1964 to prepare the way for King and SCLC, who would arrive in January. We have seen that even before the arrival of the Bevels, the Lafayettes had already done substantial groundbreaking work, and by the time they left Selma, they had accomplished three important things that were most beneficial to King and SCLC: 1) In what was probably the most important achievement, the Lafayettes broke through the fear barrier among black residents, and established a foundation for beginning a movement;[23] 2) They assisted and inspired local blacks and their ministers to become more active in fighting for the right to vote; and 3) They unwittingly proved to movement leaders such as King that Selma was indeed one of the toughest Deep South cities, a showpiece of racial segregation as far as whites were concerned.[24]

Sixteen-year-old Princella Howard went to Selma with an SCLC staff person in late August 1964. Their assignment was to meet with SNCC leaders to determine whether the project there warranted human and other resources that SCLC could provide. Howard recalled that they were assured that "this was the next place . . . this is it!"[25] But even so, once SCLC arrived in Selma, it was still just as dangerous as when SNCC activists first arrived three years earlier, although significant progress had been made with many of the local blacks, who were no longer stymied by fear.

It is of interest to point out that Bernard Lafayette and other SNCC activists such as Bob Moses and John Lewis, along with the Bevels, had already figured out from their earlier work in Mississippi, that passage of a civil rights bill, important as that would be, would not be

---

23. Powledge, *Free at Last?*, 616.
24. Halberstam, *The Children*, 429.
25. Ellen Levine, *Freedom's Children: Young Civil Rights Activists Tell Their Own Stories* (New York: G. P. Putnam's Sons, 1993), 117.

sufficient if blacks in the South did not also have the right to register, vote, and have their votes count.[26] This was an example of the youth being more in touch with the pulse of what needed to happen than much of the older, more "acceptable" leadership in SCLC and other more traditional and conservative civil rights organizations. To King's credit, it did not take long before he too saw the truth in the need for a voting rights bill.

We saw in chapter 3 that it was Martin Luther King's and SCLC's good fortune to have James Bevel as a staff member. Bevel had a piercing analytical mind and had quickly developed into one of the best strategists in King's inner circle. In addition, we saw that more than the other staff members, Bevel was able to relate well with SNCC activists and other youths, and thus served as a kind of liaison between them and SCLC. Bevel was also a powerful and passionate personality who excelled at making older leadership types—in and out of SCLC—uncomfortable. He frequently made them feel that they were much too conservative and timid for what really needed to be done in movement work. This played well to King's dialectical method, by which he examined and gave both the thesis and the antithesis their day in court, as he worked toward a synthesis. Frequently, what King deemed to be the solution to a problem or issue was found by combining the strengths of the suggestions offered in favor of (thesis) and against (antithesis) various ideas and proposals put forth by his staff and other civil rights leaders.

Bevel also made SCLC's president uncomfortable at times. However, King respected him a great deal and depended on his analyses, fresh ideas, courage, and persistence. Because King had to work with a large board of directors, comprised of primarily conservative black Baptist pastors, he frequently found himself in a

---

26. Halberstam, *The Children*, 442.

real struggle when trying to push through some of his proposals. He also had to fight with his staff, so that even when Bevel would bring him into the loop about what SNCC leaders saw as important next steps, King often had to delay his own action because he had to work through his staff and a sometimes difficult board. All of this is to say that like the young activists in SNCC, King too had a strong sense before 1965 that the passage of a civil rights bill would not be sufficient to guarantee that Southern blacks could vote. He sought to make this point to President Lyndon B. Johnson upon his return from Oslo, where he was awarded the Nobel Peace Prize.[27] Before they had been in Selma for long, King was convinced that a voting rights bill would have to be passed. Writing from a Selma jail, King said:

> By jailing hundreds of Negroes, the city of Selma, Alabama, has revealed the persisting ugliness of segregation to the nation and the world. When the Civil Rights Act of 1964 was passed many decent Americans were lulled into complacency because they thought the day of difficult struggle was over.
>
> Why are we in jail? Have you ever been required to answer 100 questions on government, some abstruse even to a political scientist specialist, merely to vote? Have you ever stood in line with over a hundred others and after waiting an entire day seen less than ten given the qualifying test?
>
> This is Selma, Alabama. There are more Negroes in jail with me than there are on the voting rolls. . . .[28]

As in Birmingham, King's intention was to fill the jails to overflowing in Selma. When he was first arrested on February 1, approximately a thousand demonstrators, many of them children and

---

27. Carson, ed., *The Autobiography of Martin Luther King, Jr.*, 270.
28. Quoted in Sanford Wexler, *An Eyewitness History of the Civil Rights Movement* (New York: Checkmark Books, 1999), 231. From King, "A Letter from Martin Luther King from a Selma, Alabama Jail," an SCLC solicitation advertisement in the *New York Times* (February 5, 1965).

young people, were arrested. By February 3, about five hundred more demonstrators had been arrested. The jails in Dallas County were overflowing.

King's job was to do what he could through nonviolent direct action to support President Johnson's political efforts to bring a strong voting rights bill into law.[29] King vowed that they were "going to bring a voting bill into being in the streets of Selma, Alabama."[30] Indeed, Johnson himself acknowledged the immense value of the efforts of blacks and King, in particular, in the trenches.[31] As he had provided leadership in getting the 1964 Civil Rights Bill passed, Johnson also led the charge to get a Voting Rights Bill passed. He did much to challenge the nation's moral sense about the denial of voting rights for any segment of the nation's people. "All Americans should be indignant when one American is denied the right to vote," Johnson said in a press release on February 4, 1965. "The loss of that right to a single citizen undermines the freedom of every citizen. This is why all of us should be concerned with the efforts of our fellow Americans to register to vote in Alabama. . . . I intend to see that that right is secured for all citizens."[32]

The Children of Selma

King's adoration for, and tenderness toward the children, and his desire for their involvement in the demonstrations were as evident in Selma as in Birmingham and other civil rights campaigns. Indeed, we have seen that even before the Birmingham campaign stalled, he claimed to have been pondering the idea of utilizing children in

---

29. Carson, ed., *The Autobiography of Martin Luther King, Jr.*, 276.
30. Quoted in Wexler, *An Eyewitness History*, 231.
31. Nick Kotz, *Judgment Days: Lyndon Bains Johnson, Martin Luther King, Jr., and the Laws That Changed America* (Boston/New York: Houghton Mifflin, 2005), 311, 314.
32. Quoted in Wexler, *An Eyewitness History*, 231.

the demonstrations. This was not merely a strategic move, although we saw that the use of children in Birmingham proved to be an ingenious tactic. As one who was inclined to think things through, King pondered the meaning of children as human beings and what that must mean for them in the social struggle for civil and human rights. He knew that as their parents and other black adults suffered racial and other forms of injustice, the children also suffered, and were aware that they had to contend with things their white counterparts did not. Although they were not as mature in their thinking and outlook on life as adults, black children and young people were not only aware that their parents were being mistreated, but that their own humanity was being systematically undermined by racism and discrimination. Indeed, as a boy, King observed how the rude treatment by a shoe salesman, and then a police officer, had angered and embarrassed his father. Although a child, King knew instinctively that being treated that way was degrading to his father, and to all black people.

Martin Luther King knew that every Afrikan American, regardless of gender, class, and age, was being adversely affected by racism. It was therefore not difficult for him to arrive at the view that children, who had a sense of being unjustly treated because of their race, have every right to participate in organized efforts to eradicate the causes of such treatment. He knew, and preached, that children are no less sacred before God than adults. Remembering his experience in Birmingham, King's major concern about utilizing children in the Selma demonstrations was, first and foremost, their safety. He was also concerned about the criticisms he would very likely encounter from parents and other adults for putting children in harm's way. Nevertheless, intellectually and even strategically, he was convinced that involving the children in the demonstrations was the right thing to do. Many of the children took it upon themselves to participate in the demonstrations, regardless of the possible consequences. Such behavior only confirmed for King that the children not only had a major stake in the struggle against racial injustice, but they had a strong awareness of being mistreated and subjected to discrimination. It was reasonable, therefore, to openly allow—indeed invite—their participation in the mass prayer meetings and the demonstrations.

Black children in Selma, like those in Birmingham, were up to the challenge, and performed courageously and devoutly in the demonstrations. On February 1, not long after King and SCLC arrived, five hundred children marched to the county courthouse along with two hundred fifty adults, including King. The children carried protest placards written in crayon. They were all arrested outside the courthouse. The next day, several hundred more children marched and were arrested. The children were really quite amazing. In fact, it was reported that when the racist Sheriff Clark checked into the hospital for exhaustion, a group of black children prayed outside the hospital for his speedy recovery, a gesture that Clark did not acknowledge.[33]

Like Bull Connor, Jim Clark was not in the least hesitant to subject black children to police brutality. John Lewis recalled that just such an incident occurred a few days after a contingent of fifteen liberal U.S. congressmen arrived on February 5 to get a firsthand look at what was happening in Selma. Lewis wrote about the incident in his memoir.

> The day those congressmen came to visit, Sheriff Clark arrested some five hundred more marchers at the courthouse. Several days later he put the city in national headlines again by arresting more than 160 teenagers and sending them on a forced run of more than two miles out in the countryside. His deputies used clubs and cattle prods to keep those kids going. "March, dammit, *march!*" one officer reportedly yelled.

33. John Lewis, *Walking with the Wind: A Memoir of the Movement*, with Michael D'Orso (New York: Simon & Schuster, 1998), 315.

"You want to march so bad, now you can march. Let's *go!*" One fifteen-year-old boy said to a guard, "God sees you," and the deputy answered by clubbing him in the mouth. By the time they returned, several kids had lumps and cuts on their heads, and a few had been burned by cattle prods. One nine-year-old boy stood with tears streaming down his face—he had made the march barefoot.[34]

Lewis expressed his outrage over the incident in a hurriedly crafted statement to reporters.

> Sheriff Jim Clark proved today beyond a shadow of a doubt that he is basically no different from a Gestapo officer during the Fascist slaughter of the Jews.
>
> This is but one more example of the inhuman, animal-like treatment of the Negro people of Selma, Alabama. This nation has always come to the aid of people in foreign lands who are gripped by a reign of tyranny. Can this nation do less for the people of Selma?[35]

At any rate, those young children were devoted to the cause of freedom, and all had a sense that it was a just and righteous cause. Indeed, they had a sense that the God of the universe was not pleased with the actions and behavior of Sheriff Clark and his racist henchmen; that God's justice trumped the injustices being done to blacks. "God sees you," the young boy had said to the deputy. "God sees you."

A native of Selma, Sheyann Webb was a resident of the George Washington Carver housing projects when Martin Luther King arrived on the scene. Introduced to King as "his smallest freedom fighter,"[36] Webb was the first of the Selma children to get involved in the voting rights campaign.[37] As an eight-year-old, she was walking

---

34. Ibid., 314.
35. Ibid., 315.
36. Quoted in Raines, *My Soul Is Rested*, 204.
37. Sheyann Webb and Rachel West Nelson, *Selma, Lord, Selma: Girlhood Memories of the Civil Rights Days*, as told to Frank Sikora (University: University of Alabama Press, 1980), 25.

to school one day when she saw a large group of blacks and whites talking together at the Brown Chapel A.M.E. Church, the place where the mass prayer meetings were being held. This mingling of blacks and whites together seemed odd to the eight-year-old, in light of what she had grown accustomed to seeing in the racially divided city. Blacks and whites were usually segregated, and were seldom seen engaging each other in civilized interracial conversation. This was not the case at Brown Chapel that day, however. "I had never seen [blacks and whites] in a friendly or social environment where they were actually communicating,"[38] Webb recalled. Out of curiosity, and not thinking about being late for school, she went over to the crowd and followed them into the church. Once there, she heard Hosea Williams speaking about voter registration from the pulpit. She remembered him talking about Martin Luther King, who she knew nothing about at the time. Nor did she know anything about voter registration, but she remembered it as "something that seemed exciting." It made the young girl feel that something big was about to happen in her hometown.

When Sheyann Webb told her parents about her experience, they strongly admonished her to not pursue the matter further, and ordered her to stay away from the church. They knew about King, but told her to forget about him too. Being a child, of course, this only further aroused her curiosity. While playing near the church with her nine-year-old friend Rachel West one day, she saw several nice-looking cars drive up. This too was unusual, since black residents did not often see such cars in their impoverished neighborhood. Reflecting on the experience after forty years, Webb recalled that one of the men spoke to them and asked their names. When they responded, the man introduced himself as Martin Luther

---

38. Levine, *Freedom's Children*, 123.

King. Excited, the girls followed the men into the church. When one of the men told them to leave, King intervened and said they could stay.[39] Webb recalled that King expressed the view that there was nothing they would talk about in the church that day that did not also concern the children, and that is why he invited them to stay. When the meeting ended, King reportedly told the girls that he hoped to see them again when he returned. The girls were deeply moved by this gesture. Webb reflected: "Just the idea that he had the patience. He didn't throw us aside, or anything. He gave us the attention."[40] This was a testament to King's humanity and his genuine concern for the well-being of children and youth. Against the instructions of her parents, Webb and her friend Rachel began attending the mass meetings. Periodically they would go up to the pulpit and King would place them on his lap.[41]

Even at eight years of age and a third-grader, Sheyann Webb had a sense of her parents' fear as well as that of her teachers regarding involvement in the voter registration project. Not unlike Anne Moody's experience when she asked her mother if she had heard about the murder of young Emmett Till in 1955, Webb recalled the fear that arose in her parents whenever she asked them anything related to King's work in Selma. Such questions would always be pushed aside, until her mother finally told her that adult involvement could lead to the loss of their jobs, or worse. Consequently, neither Webb's parents nor her teachers initially got involved in the demonstrations for voting rights. They were afraid of the possible consequences, to themselves and to members of their family. Her

---

39. Ibid., 124.
40. Ibid.
41. Charles Johnson and Bob Adelman include a photograph of King with young Webb on his lap, and her friend Rachel with her hand on his left knee. This photo was taken on March 21, 1965, the day that the historic march from Selma to Montgomery commenced. See Johnson and Adelman, *King: The Photobiography of Martin Luther King, Jr.*, 189.

mother tried, unsuccessfully, to explain to young Webb that whites would fire her from her job if she participated in the demonstrations. Her parents told her about the bombing deaths of four black girl children, Addie Mae Collins, Denise McNair, Cynthia Wesley, and Carol Robertson, at the Sixteenth Street Baptist Church in Birmingham, and said that the same could happen during a mass meeting at Brown Chapel.[42]

In addition, Webb and her father had attended the funeral of Jimmy Lee Jackson in Marion, Alabama, not far from Selma. On the night of February 18, 1965, a small group of demonstrators in Marion were attacked by the police, and Jackson, a twenty-six-year-old, was mortally wounded by a state policeman as he tried to shield and protect his mother who had been clubbed. Martin Luther King was angered by this senseless murder. One could sense the anger in his eulogy of Jackson, when he said that the murder had been caused "by every lawless sheriff, every racist politician from governors on down, every indifferent white minister and every passive Negro who 'stands on the sidelines in the struggle for justice.'"[43] A few days after Jackson's funeral, King announced that there would be a march from Selma to Montgomery in protest of police brutality and the denial of voting rights. Albert Turner, longtime resident of Marion, maintains that the idea to march to Montgomery was actually that of black activists in Marion. They had wanted to march from Marion to Montgomery, but were told that "that was too far and that it would be much more dramatic to go from Selma, instead of Marion."[44] Turner believed that the demonstration in Marion that led to the murder of Jimmy Lee Jackson was worse than the "Bloody Sunday" tragedy, because it was a night demonstration.

42. Levine, *Freedom's Children*, 126–27.
43. Wexler, *An Eyewitness History*, 218.
44. Quoted in Raines, *My Soul Is Rested*, 195.

Once the police attacked the demonstrators, they reportedly shot out and/or turned off all lights, and commenced to randomly beat the demonstrators. No one could see anything, and this included news photographers with cameras.[45] In any case, Jackson's death, the first in the voter registration campaign in the Black Belt, was a stimulant for renewed protests and demonstrations. We will see momentarily that, unfortunately, the shooting death of this young black civil rights activist did not receive the national attention and outrage that was expressed when white civil rights activist, Reverend James Reeb, was struck with a pipe and mortally wounded after the second march to the Edmund Pettus Bridge.

"Bloody Sunday"

Sheyann Webb, although a young child, would not be deterred. She continued to defy her parents by attending the mass meetings and participating in the demonstrations along with her friend Rachel. She and Rachel even participated in the infamous "Bloody Sunday" march on the Pettus Bridge on March 7, 1965, even though some marchers complained, saying that they were "too small." This was the first attempted march from Selma to Montgomery. Because of the tensions between SNCC and SCLC, the former's executive committee voted to not participate in the march, but decided that any individual SNCC member who desired to do so could. John Lewis felt that he had to participate, since doing so would reveal his solidarity with the local residents and their struggle. Although he could not represent SNCC, he decided to participate as a concerned citizen. On the day of the march, about five to six hundred black and white people showed up near the church. Martin Luther King

---

45. Raines, *My Soul Is Rested*, 189.

and Ralph Abernathy had gone home to Atlanta to be present in their respective pulpits that Sunday. When the people showed up at Brown's Chapel, King was phoned at his church and asked whether the march should proceed. King gave the green light, with the understanding that the leaders of the march would be Hosea Williams (representing SCLC) and John Lewis (who King did not know at the time was representing only himself).

According to Albert Turner, more than 50 percent of the marchers had driven over from Marion "with the intentions of going on to Montgomery that Sunday."[46] The marchers got as far as the Pettus Bridge, which spans the Alabama River and leads away from Selma. On the other side of the bridge they were stopped by local and state police and Jim Clark's posse. They were given the order to turn back. Before the nonviolent marchers could really react, they were attacked by the posse and police on horseback and on foot. Many of the marchers were beaten bloody by clubs and whips. Many recalled the awful sound of the wooden clubs contacting human skulls. As had happened multiple times during the Freedom Rides, John Lewis was once again beaten unconscious. The people were tear-gassed and beaten all the way back to the church. During the melee, Sheriff Clark's voice was heard shouting: "Get those goddamned niggers! And get those goddamned *white* niggers."[47]

Looking back as an adult, Sheyann Webb recalled being simply "terrified" when the marchers were attacked. It was an experience she would never forget, and even as an adult she sometimes had nightmares about it. She remembered seeing the horsemen riding toward her at a full gallop. The riders all had on "those awful masks." Having thrown tear gas canisters, they rode right through the clouds of smoke. "Some of them had clubs, others had ropes or whips,

---

46. Quoted in ibid., 195.
47. Quoted in Lewis, *Walking with the Wind*, 331.

which they swung about them like they were driving cattle," said Webb. "I'll tell you, I forgot about praying, and I just turned and ran. And just as I was turning the tear gas got me; it burned my nose first and then got my eyes. I was blinded by the tears. So I began running and not seeing where I was going."[48] She recalled the horrible sight of both women and men being beaten like they were of no value whatever. Webb did not stop running until she got home. Once there, she saw horsemen still chasing and hitting people. When she got to the family apartment and tried telling her parents what happened, her father, like some other men in the apartment complex, was furious to the point of getting his shotgun and heading out the door to shoot any horseman he saw. His wife was finally able to get him to calm himself enough to put the shotgun away. Sheyann Webb recalled: "They had beaten us like we were slaves."[49]

Rachel West recalled being chased by horsemen as she ran toward her apartment. "My legs didn't seem to be moving," said West—"it was like in a bad dream when you are chased by something and can't run. Well, just as I got to the yard this white guy named Frank Soracco came by me and he was moving fast. And I must have been crying out because he stopped and just swept me up and carried me under the armpits and kept moving."[50] West knew that Soracco was terrified, for once they got to her family's apartment he "headed straight into our front door, dropped me, then ran up the steps to the bathroom and locked the door."[51] West was certain that the horsemen wanted to kill Soracco more than anybody, since he was a white man who had chosen (with other whites) to struggle with blacks for their freedom and civil rights.

---

48. Webb and West Nelson, *Selma, Lord, Selma*, 96.
49. Ibid., 97.
50. Ibid., 100.
51. Ibid., 101.

Both Webb and West recalled that they had done nothing to deserve the way they and the people had been treated by law enforcement officers that day. There was a cloud of fear over the apartment complex and the church. But later that evening they returned to the church. West remembered that the faces of the people were unforgettable. "They were like masks. Some of them were still crying, but they all just sat there staring to the front. I had never seen such looks before. They were hurt, they were angry, they were outraged. The smell of tear gas was everywhere; it was in their clothes, in their hair. It stung my eyes."[52] Initially, no one sang, no one prayed. There was just sobbing and blank stares throughout the church.

But even so, the church, Brown Chapel, was the place to be. After so much crying, the moaning that many had been doing eventually turned into humming, "Ain't Gonna Let Nobody Turn Me 'Round." The girls had not heard it hummed that way before, but it caught on, and before long they were singing the words: "Ain't gonna let George Wallace turn me 'round." And, "Ain't gonna let Jim Clark turn me 'round." "Ain't gonna let no horses . . . ain't gonna let no tear gas—ain't gonna let nobody turn me 'round. *Nobody!*"[53] The singing got louder and more spirited as more and more people entered the church, many with bandaged heads. Something was happening in the church that the people could not explain. Sheyann Webb reflected:

> We was singing and telling the world that we hadn't been whipped, that we had won.
>
> Just all of a sudden something happened that night and we knew in that church that—Lord Almighty—we had really won, after all. We had won!

---

52. Ibid., 102.
53. Ibid., 105–6.

> I think we all realized it at the same time, that we had won something that day, because people were standing up and singing like I'd never heard them before.[54]

Once again, we see how the power of song lifted the people's spirits and renewed their commitment and determination to hold on and to press ever forward, refusing to be turned around. And it was no small thing that black children and youth were present to witness the low of things, the inhumane treatment they had been subjected to, as well as the resilience of black people in the face of tremendous odds.

Contrary to Albert Turner's claim that those who had driven over from Marion intended to march all the way to Montgomery on March 7, Wilson Baker and John Lewis recalled that there was no real indication that this was the case. Baker recalled, for example, that there were women who had shown up in high heels. For the movement's part, Lewis said they had not really drawn up the plan and completed logistics for a march to Montgomery.

The Bloody Sunday tragedy had a significant unintended consequence for the movement. The parents of eight-year-old Sheyann Webb, and many other black adults, including black schoolteachers, who had not participated in the demonstrations, began attending the mass meetings and demonstrating. Without question, a little child had once again led the way. As in Birmingham and other campaigns, black children and youth had been a formidable force, and Selma was no different. They had understood that what was happening in Selma and other Black Belt towns was as much about them, as black adults.

Not unlike Bull Connor, Jim Clark had unwittingly (and no doubt much to his chagrin) played right into the hands of King, which is quite ironic, since he had the advantage of knowing what happened

---

54. Ibid., 106.

to Bull Connor and Birmingham's image when Connor used excessive force on demonstrators, including children. Resorting to brutal violence against the demonstrators merely angered and provoked black nonparticipants and led to the involvement of substantially larger numbers of black residents. In addition, Clark's miscalculation, just like Bull Connor's, led to a massive outpouring of northern white goodwill, federal government intervention, and massive news media coverage. Furthermore, when Martin Luther King sent out the call to white liberals and others in the North to join the second march from Selma to Montgomery, there was an overwhelmingly large positive response. King was convinced that "Selma is to 1965 what Birmingham was to 1963."[55]

Martin Luther King's sister, Christine King Farris, recalled that at one point in Selma, a group of thirty-two teachers tried to register to vote. All were terminated by the school board.[56] Andrew Durgan, longtime schoolteacher in Selma, remembered that when the demonstrations started, black students defied him and other teachers and marched. The students called their teachers unkind names—"cowards" and "toms." After the Bloody Sunday incident, Durgan himself was compelled to join the demonstrations. Risking dismissal, he led black teachers in a mass march on the Dallas County Courthouse. "In the entire history of the Movement, it was the only time black public school teachers—the heart of the black middle class in most Southern towns—demonstrated in force. Later, when the march moved out for Montgomery, he was in the front ranks."[57] Frederick Reese, another black teacher, led 99 percent of the teachers to the county courthouse on a different day to ask if the board of registrars would have the board office open so teachers could register.

---

55. Quoted in Wexler, *An Eyewitness History*, 236.
56. Christine King Farris, *Through It All: Reflections on My Life, My Family, and My Faith* (New York: Atria, 2009), 116.
57. Quoted in Raines, *My Soul Is Rested*, 225.

They were refused admittance by Sheriff Jim Clark. Significantly, Reese recalled that after the teachers' demonstration, "all kinds of groups" got involved. "The undertakers got a group and they marched. The beauticians got a group and they marched. Everybody marched because the teachers had more influence than they ever dreamed in the community."[58]

Selma black students were ecstatic when they saw their teachers finally participating in one of the marches.[59] The children had led the way, and their teachers, as their parents and other previously nonparticipating black adults, were moved to step up to the plate. Sheyann Webb reflected: "What impressed me most about the day that the teachers marched was just the idea of them being there.... They were just as afraid as my parents were, because they would lose their jobs. And it was amazing to see how many teachers participated."[60] Webb was also among the demonstrators in the march from Selma to Montgomery that began on March 21. When King saw her, he inquired as to whom she was with, and placed her in the care of his staff. Looking back on that period, Webb said: "They put me in a van and I came on over to Montgomery with one of his secretaries. Dr. King told his assistant that my parents had to be contacted and told that I was in their care, and that I was okay."[61] This was more than a gesture on the part of King. His action was one of genuine concern for the well-being of a young child who was without parental supervision and who was fighting for her freedom.

---

58. Quoted in Hampton and Fayer, *Voices of Freedom*, 219.
59. Webb and West Nelson, *Selma, Lord, Selma*, 35.
60. Quoted in Hampton and Fayer, *Voices of Freedom*, 219.
61. Levine, *Freedom's Children*, 129.

"Turnaround Tuesday"

Martin Luther King was not unmindful of the tensions between SCLC and SNCC. Moreover, he respected his youthful colleagues enough to listen to their argument after the Bloody Sunday tragedy that they should proceed to march to Montgomery from Selma, even before federal judge Frank Johnson ruled on their request for an injunction to continue the march.[62] Andrew Young maintains that, King listened to their argument, but decided to march (on Tuesday, March 9), only to the point on the Pettus Bridge where the Bloody Sunday incident occurred, kneel and pray, and then turn back toward Selma. What Young failed to convey, however, is that King had not in fact informed SNCC leaders of the plan to march only to the point on the Pettus Bridge.[63] It was later found that only a very few of King's closest staff members were aware of the compromise that was worked out prior to the march.[64] Ralph Abernathy confirmed that a compromise had in fact been agreed upon. As Abernathy remembered it, Governor Leroy Collins, chairman of the newly created Community Relations Service Under the Civil Rights Act of 1964, actually offered up the idea during negotiations; the idea that marchers would march only to the place where the Bloody Sunday melee occurred. It would be a "symbolic" act, "a reenactment" of the previous march. According to Abernathy, Collins then said: "Then you could voluntarily turn around and walk back to the churches, obeying a federal injunction, telling your people that you had made your point."[65] When King asked Abernathy what he thought about it, he agreed that it was a good

---

62. Andrew Young, *An Easy Burden: The Civil Rights Movement and the Transformation of America* (New York: HarperCollins, 1996), 360.
63. Carson, *In Struggle*, 159.
64. Lewis, *Walking with the Wind*, 334.
65. Quoted in Ralph Abernathy, *And the Walls Came Tumbling Down: An Autobiography* (New York: Harper & Row, 1989), 337–38.

compromise. "Either route incurred risks and criticisms," Abernathy said. "But this way we could salvage something for tomorrow [march day] and still obey Judge Johnson, who, we were certain, would clear the highway for us by next weekend."[66] Unfortunately, King, despite the fact that he was viewed as a *moral leader* by many, stuck to his story that "no prearranged agreement existed." Moreover, he said, "There was no talks or agreements between Governor Collins and me. . . ."[67] The facts do not support this claim.

Understandably, many SNCC activists were infuriated and disappointed with King's tactic, and viewed his action as a sellout.[68] In addition, many of the Northerners who King invited to join the march felt the same. At the very least, they were confused by his decision. After all, said John Lewis, "they had come to put their bodies on the line, and now they were backing down, retreating, going home."[69] The incident was emblazoned in the memories of SNCC activists as "turnaround Tuesday."

King tried hard to explain the turnaround, but virtually no one was buying it, or understood it better, once he tried to explain his reasoning. SNCC leaders openly expressed their disappointment and sense of being sold out. Even many of those who arrived from other parts of the country to participate in the march could not understand what led King to turn around. Orloff Miller, a Unitarian minister from Berkeley, California, was one of these. Miller recalled that once the marchers had returned to Brown's Chapel, King tried to explain the turnaround, but much to the chagrin of many of the marchers, "we never fully understood what had gone on behind the scenes,"[70] said Miller. Because King also inquired of those present whether any

---

66. Abernathy, *And the Walls*, 338.
67. King, "Behind the Selma March," in *A Testament of Hope*, 130.
68. Powledge, *Free at Last?*, 624.
69. Lewis, *Walking with the Wind*, 334.
70. Quoted in Hampton and Fayer, *Voices of Freedom*, 231.

of them would be able to remain for a few more days, many got the impression that yet another march to Montgomery was being planned. This, itself, undoubtedly suggested to some that from the beginning, King had not intended to violate the federal injunction. Because one of his Unitarian ministerial colleagues, James Reeb, of Boston, was killed by white-supremacist thugs that night, Miller came to see that Tuesday as "the 'Turnaround Day'—not only of the march, but also of how America saw the civil rights struggle. Because when Jim Reeb, a white clergyman from the North, was killed in Selma, people suddenly sat up and took notice and from then on things changed in the movement. . . . People went to Washington and they [put pressure] on President Johnson."[71] The same did not happen when Jimmy Lee Jackson was murdered in February.

King himself maintained, publicly, that he had made no deal or compromise with authorities that led to the turnaround. He admitted that Governor Collins, and John Doar of the Justice Department, met with him to try to dissuade him from violating Judge Johnson's injunction against marching. "I explained to them why, as a matter of conscience, I felt it was necessary to seek a confrontation with injustice on Highway 80," King said later. "I asked them to try to understand that I would rather die on the highway in Alabama than make a butchery of my conscience by compromising with evil."[72] King was adamant in stressing "once again that no prearranged agreement existed," at least that he was involved in.[73]

This is all very interesting, considering that Andrew Young, then executive director of SCLC, stated years later that a compromise of sorts had in fact been reached. Forbidden to march by federal

---

71. Juan Williams, *Eyes on the Prize: America Civil Rights Years, 1954-1965* (New York: Viking, 1987), 277.
72. King, "Behind the Selma March," in *A Testament of Hope: The Essential Writings of Martin Luther King, Jr.* ed. James M. Washington (New York: Harper & Row, 1986), 130.
73. Ibid.

judge Johnson, King was in a real pickle since the federal courts were generally more supportive of the movement than local and state courts. King, therefore, really did not want to violate the federal injunction, and yet he was compelled by conscience to do something. This was invariably the great challenge of his decision-making process: balancing the demands of conscience with political feasibility and the politically possible in any given moment. It was a terrible tension in which he lived daily, but one from which he could not escape. In the case of the second march, he had invited many supporters from around the country to join him, and very many had already arrived in Selma. Young remembers it this way:

> So we were in the delicate position of having people who had come down wanting to march, but for them to march would have meant that we would have turned the movement around. Since the police—the troopers—weren't going to let us march anyway, we worked out a compromise that we would go up to the place where people were beaten, have our prayers, and then turn around and come back. There were some people who wanted to insist on another confrontation. But Martin made a deliberate distinction between federal judges and state court judges. He said that from 1954 the only ally we've had has been the federal courts. And we have to respect the federal courts, even when we disagree with them. So he just refused to violate any federal court order.[74]

It should also be noted, however, that when King appeared in Judge Johnson's court the day after the second march ("turnaround Tuesday"), he as much as confessed that a compromise had in fact been agreed upon with federal officials. King told the judge "that 'there was a tacit agreement at the bridge that we would go no further,' an admission which saved him from a contempt citation but made him appear less than frank in denying the existence of a prior agreement with Collins."[75] King told the judge that he felt

---

74. Quoted in Hampton and Fayer, *Voices of Freedom*, 231–32.

morally obligated to respond to the "Bloody Sunday" incident and the police officials who caused it. He had to make a moral witness by demonstrating their resolve, but said that it was not his intention to violate the injunction by marching to Montgomery.[76]

A great deal has been made of the fact that once King got to the point at the foot of the Edmund Pettus Bridge where all of the state troopers, local police, and posse were, the line of officers seemed to part, as if to allow the marchers to proceed on to Montgomery. Rather than proceed, King and the marchers kneeled, prayed, and turned around. It has never been satisfactorily explained why that opening occurred in the line of police officers. Critics contend that the door was open for King to proceed with the march, and yet there is no reason to believe that the line would not have closed as quickly as it opened had King tried to go forward. And of course, it might well be that the enemies of the movement knew full well that King was under federal injunction not to march, and they may have been baiting him to violate Judge Johnson's order. We cannot know for certain. What we know is that King turned around, and having done so, he had to endure massive criticism from many quarters. John Lewis described King's account of the march "as a 'transparent misrepresentation of the facts.'"[77] But looking back, many years later, Lewis acknowledged that he had no problem with King's decision to turn around. "I thought it was in keeping with the philosophy of the movement, that there comes a time when you must retreat, and that there is nothing wrong with retreating. There is nothing wrong with coming back to fight another day. Dr. King knew—we all knew—that Judge Johnson was going to give us what we were

---

75. Quoted in Adam Fairclough, *To Redeem the Soul of America: The Southern Christian Leadership Conference & Martin Luther King, Jr.* (Athens: University of Georgia Press, 2001 [1987]), 246.
76. Williams, *Eyes on the Prize*, 275.
77. Quoted in Fairclough, *To Redeem the Soul of America*, 466 n. 58. From *Saturday Review*, April 3, 1965, 16–17, 57.

asking for if we simply followed procedure, followed the rules."[78] As SNCC goes, however, Lewis was in the tiny minority. Most others, led by James Forman, were fed up with SCLC and King, and therefore moved out of Selma and concentrated SNCC resources on demonstrations at the state capitol in Montgomery.

One would think that King, aware of the already-mounting tension between SNCC and SCLC, would have sought to be more transparent with the youthful activists. And yet, if a compromise was in fact reached with government authorities (as appears to have been the case), it is possible that King did not feel that he could trust SNCC leaders to remain silent about it until after the march. At any rate, by agreeing to the compromise, King revealed his respect for the federal courts. His action, no matter how much it confused and offended student activists, local leaders, and supporters from the North, allowed him to avoid "offending Lyndon Johnson," and allowed him to avoid what most likely would have been a bloodbath worse than what occurred on Bloody Sunday. "Had King pressed on with the march, the president told Collins afterwards, 'the blood would be running knee-deep in the ditches.' It would not have been that bad, Collins, thought, 'but it would have been bad.'"[79] The short of it is that King had to do something that day, and for him, at least, it had less to do with saving face politically, than making a moral witness against racism and the violence of Bloody Sunday. It also had much to do with making a moral witness in favor of respecting and obeying federal injunctions, since barring a few exceptions, federal courts had been supportive of civil rights efforts. Generally, federal courts failed civil rights leaders' expectations in those instances in which the Kennedy administration, in a political move to appease southern politicians, appointed a number of federal

---

78. Lewis, *Walking with the Wind*, 335.
79. Quoted in Fairclough, *To Redeem the Soul of America*, 246.

judges early on without paying close attention to their racial attitudes and practices. In such cases, knowingly or not, the administration appointed southern white supremacists to the bench. Two of the most notorious of these, who worked hardest to deny blacks the right to vote, were W. Harold Cox of Jackson, Mississippi (thought to be the worst of the racist federal judges, and did not hesitate to use the term "nigger" on the bench), and J. Robert Elliot of Columbus, Georgia (who, during Robert Kennedy's tenure as attorney general, ruled against blacks in more than 90 percent of civil rights cases brought before him).[80]

Selma to Montgomery

In the Selma-to-Montgomery march that commenced on March 21, 1965, Martin Luther King believed that he had seen one of the few times that the church stood up to be counted. It was as solid an interreligious, interdenominational event as he had witnessed in the movement to that point. Reflecting on the march, he said that "we had one of the most magnificent expressions of the ecumenical movement that I've ever seen."[81] This said much to him that was positive about the church, at least in this instance. "The march gave new relevance to the gospel," King said. "Selma brought into being *the second great awakening of the church* in America. Long standing aside and giving only tacit approval to the civil rights struggle, the church finally marched forth like a mighty army and stood beside God's children in distress."[82] It was an instance of the church's acknowledgment of the centrality of the social gospel in its ministry.

---

80. Powledge, *Free at Last?*, 386. See also 380, 387.
81. Carson, ed., *The Autobiography of Martin Luther King, Jr.*, 287.
82. Ibid. (my emphasis).

It is not often mentioned that as the marchers neared Montgomery, word came through John Doar of the Justice Department that there was a credible threat against King's life. Doar asked Andrew Young whether they could drive King to the state capitol from the city limits, but King made the decision to walk in with the other marchers. Young and other SCLC staffers did the best they could to provide what protection they could, by surrounding King with black men in dark blue suits like the one King was wearing. These men were all placed on the front row with King. In addition, most of the men were about King's height.[83] This was one instance in which blacks hoped that many whites truly did believe that "all blacks look alike."

King's life was threatened so often that one must wonder how he was able to cope and continue on with movement work. He thought about death philosophically, but it appears that one of his best coping mechanisms was humor. Andrew Young makes the point well.

> Martin had a way of making fun out of any dangerous situation. He talked about going down to Selma. We knew the kind of people that were there. And he started preaching everybody's funeral. He was saying, "We were lucky in Birmingham, all of us got out alive." But some of us weren't going to make it out of Selma. And he'd go around the room sort of saying, "Well, Ralph, now if they get you . . ." and then he'd preach Ralph Abernathy's sermon for about five minutes. He just made fun of saying all the embarrassing things he could think of saying, pretending that he was preaching our eulogies and our funerals. That was the way that we dealt with the anxiety and the fear and the tension, by joking about it and laughing about it.[84]

This is something that most white people have *never* understood about blacks; that they have *always*—since the time of American

---

83. Hampton and Fayer, *Voices of Freedom*, 239.
84. Quoted in ibid., 214–15. Preeminent King scholar, Lewis V. Baldwin, believes that humor was so important for King that his is presently assembling some of his most important humor in a small soon to be published collection.

enslavement—had survival and coping mechanisms such as humor and horseplay that have helped them to survive whatever has been thrown at them. Indeed, when King arrived in Memphis on April 3, 1968, there was a credible threat to his life, which he spoke about in his last speech that night at Mason Temple. Just hours before his assassination he spent a portion of the afternoon engaging in horseplay with Andrew Young, Abernathy, and others in his motel room.

As noted previously, after "turnaround Tuesday," SNCC leaders departed for Montgomery to lead demonstrations at the state capitol. John Lewis did not feel that some of those demonstrations were in keeping with movement strategy, since some of the students taunted the police and posse men.[85] Most of the demonstrators were students—mostly black, but some white as well—from local colleges. At the conclusion of one of their demonstrations, the students were brutally attacked and beaten by state troopers and posse men on horseback. King and SNCC leader James Forman led a demonstration at the capitol in protest against the attack. At that time, Sheriff Mac Butler apologized for the attacks.[86]

Upon arrival at the state capitol on March 25, King and the marchers from Selma were greeted by a crowd of more than 25,000. King told the large crowd that by gaining the right to vote, blacks could become equals to whites in terms of civil rights. He applauded the many religious persons, clergy and laypeople, from all over the country who joined with them in the Selma campaign. He praised President Johnson, a Southerner, who "had the sensitivity to feel the will of the country, and in an address that will live in history

---

85. Lewis, *Walking with the Wind*, 335.
86. After the peaceful march to the capitol and his speech in a driving rain, King and other black leaders went into the courthouse to confer with Sheriff Butler and John Doar of the Justice Department. See Jim Bishop, *The Days of Martin Luther King, Jr.* (New York: G.P. Putnam's Sons, 1971), 392.

as one of the most passionate pleas for human rights ever made by a president of our nation, he pledged the might of the federal government to cast off the centuries-old blight."[87] King told the crowd of his certainty that segregation was on its deathbed in the state of Alabama. Although he insisted that they were on the move, and that they refused to allow anything to stop their forward progress, he also reminded them of the hard realism that they "are still in for a season of suffering" in much of the Deep South.[88]

At the conclusion of King's speech, a delegation of eight march leaders were selected to deliver a petition to Governor Wallace, asking him to remove all existing obstacles to voter registration in the state of Alabama. Prevented by state police and posse men from delivering the petition, an aid to the governor agreed to take it to him. Tragically, the day would end on the dreadful note of the murder of Viola Liuzzo, a Detroit mother and wife who had responded positively to King's call to the North for volunteers to participate in the march from Selma to Montgomery. Mrs. Liuzzo was one of the volunteers helping to transport people back to Selma, when she was shot twice in the face by a carload of Klansmen as she was driving back to Montgomery to transport more people.

The Voting Rights Bill and the Pettus Bridge Connection

Ironically, the voting rights campaign in Selma and the white violence and resistance to it did much to ensure passage of the Voting Rights Act of 1965. Wilson Baker recalled a conversation he had with Attorney General Nicholas Katzenbach about numbers of people the Justice Department expected would be registered to vote

---

87. King, "Our God Is Marching On!," in *A Testament of Hope*, 228.
88. Ibid., 229.

if the Voting Rights Bill passed. "What do you mean *if* it passes," Katzenbach snapped. "You people passed that on that bridge. You people in Selma passed that on that bridge that Sunday." Katzenbach went on to say, "You can be sure it will pass, and because of that, if nothing else."[89] White violence against blacks on the Pettus Bridge contributed much to the passage of the Voting Rights Bill. Katzenbach expected that there would be at least ten thousand blacks registered once the Voting Rights Bill passed. It wound up being closer to fifteen thousand, making it possible for Baker (the moderate racist) to defeat Jim Clark (the blatant, hardcore racist) for the office of sheriff.

It is strange indeed, how whites fought so hard to deny blacks their civil rights and voting rights, but then benefited just as much once such rights were granted. This has been a long-established pattern in the U.S. White moderates and hardcore racists alike in Selma, the Black Belt, and other Deep South cities benefited mightily from the Voting Rights Act in some ways. None said it better than Fred Powledge.

> Almost before Lyndon Johnson's signature was dry on the Voting Rights Act of 1965, white politicians in the South started courting the Negro vote. Several Southern congressmen who had voted against the legislation when it passed the House changed to "Aye" when it returned from the Senate and it was obvious that the bill would pass. It was surprising even to cynics who were familiar with the Southern white politician's facility for shamelessly adjusting to rapid change.[90]

In agreement with President Johnson, King said that the Voting Rights Act was "one of the most monumental laws in the history of American freedom."[91] He also told the President it was ironic that

---

89. Quoted in Raines, *My Soul Is Rested*, 215.
90. Powledge, *Free at Last?*, 630.
91. Carson, ed., *The Autobiography of Martin Luther King, Jr.*, 289.

"after a century, a white southern President would help lead the way toward the salvation of the Negro."[92] Indeed, it might well be that Lyndon Baines Johnson, more than any other president, identified himself and his administration with blacks' cause for freedom.[93] More so, in his address to Congress announcing the Voting Rights Bill, Johnson conceded that blacks were the real heroes and "she-roes" of the struggle for voting rights, saying: "His [blacks'] actions and protests, his courage to risk safety and even to risk his life, have awakened the conscience of this nation. His demonstrations have been designed to call attention to injustice, designed to provoke change, designed to stir reform. He has called upon us to make good the promise of America."[94] Indeed, acknowledging the difficulty of bringing about social change through democratic process, the president also made it clear that the Bloody Sunday tragedy and the murder of Reverend James Reeb was not just a tragedy for Selma and the Black Belt. Rather, he said, it "was an American tragedy."[95] The president's main blunder in his momentous speech was his failure to acknowledge similarly the tragedy of the murder of Jimmy Lee Jackson, who happened to be black. Johnson's moral sentiment was in the right place, but his own deeply entrenched racism blinded him to his and his administration's failure to express the same level of moral outrage in the Jackson tragedy, as that of Reeb.

Growing Tension between SNCC and SCLC

We have seen that SNCC youths did not like the fact that in Selma, as in Albany, and various places in the Mississippi Delta, they went

---

92. Quoted in Kotz, *Judgment Days*, 314.
93. Ibid., 313–14.
94. Quoted in ibid., 311.
95. Wexler, *An Eyewitness History*, 236.

in and did the thankless groundbreaking, quite dangerous work, and SCLC came in later and got most of the credit, media attention, and the lion's share of financial contributions. We also saw that by all accounts, including King's, the Albany campaign was not the "success" he had hoped for. Although unwilling to name Albany as a complete failure, King readily admitted to Alex Haley that they made the grave mistake of protesting "against segregation generally rather than against a single and distinct facet of it. Our protest was so vague that we got nothing, and the people were left very depressed and in despair."[96] Is it no wonder that after Albany, King was looking for a place to test nonviolent direct action? Nevertheless, King was sensitive to the charge that he and SCLC tended to come in only after SNCC had done the groundwork, and then take over. Some SNCC youths, for instance, James Forman, got so worked up over this that they insisted on challenging King's leadership. Stokely Carmichael strongly disagreed with Forman and others in this regard. Instead, he offered a strong rationale for creatively using and exploiting the energy and excitement that King tended to generate, particularly among older, lower-class, religious blacks. According to Carmichael:

> People loved King. . . . I've seen people in the South climb over each other just to say, "I touched him! I touched him!" . . . I'm even talking about the young. The old people had more love and respect. They even saw him like a God. These were the people we were working with and I had to follow in his footsteps when I went in there. The people didn't know what was SNCC. They just said, "You one of Dr. King's men?" "Yes, Ma'am, I am."[97]

As an illustration of Carmichael's point about the way rural blacks felt about King, Maria Gitin, a white civil rights veteran who did voter education-registration work in the dangerous Wilcox County,

---

96. King, "Playboy Interview," in *A Testament of Hope*, 344.
97. Quoted in Carson, *In Struggle*, 164.

Alabama, recalled that when she and other college volunteers went to the homes of rural blacks for the first time they would say: "Dr. King sent us." That was generally all they needed to do in order to be accepted by residents.[98] In any case, Carmichael was focused on what was best for the local people in the most concrete sense. His argument was that, anything that King did that helped SNCC in any way to work cooperatively with the local people to gain voting rights should be utilized. At least in this instance, Carmichael saw clearly that in the end, it was more about the well-being of the people of Lowndes County and other Black Belt counties, than seeking to score points or victories over King's leadership. And yet, unquestionably, not all SNCC youths felt this way, as indicated by Forman's stance. However, if the real aim was to serve the local people in their bid for civil and voting rights, then Carmichael's was indeed the wiser stance.

Conclusion

From very near the beginning of his civil rights ministry in Montgomery, Martin Luther King did not hesitate to lavish praise on the positive contributions of black youth to the cause of freedom and human dignity. In a 1958 interview at Bennett College in Greensboro, North Carolina, he praised the nine black children (six females and three males) who integrated Central High School in Little Rock, Arkansas in 1957. He said that they stood up "with so much courage and yet so much dignity in the midst of all of the abuses that they've had to confront."[99] Never wanting to steal

---

98. As noted in chapter 4 (n. 117) Gitin shared her recollection of this when she read selections from her book of stories about the work in Wilcox County, *This Bright Light of Ours*.
99. Clayborne Carson et al., eds., *The Papers of Martin Luther King, Jr.* (Berkeley: University of California Press, 2000), 4:365.

the thunder of his youthful colleagues, King always expressed appreciation for their courage, creativity, and willingness to take their destiny into their own hands. He did not always agree with them, or they with him, but by and large there was mutual respect between them. Many of the youths understood that by virtue of who King was and his own level of devotion to the cause, there were things that he could do that they could not do as well, such as attract monetary donations, media coverage, celebrity support, and the attention of the federal government. The wise ones among the youthful activists sought to take advantage of King's status, not for themselves, but for those they sought to help liberate. King understood that there were things the young people could do that were just as important, such as bring in large numbers of youthful demonstrators who filled the jails in Birmingham and Selma. Nor was he unmindful of the fact that the youthful activists tended to be more adept at doing the all-important groundbreaking work in local communities, no matter how dangerous they were.

Martin Luther King was not the only one to acknowledge the courage and contributions made by black youth in the struggle for civil and human rights. Nor were blacks the only ones to praise them. In a statement that King surely would have applauded, Benjamin Spencer, a white Kentucky college professor, said in 1963: ". . . Heroism has not gone out of American life, but, ironically, it seems to me, it has been most magnificently displayed by the young Negro children of the South during the past five years."[100] Probably no one appreciated the role and contributions of black children and young people more than Martin Luther King.

Without question, King would have been very pleased at how some of the youths with whom he had been affiliated in the

---

100. Quoted in Mary King, *Freedom Song* (New York: William Morrow, 1987), 161.

movement turned out. A case in point is Sheyann Webb, the young eight-year-old who was the first child to get involved in the Selma demonstrations, and who was befriended by King. In high school, Webb was a consistent honor-roll student, and went on to earn a degree at what is now Tuskegee University. While King would be proud of her accomplishments, he would also resonate to her frustration over the failure of black residents of Selma to vote in the 1970s. When Webb turned eighteen in 1974, she said that the first thing she did was register to vote, fulfilling a promise she made while still a child. However, she laments: "But you'd be surprised how many people haven't done it. After all we went through back in 1965. I worked on a voter registration drive in 1974 in Lowndes County. They [blacks] still live on the land that used to be plantations. It made me sick. They told me they didn't have any use in registering. I couldn't believe it. Dr. King put his life on the line for them and they tell me that. It seemed like he died for nothing, in some cases."[101]

Webb knew that in light of what King tried to do and what he so staunchly believed, were he alive today, he too would be disappointed that so many of his people throughout the country do not exercise their right to vote, particularly those who were children in movement days. Far too many blacks seem to be overcome with apathy and a sense of not having anything to keep them going, unlike during movement days when blacks, young and old, seemed instinctively to see purpose in fighting for the right to be human beings and to be free. In the second decade of the twenty-first century, far too many blacks seem to just passively exist from day to day. Indeed, as far back as 1958, King named *apathy* as one of the great challenges that blacks had to overcome. "Even where the polls are open to all, Negroes have shown themselves too slow to exercise

---

101. Webb and West Nelson, *Selma, Lord, Selma*, 133–34.

their voting privileges," he said.[102] King saw it as an obligation for blacks to vote, and to contribute constructively toward citizenship. He challenged black leaders to be intentional about working to alleviate complacency among their constituents.

The problem that frustrated Sheyann Webb in 1974 was not new in black communities. But fortunately, whether during, before, and after young Webb's childhood involvement in the voting rights campaign in Selma in 1965, there have always been blacks who rejected complacency, and chose rather to relentlessly pursue their freedom and civil rights. Frequently, as in the case of the Selma campaign, these have been "ordinary people" who were determined and committed to gain their rights and freedom.[103]

As we approach the end of this book, it is important to remember that Martin Luther King Jr. was never eager to engage in direct public confrontation with his youthful colleagues in the movement, even when they did not hesitate to criticize him publicly, as some SNCC activists and black power advocates did. King preferred, generally, to settle differences with young people in private, a view that SNCC leader John Lewis shared.[104] For example, in King's case, he declined to sign his name to the *New York Times* advertisement by Bayard Rustin to publicize the divisions between more moderate civil rights organizations such as SCLC, and some of the more militant ones managed and led by young blacks in organizations like SNCC. Within forty-eight hours of the appearance of the *New York Times* advertisement, King went on record to state his own position, saying: "Some consider certain civil rights groups conclusively and irrevocably committed to error and wish them barred from the movement. I cannot agree with this approach because it involves

---

102. Martin Luther King Jr., *Stride Toward Freedom* (New York: Harper & Row, 1958), 222.
103. Webb and West Nelson, *Selma, Lord, Selma*, 139.
104. Lewis, *Walking with the Wind*, 336.

an acceptance of the interpretation of enemies of civil rights and bases policy on their distortion. Actually, much thinking, particularly by young Negroes, is in a state of flux."[105] King knew that young people were dedicated to the movement, and that their thinking was fluid and thus was susceptible to change. He therefore wanted to do nothing that would kill their spirit and sense of determination in the struggle for freedom and equality. He would not speak to reporters about disagreements between SCLC and SNCC. For all intents and purposes, these were "family" matters, and for King, they should be kept in the family.

There are a number of important stories that beg to be told regarding black and white youth during and beyond the movement years. One of these has to do with what black students, from elementary school to college, thought about their white peers in Montgomery and other places in the Deep South. Some black youths believed that a few of their white peers were sympathetic to their cause, but did not have the courage to join in with them. They were the "good" white people who knew right from wrong, but lacked the courage to do the right thing. In other instances, such as the sit-ins in Greensboro, and other places throughout the South, some white college students quickly joined with black students, enduring the same harassment, violence, and dehumanizing treatment. This was also the case of the Freedom Rides, and Freedom Summer. Indeed, as with Freedom Riders James Zwerg and Bob Zellner, committed white youth were frequently beaten more severely than their black peers as a way of making an example of them for supporting blacks' cause. Indeed, there is evidence that racist whites hated the Zwergs and Zellners even more than they hated blacks. One wonders—I

---

105. "Dr. King Clarifies His Racial Stand," *New York Times*, October 17, 1966.

wonder—whether such committed whites exist in the United States today. I would surely like to meet and join forces with them.

And what is to be said about the white students and nonstudents who were every bit as vicious and racist as their parents and other white adults in their behavior toward any who participated in the civil rights campaigns from Montgomery to Memphis, and beyond? Who can forget the horrific photographs of jeering, taunting, white youths, their parents, grandparents, and other white adults during the Birmingham campaign, the sit-ins and Freedom Rides, Selma, St. Augustine, Florida, and Cicero, Illinois, as blacks and some whites—students and adults—demonstrated nonviolently and courageously? Who can forget the photographs of black and white youths bleeding profusely after being attacked and savagely beaten with clubs and bottles by other white youths and adults? I often wonder what came of those jeering, racist white youths. To what extent did they and their posterity continue their racist ways? More than a few must have done so, since many of the things that blacks and committed whites fought for during the civil rights era are the same things that their children, grandchildren, and great grandchildren are fighting for today, that is, racial equality, and the freedom and life-chances needed to live a life worth living in a racism-free society.

And what of the children and grandchildren of powerful and privileged white racists such as Commissioner Bull Connor, Governors George Wallace, Orval Faubus, and Ross Barnett (of Alabama, Arkansas, and Mississippi, respectively), and Sheriffs Laurie Pritchett and Jim Clark?[106] To what extent did their posterity simply carry on their racist beliefs, policies, and practices, albeit in subtler, more politically correct ways today? To what degree did they

---

106. See John Blake, *Children of the Movement* (Chicago: Lawrence Hill, 2004), for discussions on the children of George Wallace, Ross Barnett, and Joe Smitherman (former mayor of Selma).

uncritically defend their parents' and grandparents' behavior toward blacks? Who among them had the courage to critique the stance of their parents and grandparents, and to work toward a fully antiracist nation, with equality for all? In any case, the story of what black and white youths thought of each other during the movement years is one that is waiting to be told,[107] as is the story of what happened to the children and grandchildren of white supremacists from movement days.

In addition, I cannot help wondering about what has come of the children of some of the key civil rights leaders. For many years, the children of Martin Luther King were in the public spotlight, but what of the children of Fred Shuttlesworth? James Bevel and Diane Nash Bevel? Andrew Young? Ralph Abernathy? Malcolm X? Stokely Carmichael (Kwame Ture)? To what degree were these civil rights children influenced by the work of their parent(s) and are carrying on that work today?

Another story that has not been adequately told is the extent to which it was sometimes black children who taught black adults about the difference between Southern white racists and Northern white freedom fighters. The latter, such as many of the hundreds of white college students who participated in Freedom Summer and SCOPE, were genuinely dedicated to fighting with blacks for their freedom,[108] because they saw blacks' freedom as integrally linked to their own. Surely this was yet another instance of black children leading the way in some of the civil rights campaigns. Southern black youth often helped their adult counterparts to see that not all white people were the same; that many of those who came from the North to help in

---

107. For reactions of blacks to their white peers, see Ellen Levine, *Freedom's Children*, 4, 53, 54, 57, 101–2.
108. See Levine, *Freedom's Children*, 72, 73, 76. See also Halberstam, *The Children*, 406. Here the author discusses Bob Zellner as the only white leader in SNCC during the voter registration campaign in McComb, Mississippi.

voter registration campaigns during Freedom Summer and in Selma, for example, were willing to give their lives for the cause. These were qualitatively different from the white people that most black youth had grown up with in the Deep South. It is critical that this history be kept alive and taught for the benefit of present-day youth of all racial-ethnic backgrounds, in the hope that it will inspire them to take up their own causes rather than to passively and complacently sit back, thinking that there is nothing they can do. Among other things, I address this in more detail in the next chapter.

6

Who Will Carry the Freedom Struggle Forward?

This book began by acknowledging that historically, blacks believed that their children had a certain place and expected them to remain in it. Childrearing itself was intentionally devoted to teaching this. From the time of slavery in the United States the very survival of black children and their parents frequently depended on how well the children understood their sense of place in the black family, and the importance of remaining silent around whites as to what transpired in the enslaved quarters. Not a few black parents were severely whipped because a black child innocently shared with white children conversations they overheard in the enslaved quarters. Needless to say, the expectation that children acknowledge and remain in their place generally meant that they were taught to be both obedient and respectful not only of their parents and adult extended family members, but other adults as well. Essentially, children were to be seen, but not heard. More often than not, they were even discouraged from asking questions of adults. The point was not to stifle their sense of curiosity, but to teach them the importance of controlling their tongue. Parents' sense was that if their children could do this at home, they likely would be successful at it when around white people. Black parents were interested in protecting and saving their children, not in requiring that they be silent and passive for the sake of being silent and passive. More than a few Afrikan Americans have spoken of the effect of such childrearing on them in later life, particularly the difficulty they have even in their adult years of speaking up. While none can deny the adverse effects of early black childrearing that required children to hold their tongue in the presence of adults, it is also the case that the lives of many black children were spared because of it.

Unfortunately, in many instances Afrikan Americans, when they discovered the problematic with this aspect of childrearing, tended to make adjustments by overcorrecting the problem. Beginning approximately a generation ago, many black parents began giving their children a great deal of leeway regarding what they could and could not do in the presence of adults. Before long it was clear that a different parenting style was in play and that children were no longer required to be silent, to keep a certain place in the presence of adults, and to obey and respect their parents and other adults. All of this was done under the guise of not wanting to break the child's will or to stifle her voice. In my estimation, Martin Luther King was not wrong to take issue with this *childrearing without consequence* approach, where the child is essentially allowed to do whatever he wants to do, without fear of consequence. King reacted to such approaches to parenting in his "Advice for Living" column in *Ebony* magazine in 1958:

> But freedom can very easily run wild if not tempered with discipline and responsibility. This almost "lunatic fringe" of modern child care has

been responsible for most strange and fantastic methods of child rearing in many American homes. The child is permitted to almost terrorize the home for fear of having its individuality repressed. Somewhere along the way every child must be trained into the obligations of cooperative living. He must be made aware that he is a member of a group and that group life implies duties and restraints. . . . The child must realize that there are rules of the game which he did not make and that he cannot break with impunity. In order to get all of these things over to the child it is often necessary to subject the child to disciplinary measures.[1]

It is understandable that adjustments to parenting in the enslaved quarters was in order, and also after the Civil War with the emergence in 1866 of the Ku Klux Klan and during and beyond the Reconstruction years. But when the adjustment began in the other direction, too many black parents went too far. Indeed, it is not uncommon today to see parents, male and female, literally struggling to get a young child under control in a department store or other public arena. I long ago lost track of the number of times I have witnessed such parents tell their young child to stop doing something, only to have the child continue in utter defiance. The tool of correction for the parent is to begin counting, which seldom gets the desired result. There was a time when I would only see white parents resort to such measures. In more recent years I have seen more and more Afrikan American parents adopt such tactics. My concern about this is that it is still the case that black children, and blacks generally, continue to be up against it in ways that white children and their parents are not. Black boys, for example, are still too often subjected to unnecessarily rough treatment by local police, and to a much, much larger extent than white boys. This suggests to me that black parents must again become vigilant in rearing black children such that they understand the need to behave in a certain

---

1. Clayborne Carson et al., eds., *The Papers of Martin Luther King, Jr.* (Berkeley: University of California Press, 2000), 4:374.

way, control their tongue, and always be aware of the existence of racism, especially when away from home.

As I express these concerns, I am not unmindful that just as black youths of the civil rights movement managed to find both their voice and place in the struggle, the very same will need to happen regarding present-day youths. I am confident that they will do this, and that they will do so in alliance with informed and sensitive youths of other communities who resist injustice of various kinds. Indeed, we saw an illustration of such youth reaction to the not guilty verdict in the George Zimmerman case, a point to which I return subsequently.

Afrikan American youths need to know that they matter and that what they do, as well as what happens to them, matters.[2] I say this because these are among the most endangered youths in the nation. They continue to be among the most undereducated, underemployed, and unemployed, disrespected, and virtually ignored youths in the country when it comes to life-chances. In addition, and particularly among the males, they are the victims of homicide more than any other group in the U.S. Many of the homicides are intracommunal, and far too many are still a result of questionable police shootings, all of which suggests a cheapening of young black lives. And then there is the matter of the highly suspicious shooting death of seventeen-year-old Trayvon Martin by George Zimmerman in Florida, and the nonstellar prosecution of the case that surely helped lead to a not guilty verdict. This cheapening of the lives of young Afrikan American males is all the more reason that young people, particularly those of color, need to know that the practical world they live in is such that they dare not sit back passively and

---

2. I know full well that the same applies to Hispanic youths, but I am also aware that Hispanic scholars such as Juan Gonzalez, Carmelo Alvarez, Tercio and Débora Junker, Harold J. Recinos, the late Ada María Isasi-Díaz, and others have given voice to this issue.

merely wait, hope, and trust that someone else—adults or otherwise—will address the problems that deny them the right and opportunity to obtain a life worth living, including a decent and reasonably safe neighborhood in which to live, decent housing, adequate food and clothing, healthcare insurance, quality education, and so forth. Many young people (in all social classes) during the civil rights movement years figured this out. That is, they decided that their involvement in the struggle for civil rights and justice was their decision to make, and no one else's; that they must take their own life and future into their own hands. Whether they were trained in the methods of nonviolence or not, those young people understood that their involvement would be costly, but they prepared themselves to face the consequences of their actions, for example, having to go to jail, and possibly even being made to disappear and their bodies never to be found. They understood, and in a way that far too many present-day young people do not, that they were fighting not merely for themselves, but for those coming after them. They were fighting not simply for the present, but for the future. Some realized the very real possibility that they would not be around to benefit from their dedication and sacrifices, but they were driven by the idea of doing what they could to make things better for others. They knew, as Alice Walker once said, that the world was not as good as it could be, and that it was their responsibility to make it better. Somehow, if young people today are to have a future worth living (not dying!) for, they would do well to study young people's involvement in the civil rights movement of the 1960s.

One of Martin Luther King's staple sayings, borrowed from his predecessor at the Dexter Avenue Baptist Church, Vernon Johns, was that, if an individual has not found something worth dying for, he is not fit to live.[3] Understandably, King was essentially challenging people to get involved in the struggle for freedom and civil rights, believing that some things are so important and precious that people should be willing to fight for them, and if need be, die. Freedom and civil rights were so important in his view, that they were truly worth struggling and dying for. Today, however, in the early years of the twenty-first century, I think we need to change our emphasis to focus more on the idea that *if an individual has not found something worth living for, he isn't fit to die*; is not fit to go to an eternal rest; to be in the distinguished company of honored ancestors. Such a person is not fit to be in the company of that "great cloud of witnesses" until he has found and endeavored to achieve his noble purpose in life. To be allowed to rest eternally in the presence of the ancestors, the great cloud of witnesses, is an honor that must be earned by the way one lives out his life in this world. That alone is his ticket to join such a noble company of spirits. He must, by virtue of his actions in this world, show himself worthy, that is, fit to die to be in such company.

From my perspective, the most tragic phenomenon of the late twentieth century, and the first years of the twenty-first, is intracommunity violence and homicide among young Afrikan American males. In a number of major urban centers, with the Southside of Chicago still leading the way, this phenomenon has gotten completely out of control and officials seem to have no clue as to how to get the violence stopped (nor am I convinced—because of enduring racism and the complexity of the problem—that white officials could stop it, even *if* they truly desired to do so). In any event, it occurs to me that the question to be asked of many young black males today should have less to do with what they are willing to die

---

3. In the sermon, "It's Safe to Kill Negroes in Montgomery," Vernon Johns said: "No man is fit to be alive until he has something for which he would die." Quoted in my book, *An Extremist for Love: Martin Luther King, Jr. as Man of Ideas and Nonviolent Social Action* (Fortress Press, 2014), 154. (The quote from Johns is taken from Charles E. Cobb Jr., *On the Road to Freedom: A Guided Tour of the Civil Rights Trail* (Chapel Hill: Algonquin Books, 2008, 213; from http://www.vernonjohns.org.) King very likely heard Benjamin E. Mays, his mentor at Morehouse College, utter similar words.

for, and everything to do with what they are willing to fight to live for. Young black males are already dying in massive numbers all over the country for as little as a pair of stolen tennis shoes, or a stare down, that is, because they looked at somebody a certain way, or somebody looked at them a certain way.

I am convinced that people who have a strong sense of self-worth and respect for others do not kill other members of their community, or even allow themselves to be subjected to unnecessary violence and killing over something as insignificant as a dirty look or a pair of tennis shoes. Too many young black males are all too susceptible to dying for that which is trivial and has little real value. Sadly, and just as tragic, this is too often due to poor choices available to them. Young black males do not control the education system, and the availability of living-wage jobs, for example. They and their parent(s) too often have little to no choice about where they live and the house in which they live. Institutional racism and economic injustice so severely limits the choices of young black males that virtually every available alternative has potentially deadly consequences. The question, it seems to me, is whether young black males can find their way to see the reason in sacrificing their lives for a life truly worth living, even though they know that the present socioeconomic arrangement in this nation does not favor a quality life for them. Somehow the hope must be that they will, in increasingly greater numbers, choose life (Deut. 30:19), despite the very real odds against them. It is imperative that they not only choose life, but that they devote their lives to achieving a life worth living, not only for self and immediate loved ones, but for the community.

And yet, this is easier said than done, primarily because this nation is still essentially racist to the core, a point that Martin Luther King acknowledged time and again throughout his civil rights ministry, placing particular emphasis on it near the end of his life. In the posthumously published essay, "A Testament of Hope," King, pondering the problem of racism and the challenge of achieving full equality in this country, concluded: "The problem is so tenacious because, despite its virtues and attributes, America is deeply racist and its democracy is flawed both economically and socially."[4] He was convinced that the vast majority of whites are "still poisoned by racism, which is as native to our soil as pine trees, sagebrush and buffalo grass."[5] According to King, white supremacy was so deeply embedded in this country that he believed it would take many years, certainly more than a generation, before race would no longer be a major factor in how the nation relates to Afrikan Americans. The late legal scholar-civil rights activist, Derrick Bell (1930–2011), was absolutely right when he argued that blacks are the only people in the United States who are "burdened with the legacy of slavery and segregation in a land of freedom that, over time, has undermined the sense of self-worth for many black people."[6] Bell argues that as a result of this legacy, many whites are of the view that blacks should be on the bottom, presumably their rightful place.

Those who come to positive decision about carrying the struggle for freedom and justice forward will need fortitude and all that that term implies: determination, courage, endurance, strength, and *stick-to-itiveness*. During the civil rights struggle, those who held the reins of power and privilege, and benefited most from the injustices done to others, generally did not yield or share their power and privilege willingly. Moreover, historically, such individuals exhibited no shame for their behavior. "Men will not cease to be dishonest, merely because their dishonesties have been revealed or because they

---

4. Martin Luther King Jr., "A Testament of Hope," in *A Testament of Hope: The Essential Writings of Martin Luther King, Jr.* ed. James M. Washington (New York: Harper & Row, 1986), 314.
5. Ibid., 316.
6. Derrick Bell, *And We Are Not Saved: The Elusive Quest for Racial Justice* (New York: Basic Books, 1987), 122.

have discovered their own deceptions," declared theological social ethicist Reinhold Niebuhr. "Wherever men hold unequal power in society, they will strive to maintain it. They will use whatever means are most convenient to that end and will seek to justify them by the most plausible arguments they are able to devise."[7] It is no different today, which means that any struggle for justice will likely be a long and protracted one, with sometimes very harsh consequences for those who are unjustly treated in society.

In chapter 2, we were introduced to Jim Zwerg, a white college student from Beloit College in Wisconsin, who had grown up in Appleton. Zwerg volunteered to be an exchange student at the all-black Fisk University in Nashville. This was when he got caught up in the civil rights activism of the Nashville youth activists, many of whom were either in college, or had dropped out to devote fulltime to the cause. Zwerg joined (now longtime Congressman) John Lewis and other youth activists to continue the Freedom Ride after another group of Riders had been brutally attacked outside Anniston, Alabama, and CORE director James Farmer had called the Ride off. Under the leadership of Nashville youth activist, Diane Nash, the youthful activists insisted that precisely because of the brutal attack on the Riders and the firebombing of their bus, the Ride must continue. The youths effectively argued that there must be no indication to would-be white-supremacist mobs that in order to stop a civil rights campaign in its tracks all they need do is use violence against the demonstrators. The youth activists won the day, and were allowed to continue the Ride. Once they left the Birmingham bus terminal and arrived at the bus station in Montgomery, Zwerg and others were savagely attacked by racist thugs as they left the bus. Zwerg boldly left the bus first, and was likely beaten worse because

---

7. Reinhold Niebuhr, *Moral Man and Immoral Society* (New York: Scribners, 1932), 34.

he was white, since in the warped minds of white supremacists the worst thing a white person could do was to support and participate in the freedom struggle with blacks to make freedom and democracy a reality for all. Zwerg's injuries were such that he was hospitalized and unable to continue with his Freedom Ride colleagues. From his hospital bed he displayed the fortitude that had already characterized his sister and brother Riders. He told an interviewer that the Ride must continue, even if some had to die. This was the motto of the youthful Riders. Diane Nash had said: "Mob violence must not stop men's striving toward right. Freedom Rides and other such actions must not be stopped until our nation is really free."[8] These were young people who would not be deterred by violence; not even the death of their activist peers.

Because of his stance and his involvement in the struggle for justice, Zwerg was disowned by his Christian parents who, as he recalled, were the very ones who instilled in him Christian values such as respect and love for human beings. Apparently, like so many white Christians, Zwerg's parents stressed only the abstract notion of respect and love for human beings, which generally means to love and respect human beings in general. According to this line of reasoning it is the abstract human being, the universal human being that one is to love, not specific or particular flesh-and-blood human beings. This makes it possible to say that in general one loves (or should love) human beings, but when it comes to specific human beings, for instance, human beings with black skin, well, that's another matter altogether. Throughout history, and especially history in the United States, to only love human beings in general has too often meant that it is permissible to ignore or even hate specific concrete groups of human beings. The more one loves human beings

---

8. Diane Nash, "Inside the Sit-Ins and Freedom Rides: Testimony of a Southern Student," in *The New Negro*, ed. Mathew H. Ahmann (New York: Biblo & Tannen, 1969), 53.

in general, according to a character in Dostoevsky's book, *The Brothers Karamazov*, the less she loves concrete individual human beings.[9] This, unfortunately, is the stance of far too many Christians.

In any case, young, conscientious Jim Zwerg had apparently taken his parents quite literally. Because he was a Christian, he took what they said to mean that he was to love and respect human beings as such. Since his parents did not qualify the statement, he assumed that the reference was to all people, regardless of gender, race, or class. He learned what his parents truly meant when he joined the Freedom Ride. It must have taken a real sense of determination, courage, and fortitude for young Zwerg to continue in the struggle for civil rights and freedom for all, after he discovered that his parents did not include blacks in the Christian teaching on love.

During a reunion of Freedom Riders in the early years of the twenty-first century at the Birmingham Civil Rights Institute and Museum in Alabama, Jim Zwerg broke down and cried when he saw his battered, bleeding face on a video. He cried because upon seeing the video again he was reminded that countless numbers of blacks had been beaten even more severely than he, and even murdered—some of their bodies never even found—on the civil rights trail, and yet it was he and a few white activists who seemed to get so much of the publicity, even today. So he broke down, right there in that public setting, with all kinds of people looking on, and cried. An Afrikan American veteran Freedom Rider, Jim Davis, went over and embraced Zwerg and said: "Jim, you don't realize that it was your words from that hospital bed that were the call to arms for the rest of us."[10] The two grown men stood there in an embrace, crying like babies. No doubt as they stood there, they remembered how

---

9. Fyodor Dostoevsky, *The Brothers Karamazov*, trans. Andrew H. MacAndrew (New York: Bantam, 1981), 65.
10. Quoted in John Blake, *Children of the Movement* (Chicago: Lawrence Hill Books, 2004), 36.

black and white young people struggled and suffered together for freedom and civil rights, only to find that many years later there was still so much to be done. If there is to be continued progress, young people today will have to be at least as devoted to the struggle as their predecessors during the civil rights movement. In addition, the lives of blacks and whites continue to be so integrally intermingled in the United States that it is virtually impossible for either group alone to succeed in establishing the beloved community wherein every individual person will be respected by virtue of being a person, and where the needs of all are met before any has the right to collect and store away surplus goods.

But in order to establish such a community, civil rights youths had a good sense that strong alliance-building needed to occur. Somehow, blacks and whites had to figure out how to bond in coalition around strong common interests and goals. Such efforts among black and white youth of the civil rights era did not go unnoticed by Martin Luther King, who was always quick to support and cheer their efforts in this regard and to encourage them to keep at it. When black youth initiated the sit-in movement and also insisted on the need for the Freedom Rides to continue, white youth of conscience and goodwill quickly joined in alliance with them, and this, King recalled, stirred and "aroused the conscience of the nation." This was all done by young people who saw the nation and world as they were, and made the decision to do something about it, with or without the support of adults. Neither group of youths, white or black, did a good enough job of addressing the racial aspects of the coalitions they formed, which is why none of them held together after the 1960s. However, it was a moment in history from which youth of today can learn valuable lessons, in the event they are able to see the wisdom of building coalitions with groups that share similar interests in beloved community-making. Indeed, it might well be the case that some configuration of today's youth can show us how to achieve the beloved community.

Martin Luther King himself wrote and spoke frequently about the importance of fortitude, which he characterized as the "determined refusal not to be stopped," noting that such determination "will eventually open the door to fulfillment." King went on to say: "This refusal to be stopped, this courage to be, this determination to go on in spite of, is the hallmark of any great movement."[11] This was the Martin Luther King who said, just months before he was assassinated, that although he was not completely optimistic, neither was he ready to concede defeat. Although King stressed the importance of individual fortitude and determination in the freedom struggle, he emphasized just as strongly the existence of systemic problems that make it so difficult for many in the general population to obtain a quality-of-life existence. King always knew that blacks' predicament can never be tied solely to individual choice as long as systemic racism and economic deprivation exists on a massive scale.

To the extent that he trusted and had faith in God and the future, he had faith that human beings can make the world better than it is. The key for King was his faith in God, not in human beings as such. God was the source, the ground of any faith that King had in human beings. "I have faith in the future because I have faith in God," he declared, "and I believe that there is a power, a creative force in this universe seeking at all times to bring down prodigious hilltops of evil and pull low gigantic mountains of injustice. If we will believe this and struggle along, we will be able to achieve it."[12] King's faith was in God, and through God, in human beings. Neither human beings nor God alone can abolish injustice and establish justice. Neither

---

11. Martin Luther King Jr., "The State of the Movement," presented November 28, 1967, at the Staff Retreat of SCLC at Penn Center, Frogmore, SC, King Center Library and Archives, 8, 9.
12. *The Papers* (2005), 5:418.

can establish the beloved community alone. Rather, King held, there must be ongoing cooperative endeavor between God and human beings. God will not do for human beings what they have been created to do cooperatively for themselves and in conjunction with God.

Based on the youth activism that he witnessed from Montgomery to Memphis, Martin Luther King knew that if only because of those young people's contributions, there was reason to hope that the beloved community could be achieved, or more nearly approximated. He had witnessed with his own eyes what the determination and fearlessness of committed young people could accomplish. On the contrary, and but for a few exceptions, there was much less reason to be hopeful about what adults would accomplish toward establishing the beloved community, since many of these tended to be far too conservative and timid to contribute meaningfully in this regard.

We have seen that without question, youthful activists, through their various coalitions, accomplished much during sit-ins, Freedom Rides, and numerous voter education-registration projects, most notably the Freedom Summer Project in the Mississippi Delta region and other dangerous places in the Deep South. Despite their youthful efforts toward coalition-building, it was no secret that so much negative history existed between black and white youths that even on good days their alliance was at best difficult to maintain. There were issues of trust that constantly arose, as well as the elitism exhibited by some whites (intended or not!). There was deep suspicion on the part of many blacks. And more so, the specter of racism loomed large, such that when blacks and well-meaning whites called attention to it, it led to added strain on the coalition. Some wondered, for example, how the federal government, in a democracy, could launch such a massive search for Schwerner, Goodman, and Chaney when other civil rights activists—all black—had disappeared in the Mississippi Delta and other places, and received virtually no attention. Indeed, we saw that some concluded that had Chaney, who was black, been the only missing civil rights worker the federal government would likely have remained silent and uninvolved. Some wondered why there was no national moral outrage when the half bodies of two black men, one a student at Alcorn A&M, were found as navy divers searched the river bottom for Chaney, Goodman, and Schwerner. Indeed, one of the Freedom Summer Project volunteers wrote his parents, saying: "Mississippi is the only state where you can drag a river any time and find bodies you were not expecting."[13]

In short, it was difficult for black and white youths to continue working together in common cause, but they did it better, and longer, than most, until the alliance began to break down because of increased suspicion, as well as a sense among some black youth that they needed to do some work among themselves, without whites being present. In part, at least, this is what happened to SNCC, which, from its inception, had been an interracial organization that was open to whites being in positions of leadership. In late 1967, King's assessment was that the general alliance between black and white youth activists had fallen apart "under the impact of failures, discouragement and consequent extremism and polarization. The movement for social change has entered a time of temptation to despair because it is clear now how deep and systematic are the evils it confronts," King said. "There is a strong temptation to despair of programs and actions and to dissipate energy into hysterical talk. There is a temptation to break up into mutually suspicious extremist groups in which blacks reject the participation of whites, and whites reject the realities of their own history."[14] That there was evidence

---

13. Quoted in Bruce Watson, *Freedom Summer: The Savage Season That Made Mississippi Burn and Made America a Democracy* (New York: Viking, 2010), 147.

that the old coalitions were breaking apart did not mean, for King, that coalitions were no longer important for those who intend to continue the journey toward establishing the beloved community. Indeed, for King, coalition-building for such people was all the more important, so much so that what was now needed was a forging of even broader coalitions to include previously excluded groups, such as Hispanic youth and poor youth of all races who share common interests and goals, for example, civil rights, voting rights, healthcare, jobs that pay a living wage, reasonable immigration policies and practices, quality education, and decent housing in relatively safe neighborhoods. Since Hispanics and Afrikan Americans are the largest and second-largest so-called minority groups in the country, respectively, it is most imperative that they commit to doing the very hard work of coalition-building with each other. The pastors of an Afrikan American and Hispanic church can easily begin such a process by making an intentional effort to get to know each other until such time as their congregations are fellowshiping together on a fairly regular basis. From this point the sky is the limit as to where they can go in coalition-making, and who knows what can happen between the two groups beyond that point?

What do we learn from our study of young people, Martin Luther King, and the civil rights movement that may be appropriated as we consider what needs to happen in order to advance the struggle to actualize the beloved community? A number of relevant ideas may be gleaned from the work and approach of youthful activists and King during the struggle for freedom and civil rights. The remainder of this chapter enumerates and discusses a few of these ideas: some specifically Kingian, and others derived from the youthful activists. In my estimation, the way forward will be helped much by identifying and appropriating the following ideas, whatever other steps might

---

14. King, "The State of the Movement," 7–8.

be taken and implemented. These ideas include, but are not limited to: 1) belief in a personal God and the highest estimate of the worth of human beings; 2) possession and development of character and courage; 3) need for self-acceptance; 4) role of black churches; 5) ridding Congress of racism; 6) insisting that criticizing the U.S. for its moral limitations is not unpatriotic; and 7) the need for mass civil disobedience. These are not presented in a particular order of importance, although there are points of overlap.

A Personal God and the Highest Estimate of the Worth of Human Beings

Martin Luther King was an avowed personalist, one who believed absolutely in the existence of a creator-God who is the source of all there is and is both personal and loving. Philosophically, King understood *personal* in much the same way as his personalist forebears at Boston University: possession of selfhood, self-knowledge (rationality), and self-direction (freedom). In addition, King would not have rejected John Wright Buckham's idea that virtue or worth, a fourth element of what it means to be personal, is "the crowning possession of personality. . . ."[15] Self-knowledge and self-direction, in fact, imply the worth of the individual. "A rational and free being by virtue of the very fact that he is rational and free," wrote the personalist Albert C. Knudson, "stands apart from the world of things; he is an end in himself."[16] God, on this view, is not only the source of human worth, but the chief exemplification of worth. This very God, in King's view, created human beings with a supremely high

---

15. John Wright Buckham, *Personality and the Christian Ideal* (Boston: Pilgrim, 1909), 20. King would have seen the reference to the significance of worth for the personal in Albert C. Knudson, *The Philosophy of Personalism* (New York: Kraus, 1969, originally published by Abingdon, 1927,) 82. King studied this book as a doctoral student at Boston University.
16. Knudson, *The Philosophy of Personalism*, 82.

intrinsic value, imbuing every single one with the divine image. Every human being—regardless—is infinitely precious to God, and ultimately belongs to God, and no other. These two ideas, God as personal, and human beings as inviolably precious to God, are implicit in some form or another in virtually all of King's writings, speeches, and sermons, so much so that one might quite rightly characterize him not only as a *God-intoxicated* man (as Novalis described the philosopher Spinoza), but the *person-intoxicated* man as well. At bottom a theist, King could not seem to talk about human beings (and much of anything else) in the world without also talking about God and God's expectations of them. In addition, he could not seem to talk about God without also talking about human beings and how they get on in the world. As one who believed fundamentally in a personal creator God, King was certain that God is not only the basic driving force in the universe, and the ground of all things, but also the chief conserver and enhancer of value or good.

Growing up as a preacher's kid in a southern Baptist church, Martin Luther King learned much about the personal God of his father, mother, maternal grandmother, and other faithful at the Ebenezer Baptist Church in Atlanta. Religiously, this was the God who could make a way out of no way, and did so for the faithful. It was the God who summoned every human being into existence and even called them by name (Isa. 43:1); the God who was parent when one needed a parent, a sister or brother when one needed a sister or brother. This was the God that King heard about in his father's sermons and during the family discussions around the dinner table as they consumed the delicious meals prepared by his mother and grandmother.[17]

17. Christine King Farris, King's only sister, has written about the importance of meal-time conversations at the King dining table (especially on Sundays), when she and her siblings were children. She stressed not only the value of the conversations and the variety of subjects discussed at the mandatory dinner meals, but the mouth-watering meals prepared by her

Religiously, King's idea of a personal God was that of the God who was able to grant one the power to bear that which cannot be changed, for example, a marriage that was falling apart, or an incurable disease. In King's view, this was the God that black people knew "as a rock in a weary land, as a shelter in the time of starving [*sic*], as my water when I'm thirsty, and then my bread in a starving land. And then if you can't even say that," said King, "sometimes you may have to say, 'He's my everything. He's my sister and my brother. He's my mother and my father.'"[18] From a religious or faith standpoint, God does not get more personal and loving than that. What we know is that this is the God who carried Martin Luther King along the treacherous civil rights trail and was his constant companion and help along the way. This was the God on whom he came to depend absolutely, when things were not going well for him in the movement. The abstract philosophical and theological concepts of God that he studied in seminary and during doctoral studies did not provide what he needed on a day-to-day basis in a racist, unjust nation. Although he studied the concept of the personal God as advocated by the personalist teachers who influenced him, it was the personal God of his grandparents, parents, and religious faith who promised to be with him always, even to the far corners of the universe. This was the God who promised to help him make a way out of no way.

Virtually all members of SCLC believed as King did about God as personal and loving, creator, and conserver and enhancer of value.

---

maternal grandmother. "Wonderful food was always plentiful, but never more so than on Sundays," she writes. "I can remember the table overflowing with fresh greens from the garden, baked macaroni and cheese, fried chicken, glazed ham, smothered pork chops, and corn on the cob. Desserts included cakes and pies, bread pudding, and various cobblers" (Christine King Farris, *Through It All: Reflections on My Life, My Family, and My Faith* [New York: Atria, 2009], 11). Moreover, she wrote: "These meals were filled with laughter and joy, good eating, and most important, lessons from Mother and Daddy that I still cherish" (16).

18. Martin Luther King Jr., "Why Jesus Called a Man a Fool," in *A Knock at Midnight*, ed. Clayborne Carson and Peter Holloran (New York: Warner Books, 1998), 163.

But we have seen that this was not the case with many of the youthful activists in SNCC and other youth organizations. This was especially the case of many youthful activists from the North who went South to help in the struggle. Although these youths generally were sharp intellectually and politically savvy, they were often soft on religion, church, respect for their elders, and related matters that were so important to Southern black youths who were also committed to the struggle for civil rights. Matters of religion and God did not interest northern youthful activists as much as their southern counterparts, although it would be a mistake to say that this was the case of all northern youth activists. In any event, northern youths rivaled those of the South regarding their sense of the absolute value and preciousness of human beings and the need, indeed the obligation, for all to be treated as infinitely valuable, and thus with dignity and fairness.

One need not be a theist in order to believe in the fundamental dignity of human beings, and thus the obligation to treat all with respect. Arguably, none believed more deeply and advocated more strongly for the inviolable dignity of persons than the atheistic existentialist and personalist, Jean-Paul Sartre. As a human being one has inalienable dignity, as well as certain basic rights, and this was the source of the nontheistic youths' desire to participate in the struggle for freedom and civil rights. One need not necessarily believe in a personal creator God, in order to believe in the basic worth of human beings. This made it possible for the nonbeliever to be just as devoted to the cause of civil rights and freedom as the believer. It also made it possible to forge deeper and broader alliances. As a pastor, Martin Luther King would surely have wanted all others to believe in a creator-personal God as much as they believed in the absolute dignity of human beings, but he had such an ecumenical outlook that he did not see this as a necessary prerequisite to engaging in the struggle.

One need not believe in a personal God in order to contribute to the struggle for civil rights and freedom, then or now. This was but another indicator of King's openness and willingness to work at building coalitions by including as many voices in the conversation as possible. One needed only to be committed to the civil rights and freedom of all, regardless of their religious faith or lack thereof.

King respected his youthful colleagues in the movement for their stance on the significance and dignity of every human being, as well as their commitment to working toward civil rights and freedom. They need not be in agreement about faith claims and belief or nonbelief in God. This is as important today as it was during movement days. That said, it is also important to understand that belief in a personal God was so important to King as a civil rights minister because it gave him credible cause to believe that he and other fighters for civil rights were not in the struggle alone, but had cosmic and divine companionship. One who believes this is also comforted in the thought that freedom and justice will ultimately prevail, even if one does not live to see and experience it. Those who are committed to carrying the struggle forward today should also find encouragement in this important point.

Character and Courage

Although many youths who participated in the civil rights movement were only in the first or second grade, especially during the Children's Crusade in Birmingham and during the voting rights campaign in Selma, the vast majority of them were old enough to have a sense of the meaning and importance of character and courage in the struggle and to know that both of these may be enhanced when one joins with a group to work passionately toward a common goal. Courage and character are generally required when one has to face seemingly insurmountable obstacles such as those that presented themselves to youthful activists in the movement. This applied not only to youth who were in the struggle for the long haul, but to those who participated on a more short-term basis, such as during Operation Freedom Vote, and the Freedom Summer Project in 1963 and 1964, respectively, in Mississippi. The intense and dangerous period of their involvement, although brief, was every bit as real as that experienced by long-term movement veterans. All needed courage and character to do Deep South movement work, whether long term or short term. Perhaps it will be helpful to consider the meaning of courage and character so that we have a better sense of what these entail.

My understanding of courage and character takes me back to my days as a doctoral student when I took courses in philosophical psychology and the philosophy of religion under my late teacher, the personalist Peter A. Bertocci, at Boston University. In each course we had occasion to focus on the virtues of courage and character. We understood a virtue to be a trait that is actually *chosen* by an individual. Such a person must then work to develop it. "A trait . . . represents an organization of the energies of a person that determines not so much how the environment will affect him, but how he will take his environment."[19] One may exhibit the trait of courage, which means that in situations that call for courage, he can be counted on to behave courageously, no matter what else may be occurring at the time. In order for courage or any other trait to become a virtue (or vice), however, one must choose it. All virtues (or vices) are traits, but not all traits are virtues (or vices). A trait is a virtue only if it is a product of choice. The reason for this is that "an action is moral or immoral . . . *to the extent that* it is the product of choice

---

19. Peter A. Bertocci and Richard M. Millard, *Personality and the Good: Psychological and Ethical Perspectives* (New York: David McKay, 1963), 362.

or will-agency."[20] One must acknowledge and approve "the presence of a certain disposition" in given situations in order that it may be considered a virtue (or vice). When one is faced with various conflicts and chooses to sustain a given trait, for example, courage, it becomes a moral trait or virtue ("or immoral trait or vice"), according to the line of reasoning of Bertocci and Richard M. Millard.

If courage is what Bertocci and Millard say it is—"the willingness to face insecurity and to make the sacrifices needed to achieve the goal deemed worthwhile but dangerous,"[21] there is no question that the youthful civil rights activists were not only courageous, but chose, approved, and endeavored to sustain this trait over and over again. Courage, for the youthful activists, was that special trait that we call a virtue. They chose or willed to be courageous, to press onward in the face of horrific terrorist acts against them during the sit-ins, Freedom Rides, and the many voting rights projects in the Mississippi Delta, Selma, Wilcox County (Alabama), and other places. That the youthful activists chose to be courageous did not mean that they were necessarily devoid of fear, for we saw that on numerous occasions they spoke and wrote of being afraid, sometimes even petrified to the point of not being able to leave the COFO office to go out on a Mississippi street as a result of fear. They even expressed the need to view fear as a healthy reminder of the danger involved both in their work, and the location where they were fighting for freedom. More than anything, these young people sought to avoid being paralyzed by fear. Some wrote parents and friends of "the uselessness of fear that immobilizes an individual."[22] They were courageous, even as they managed their fear, such that they were able to continue doing the work of the movement, regardless. They all possessed awareness

---

20. Ibid., 363 (authors' italics).
21. Ibid., 385.
22. Elizabeth Martínez, ed., *Letters from Mississippi* (Brookline, MA: Zephyr, 2007), 169.

of the risks and dangers involved, but they chose to continue the work anyway. Remember, before the vast majority of the college kids left Oxford, Ohio for the Mississippi Delta, they had received word of the disappearance of Chaney, Goodman, and Schwerner, and were strongly advised by Bob Moses and other COFO staffers not to remain in the program. Only a very small number opted to go home. Choosing to go to Mississippi in the face of such a tragedy was a clear indication of the virtue of courage being displayed by those youths.

When I teach my course, Prophetic and Ethical Witness of the Church, and stress the importance of ethical prophetic witness in ministry, and the need to criticize an unacceptable state of affairs in light of God's expectation that justice be done, students invariably ask: "How does one get the courage (or even increase it) to do genuine prophetic ministry, which often requires that one speak truth to the powers, which can have frightening consequences? This is an excellent question, although not the easiest to give adequate answer. Courage is that which cannot be given or handed from one person to the next. In a sense, it can be bought, but only at a substantial price to the one seeking it. It means willing to stand firm in the face of adversity and danger when one believes she is right, or that an important principle or value is being violated. There is no easy recipe or simple formula for developing and enhancing courage, I tell my students. However, there are some things that one can do to get and/or increase it. Here I find the work of William James on habit to be helpful.

In James's famous—although seemingly forgotten—lecture titled "Habit," we learn about the physiological and neurological processes involved in the formation of habits. James contends that the philosophy of habit is expressed in the idea "that our nervous system grows to modes in which it has been exercised. . . ."[23] Accordingly, "the phenomenon of habit in living beings are [sic] due to the plasticity of the organic materials of which their bodies are composed,"[24] such that when impressions are made, a path of sorts remains, thus making it easier to reproduce the same impression when similar actions are taken. Once a current has traveled a certain path in the brain, it can do so more easily the next time, and the time after that. This is essentially what the formation of habit is all about. The first few times an action occurs is voluntary, and thus requires effort or will, and steady attention. Once the action has been done a number of times and becomes habit, little to no effort and attention are needed to perform it, much like when one learns to tie her shoes. In the beginning, every step in the process requires will power, mental attention, and concentrated effort. Once one learns how to tie her shoes a certain way and has done it enough times that it becomes habit, she can then perform that same task with little to no will power or attention. She can then devote her will power, attention, or effort to other things; indeed, can even tie her shoes while simultaneously engaging in some other activity. Because of habit, one can do many important things with little effort or energy, essentially freeing one up to give steady, willful attention to other things. This, in part, is why James characterized habit as "the enormous flywheel of society."[25]

For our purpose—developing the virtue of courage, the fortitude of holding one's ground or persevering in the face of imminent danger—habit is important for precisely the two reasons elaborated in James's lecture: 1) it "simplifies the movements required to achieve a given result, makes them more accurate and diminishes fatigue,"[26] and 2) it "diminishes conscious attention with which our acts are

---

23. William James, "Habit," in his *The Principles of Psychology* (New York: Dover, 1918 [1890]), 1:112.
24. Ibid., 1:105.
25. Ibid., 121.
26. Ibid., 112.

performed."[27] The second of these is more important for our purpose. What this means is that once one has a clear understanding of the meaning of courage and desires to be a courageous individual, for example, he then engages every opportunity to perform courageous acts, until such time that doing so becomes habit, or second nature. He behaves courageously without even thinking about it. He does so because that is who he has *chosen* to become.

The first attempts to be courageous will require steady attention, concentration, or power of will, which is required in developing any habit. Something similar is required when breaking a habit as well. Once one develops the habit of being courageous, he no longer has to expend precious time, energy, and effort thinking about it. All of that energy can now be channeled to something else. He now does the thing with little or no effort, even if he also experiences fear or apprehensiveness; does it because the situation requires it, and because he wills or chooses to do it. James actually provides a helpful abstract illustration of the principle that habit diminishes the conscious attention with which our actions are performed. In an important passage he writes:

> If an act require for its execution a chain, A, B, C, D, E, F, G, etc., of successive nervous events, then in the first performances of the action the conscious will must choose each of these events from a number of wrong alternatives that tend to present themselves; but habit soon brings it about that each event calls up its own appropriate successor without any alternative offering itself, and without any reference to the conscious will, until at last the whole chain, A, B, C, D, E, F, G, rattles itself off as soon as A occurs, just as if A and the rest of the chain were fused into a continuous stream. When we are learning to walk, to ride, to swim, skate, fence, write, play, or sing, we interrupt ourselves at every step by unnecessary movements and false notes. When we are proficient, on the contrary, the results not only follow with the very minimum of

27. Ibid., 114.

muscular action requisite to bring them forth, they also follow from a single instantaneous "cue."[28]

Because one has developed the habit, the decision to respond with courage causes less fatigue since she no longer has to devote much mental energy and effort to it. So, there is less stress, and she does not have to devote much conscious attention to the matter. When one performs many smaller acts of courage, she only prepares herself to respond courageously to the much larger situations requiring courage, such as challenging the powers that be when injustice has been committed. It becomes less difficult to do this after one has intentionally performed many, many acts of courage. "The more often the process is repeated, the more easily the movement follows, on account of the increase in permeability of the nerves engaged."[29] The more times one performs acts of courage—small or large—the easier it is the next time, until one seemingly does it automatically, and with virtually no effort, when the situation calls for it.

As James approaches the end of his lecture, he says that there are generally four things involved in the acquisition and development of a new habit, or doing away with an old one. The first step requires that one bring to bear all of the forces at her disposal, and that she apply herself "with as strong and decided an initiative as possible."[30] One should gather up anything and everything in the early stage of habit formation that she believes will support those motives that have the strongest chance of helping to form the new habit. Doing so "will give your new beginning such a momentum that the temptation to breakdown will not occur as soon as it otherwise might; and every day during which a breakdown is postponed adds to the chances of its not occurring at all."[31]

---

28. Ibid., 114.
29. Ibid., 112–13.
30. Ibid., 123.

The second thing one needs to do to develop the new habit is to allow no exception to occur until the new habit is well established and secure. This will require a strong will. It is important to develop a pattern of successes at the outset. "Failure at first is apt to dampen the energy of all future attempts, whereas past experience of success nerves one to future vigor."[32] Moreover, one does well to abruptly adopt and put into practice a newly formed habit, rather than to slowly work one's self up to it, or in breaking a habit, to wean one's self off.

Thirdly, when developing the habit of courage, for example, one should always be ready to act on the very first opportunity to perform acts of courage. One must take advantage of every occasion to act. "It is not in the moment of their forming, but in the moment of their producing *motor effects*, that resolves and aspirations communicate the new 'set' to the brain."[33]

In forming a new habit, one must do all she can to keep the will or faculty of effort alive by subjecting it to exercise on a regular basis. This is the fourth thing one can do to develop a new habit or break an old one.[34] In this step, one endeavors to actually strengthen the will. Periodically one must do something for no other reason than she would rather not do it. This way, when the time comes when she needs to exhibit a strong will to act courageously, she will be able to accomplish the goal. This is what doing exercises that essentially strengthens the will can do.

The Christian individual may insist that yet a fifth element (not included in James's lecture) is needed in forming the habit of courageous behavior; that the development of such a habit is not possible through mere human effort alone. The Christian may believe

---

31. Ibid.
32. Ibid.
33. Ibid., 124.
34. Ibid., 126.

that it is possible to develop such a habit only through the help of divine grace. In a helpful way, Christian social ethicist Stephen Charles Mott defines divine grace as God's power *for* us, and also God's power *in* us. Mott characterizes the former as "the work of pardon and justification through atonement by the son,"[35] and the latter as "the work of sanctification by the Spirit of God, as well as the Spirit's work in drawing us to repentance and transforming us."[36] What is needed by those seeking to develop the habit of courageous behavior is the type of grace that is *God's power in us*, which enables us to do what we otherwise could not. Those who believe that courage is one of those things that cannot be attained and developed by human effort alone, appeal to God's grace as an added means to attaining it.

We have seen that courage is one of the things that the youthful activists in the civil rights movement exhibited in large measure. Courage will also need to be cultivated by those who desire to continue the work of moving toward the beloved community today. The youthful activists of the movement years also exhibited another trait that enabled them to stand their ground in the face of violence and possible death. They exhibited *character*, the willingness and determination to persist in doing what they believed to be right to the best of their ability.[37] Like the virtue of courage, character is not given, but is that which an individual chooses or makes, through her choices and ongoing effort. In those choices, one chooses one kind of personality, one kind of world, rather than another.[38] Through one's efforts he is able to stay the course. Young people who were

---

35. Stephen Charles Mott, *Biblical Ethics and Social Change* (New York: Oxford University Press, 1982), 27.
36. Ibid.
37. Peter A. Bertocci, *Introduction to the Philosophy of Religion* (Englewood Cliffs, NJ: Prentice Hall, 1951), 392.
38. Ibid., 455.

activists during the movement years chose the high road, as well as the beloved community, a community in which the dignity and rights of every member is respected and honored. Much like courage, character will also be a key ingredient for young people who are willing to continue the struggle for freedom and liberation today.

Need for Self-Acceptance

Nine months before the Montgomery bus boycott began, fifteen-year-old Claudette Colvin had an experience in school that was an anticipation of the Black Consciousness Movement of the mid- to late 1960s, a time when blacks expressed their pride of self, history, and culture. It was also a time of enhanced self-determination among blacks. Colvin's history teacher, Mrs. Geraldine Nesbitt, taught her students about their Afrikan heritage and the importance of blacks recognizing and proudly acknowledging their heritage as well as their natural beauty. We saw in chapter 1 that this led Colvin to stop using hair-straightening chemicals. Instead, she made the decision to wear her hair in its natural form, and began to express appreciation for her wide nose, thick lips, kinky hair, and other Afrikan features in a way and to a degree she never had before. Colvin developed a strong sense of pride in her Afrikan heritage.

Without question, Claudette Colvin understood the point of her teacher's lesson, namely that blacks stop imitating whites, and begin accepting themselves for who they were. Martin Luther King referred to it simply as the need for self-acceptance; the acceptance by blacks of both their Afrikan *and* their American heritage. Self-acceptance is an absolute necessity for people who have been traumatized by decades of systematic racism and the undermining of their race and culture. King himself was much affected by the rise of the Black Power and Black Consciousness Movements. And yet, he was quite adamant that blacks are people of two cultures—Afrika and America, and that they needed to acknowledge and express pride in both. "The problem," King said, "is that in the search for wholeness all too many Negroes seek to embrace only one side of their nature, some seeking to reject their [Afrikan] heritage or [are] ashamed of their color, ashamed of black art and music, and determining what is good or beautiful by the standards of white society. They end up frustrated and without cultural roots. Others seek to reject everything American and to identify totally with Africa. . . ."[39] King saw with a clarity that eluded many, that blacks were neither completely Afrikan, nor completely American, but an intricate and complex amalgam of the two cultures. The cultural roots of blacks extend deep in both Afrikan and American soil, a fact that movement youths increasingly came to see and appreciate, and one that black youth of today will have to come to terms with if there is to be any real chance of them saving themselves and continuing the unfinished struggle for freedom and human dignity.

Knowing whence they came and who they are will go a long way toward helping young blacks to determine where they should be going, and whether the kind of work done by their counterparts during the civil rights movement is relevant today. As in other regards, this raises the education question. If the educational system was what it should and can be, and if racism were no longer a menace in this country, no generation of youth, regardless of race-ethnicity, would go through that system without being taught the history of race relations on this soil. All would be familiar with the civil rights movement and how (mostly) blacks, and (some) whites as well, struggled and sacrificed (even their lives) for the civil rights and freedom of blacks. In chapter 4 we saw that many of the whites who participated in that struggle did so because they recognized that their

---

39. King, "The State of the Movement," 10.

own humanity and dignity were integrally linked or intermingled with that of their black counterparts, so that to fight for the freedom of blacks was to also fight for the freedom of whites.

The question before us is a simple one. Who will teach the youth of all races and ethnicities the history of race relations and the civil rights movement? Who will teach them about the huge contributions made by young people just like them? At this writing the educational system, public and private, does not do it, nor are many teachers trained to teach this history, even if they wanted to. This means that neither white nor black students are exposed to such teaching. Nor does such teaching happen in many black families as it once did, and yet this entity, the black family, is the place where every black child *should* receive their initiation to black history, black culture, and blacks' contributions to the building of this nation. Black churches can play a substantial role at this point.

The Role of Black Churches

Black churches have a responsibility to contribute in significant ways to such teaching, which most assuredly will lead to black youths developing an enlarged sense of self-acceptance and appreciation for their heritage and culture. White churches have a similar responsibility to white youths as well, but my fundamental concern is duties and responsibilities that black churches owe to the children and youth of the community they serve. More than any other organization in the black community, the black church has the resources and the means to share in educating black youths about their history, culture, and the need for self-acceptance as they do their part in the struggle to make a life worth living for themselves, as well as future generations of blacks.

Tragically, one of the saddest commentaries on black churches is the continued failure of most to invest in major ways toward efforts to save black youth and to create openings for a future that matters. Virtually every black church does *some*-thing positive for the youth in its membership and/or community. I want to be fair and acknowledge that fact. What I have in mind, and what I believe will make the most significant difference in the lives of black youth, is for black churches to annually commit a substantial percentage of their budget to saving, educating, and liberating black youth, not only those in the congregation, but those in the community where the church building is located.

The truth is, many black churches already have in their membership active and retired schoolteachers at all educational levels, and thus already have at hand one of the most important resources for the teaching enterprise. This makes it possible for churches to pay such teachers an adequate stipend or honorarium to teach black youths about their history and culture, as well as other things important to their survival and liberation. How difficult would it be to raise money to buy computers and other up-to-date technologies to aid in such teaching? To be sure, it would be a challenge, but it cannot be much more difficult than trying to raise tens of millions of dollars to build expensive church buildings. In any case, such churches do not have to limit the teaching to the history and contributions of blacks in the United States. They can also tap those retired teachers who have creative ways of teaching math and science to black kids in ways that reasonably ensure that they can learn *and* excel at these. Of course, churches can only do such things if the leadership *and* membership support it; if pastors stop espousing the nonsensical idea that God expects them to have the best of material things in life, such that they themselves pocket huge amounts out of church budgets in order to live shamefully lavish lifestyles, including the ownership of expensive houses, cars, clothing, jewelry, and such, all the while insisting that the members—many who are not well-to-do—give, give, and give to the church coffers. I mean, really, is that what the truth of the gospel requires? It sounds more like something right out of a capitalist manifesto.

In virtually every U.S. city there are black pastors who exhibit an amazing ability to raise money to build expensive church buildings. I have even known pastors to publicly boast about the cost of a new church building and the amount of money they raised to have it built. But when it comes to actually doing ministries that might make the community where the church building is located better than it is—ministries that contribute in important ways to saving and liberating black children and young people—these same pastors conveniently lack the energy and imagination to raise significant sums of money to support them. I have never heard of a black church undertaking a massive fundraising campaign to educate black youth in the ways being discussed here. (There may be such churches, but I have no knowledge of their existence.) Most black pastors seem to be imaginative and pumped only when it comes to raising money to build an expensive church building, often in the middle of a poor inner-city neighborhood, with most of the membership commuting from nicer areas of the city or nearby suburbs. When it comes to doing ministries that matter in the neighborhood, and that ultimately will support the advancement of beloved community work, imagination and will power are strangely absent in far too many black pastors. The real problem, it seems, has to do with how many pastors understand the good news of the gospel, and how they understand ministry. Too often, *good news* has to do with "what's in it, materially, for me," while ministry is to be done primarily within the walls of the expensive church building that has been constructed, with little or no attention to the community in which the building is located.

In my estimation, many pastors need to rethink their understanding of the gospel and ministry. They can begin by reexamining the expectations of the carpenter from Nazareth. If black pastors and churches do this in a serious way, I have no doubt that they can begin devising ways to contribute significantly toward black youth learning to accept themselves and their heritage, thus creating openings for them to continue the work of establishing King's ideal of the beloved community.

Criticizing the U.S. for Its Moral Limitations Is Not Unpatriotic

Part of what makes it so difficult for some people, who otherwise have a good sense of right and wrong, moral and immoral, just and unjust, to criticize the United States for questionable moral actions is the sense that in doing so one is necessarily being unpatriotic. According to this view, one must not criticize his own group, race, or country, no matter the extent of its unjust and even savage behavior. We have seen that this was not the stance of young people in the civil rights movement, however. For these were not hesitant to criticize local, state, and national governments for their failure to deliver on civil rights and freedom. Once it became clear to them that authorities on the local, state, and national levels were often complicit in the racist mistreatment of blacks, such as denial of their right to register to vote, movement youth did not hesitate to express their dismay and criticisms, and did not pass up the opportunity to take nonviolent direct action against them. These young people had such sharp, analytical minds that they were able to see through the public façade put forth by each level of government. When they saw the truth of the matter, they took immediate steps to voice their criticisms and to make their protests known, and when necessary, to engage in nonviolent direct action against injustices that they identified. They did not make the mistake of passively awaiting the permission of more traditional leadership in the movement, and they certainly were not deterred by political leaders who counseled their silence and patience.

In short, movement youths, as well as Martin Luther King, unequivocally rejected the claim by politicians and those on the religious and secular right that it was unpatriotic to criticize the nation for its injustices and perceived wrongdoings. It should not be surprising that King took such a stance, particularly in light of his commitment to the prophetic tradition of the Jewish and Christian traditions. Prophetic critique was, for King, part of the vitamin A of ministry. Moreover, King believed that the Hebrew prophets were less concerned about the moral missteps of individuals, than the injustices committed on a massive scale by powerful rulers, groups, and nations. This is precisely where King aimed his sharpest prophetic criticisms, in addition to sending the message that criticizing the United States for its social and political misdeeds was not unpatriotic. We get a clear sense of this in his address, "The State of the Movement," in late 1967, just months before he was assassinated.

> We must begin to ask why there are 40 million poor people in a nation overflowing with such unbelievable affluence? We must begin to ask why has our nation placed itself in a position of being God's military agent on earth and intervene recklessly in Vietnam and the Dominican Republic? Why have we substituted the arrogant undertaking of policing the whole world for the high task of putting our own house in order? All these questions remind us that there is a need for a radical restructuring of the architecture of American society.... For the evils of racism, poverty and militarism to die, a new set of values must be

born. Our economy must become more person-centered than property-centered and profit-centered. Our government must depend more on its moral power than on its military power. Let us therefore not think of our movement as one that seeks to integrate the Negro into all the existing values of American society. Let us be those creative dissenters who will call our nation to a higher destiny, to a new plateau of compassion, to a more noble expression of humaneness.[40]

For King, to criticize a democratic nation for its social wrongdoings is to be more patriotic than unpatriotic. Every democracy needs its "creative dissenters," he said on more than one occasion. To fail to criticize the democratic nation for its moral and political misdeeds is the true meaning of "unpatriotic." In addition, no nation is so perfect that any group should want to be uncritically integrated into the totality of its values, an idea that movement youth modeled for all to see. Indeed, we may be encouraged by the actions of Afrikan American, Hispanic, and other youths affiliated with the Dream Defenders in Miami, Florida after the "not-guilty" verdict in the George Zimmerman trial. When the verdict was issued, these young people launched a sit-in on July 16, 2013 at the Florida State House until Governor Rick Scott agreed to meet with them. This was a significant instance in which some present-day youths exhibited their willingness to carry the struggle forward; to not forget the witness and legacy of civil rights youths.[41] There is a need to see much more of this type of effort by today's youths.

Removing Racists from Congress

Both Martin Luther King and the youthful activists of the civil rights movement knew without question that the United States of America was racist at its core (i.e., structurally racist); that the nation itself

---
40. Ibid., 9.
41. See http://dreamdefenders.org/trayvonslaw/.

was conceived in racism; and that racism was the nation's "greatest moral dilemma."[42] They knew that the refusal of the local, state, and federal authorities to end the voter registration debacle throughout the South was not due merely to a lack of will, but that the lack of will was largely due to deep-seated racism and white supremacy. Prior to the 1960s and the emergence of the Black Consciousness and Black Power Movements, King and the youthful activists seemed less inclined to publicly declare that racism was a significant underlying cause of the socioeconomic and other maladies affecting the black community. After the tragic incidents in Birmingham, the Mississippi Delta, and Selma; the emergence of the Black Power and Black Consciousness Movements; as well as indisputable evidence of the white backlash against the civil rights gains in the mid-sixties, both young people and King began more persistently to name systemic racism as the underlying cause. This was quite evident among SNCC leaders such as James Forman, Julian Bond, and Stokely Carmichael.

By the mid- to late 1960s, Martin Luther King was not holding his tongue on the race question, making it clear in many speeches that the problem of achieving equality of the races in terms of life-chances for blacks was so difficult because, despite its virtues and attributes, America is deeply racist, and the idea of white supremacy is deeply embedded in all of its institutions. But King did not only name racism as a general sickness in the United States. By the late sixties he got downright specific, saying that there was a critical need to remove racists from the United States Congress. Because young people, King, and other movement people had fought valiantly for a voting rights bill and succeeded, King was convinced—rightly or wrongly—that the answer to getting racists out of Congress was through voting. "The tragic truth is that Congress, more than the American people,"

---

42. *The Papers*, (2005), 5:546.

he said, "is now running amok with racism."[43] He knew that as long as there were so many racists in Congress, civil rights and freedom would continue to be in jeopardy. The racists in Congress could be easily retired, King maintained, "if we voted in large numbers."[44] King was certain that when Congress "repeatedly denies even small measures which might bring this nation a step nearer to equality," one can only conclude that it is guilty of racial discrimination.[45]

Tragically, long after the battles and sacrifices of movement youths, King, and others in the Deep South, racism still defines the United States Congress, notwithstanding the claim to the contrary by right-wing politicians, including many moderates, and their supporters. This has been most evident during the administration of President Barack Hussein Obama. The ugly face of racism showed itself time and time again throughout his campaigns for the presidency and for reelection in 2008 and 2012, respectively. It was, and continues to be, bad enough that large numbers of white citizens have unashamedly displayed their racism. Large numbers of white, conservative members of the Senate and the House are so deeply afflicted with racism that they have done everything conceivable to prevent President Obama from governing, that is, addressing real problems endured by the masses of U.S. citizens. From the onset of Obama's administration there has been constant political gridlock in Washington, the likes of which has not existed in the history of this nation. Even if such has existed historically, it most assuredly did not exist for the reason it does today—racism and pure mean-spiritedness. This is not to say, however, that before now, racism in Congress did not exist on a massive scale. It did. The difference now is that racist members of Congress are so resentful that there

---

43. King, "The Crisis in America's Cities," Address to SCLC, Atlanta, Georgia, August 15, 1967, King Library and Archives, 3.
44. King, "The State of the Movement," 4.
45. King, Statement to the Press, November 2, 1967, King Library and Archives, 2.

is an Afrikan American in the White House that they have made it virtually impossible for the President to adequately address the needs of the middle class, let alone the systematically left-outs. They have made the utterly immoral and tragic decision to allow vast numbers of middle-class and poor people to suffer throughout the remainder of President Obama's term. Others may see this differently, but as far as I can tell, this stance by most conservatives and some moderates in Congress is motivated more by race than anything else.

In any case, *with racism still running amok in Congress*, and with no one in Washington—especially among well-meaning whites—willing to name racists for who they are, young people who desire to resume the unfinished work of the civil rights movement will have to meet this problem head on. One cannot solve the problem as long as no one will name it and call it what it is. Congressional racists want to continue their racist behavior unchallenged, while simultaneously insisting that they should not be called racists; for to do so, they argue, is nothing short of name calling and hitting below the belt, and thus a violation of the rules of civilized discourse and political correctness. Movement youths were not swayed by this, but stayed focused on trying to attain freedom and civil rights. This will also have to be the stance of present-day youths.

Since it is still too often the case that vast numbers of young people do not vote on a regular basis, one of their first tasks must be to initiate voter education and registration projects aimed specifically at voting racists out of Congress, as well as state legislatures. As it was for youthful movement activists in the Deep South, this will surely be very difficult and frustrating work, and perhaps even more so today, particularly since racists have become adept at political correctness, publicly concealing their racism, and rejecting charges of racism against them, even when they are clearly behaving as racists in legislative chambers. Although the work of voter registration will be very hard work, young people today have social media and other means at their disposal should they take up the cause.

In addition, young people have at their disposal the prophetic voices of hip hop artists who focus on sociopolitical analysis in their work. This clearly is not the case of most rappers and hip hop artists, but only of an important minority. These include, but are not limited to, rap artists such as Will.I.Am (William James Adams), EL-P (Jaime Meline), and Killer Mike (Michael Render).[46] Public Enemy was an earlier rap group that focused on sociopolitical analysis.[47] Others, such as the prophetic voices of Chuck D and KRS-One, have also been important contributors in this regard. Chuck D has aptly said that "[r]ap is now a worldwide phenomenon; . . . the CNN for young people all over the world."[48] More specifically, he refers to rap as "the Black CNN."[49] Access to such tools and prophetic critiques by socially and politically astute hip hop artists can take young people a long way toward achieving the goal of exposing and extricating the most diehard racists from Congress.[50]

---

46. I am indebted to my former student, Dr. Timothy Knight, an Indianapolis Metropolitan Police Department detective, for supplying these names. Timothy has worked long and hard trying to save at-risk young Afrikan American boys from violence and early death in the city of Indianapolis, Indiana.
47. Rebecca J. Maynard Phillips, a former student, reminded me of the role played by Public Enemy during an earlier period.
48. Quoted in Cornel West, *Democracy Matters: Winning the Fight Against Imperialism* (New York: Penguin, 2004), 174.
49. Quoted in ibid., 173.
50. I have always been aware of the so-called negative impact of hip-hop and certain rap artists on Afrikan American youths, since I hear their work on various media regularly. I had mostly written off voices in hip-hop and rap until I had the good fortune to hear a panel of young Afrikan American scholars talk about the significance of hip-hop in the post–civil rights movement era at the retirement celebration of the top King scholar in the world, Lewis V. Baldwin, of Vanderbilt University, on November 9, 2013. (The theme of the celebration was "The Voice of Conscience: Civil Rights, Post Civil Rights, and the Future Freedom Struggle.") I was deeply affected by what Professors Tim Lake (Wabash College), Keri Day (Brite Divinity School), Michael Brandon McCormack (University of Louisville), and Michael Brown (formerly of Wabash College) shared with the audience, and vowed to get up to speed on this important topic. From the beginning of my career in the academy until now, I have

"Hip-hop culture and rap music are, in many ways, an indictment of the old generation even as they imitate and emulate us in a raw and coarse manner. The defiant and insightful voices of this new generation lyrically proclaim that they have been relatively unloved, uncared for, and unattended to by adults too self-indulgent, too self-interested, and too self-medicated to give them the necessary love, care, and attention to flower and flourish. Only their beloved mothers—often overworked, underpaid, and wrestling with a paucity of genuine intimacy—are spared. They also indict the American empire for its mendacity and hypocrisy—not in a direct anti-imperialist language but in a poetic rendering of emotional deficits and educational defects resulting from the unequal institutional arrangements of the empire.

"It is important that all democrats engage and encourage prophetic voices in hip-hop—voices that challenge youth to be self-critical rather than self-indulgent, Socratic rather than hedonistic." (West, *Democracy Matters*, 184)

They should not be so naïve to think that Congress will at any time in the near future be free and clear of all racists, since there is no evidence whatever that a racism-free society is on the horizon. There is no question, however, that Congress can be less racist than it is.

always been interested in the prophetic voice. It is clear to me that some of the voices in hip-hop and rap are not merely in the business for the money, though very many of them are. The prophetic critique that some of these rap artists offers is significant for those young people who will carry the movement forward. These are voices that we need to hear; voices that more and more young people need to hear and allow their behavior to be transformed accordingly. So much more needs to be said about this. For now, suffice it to say that philosopher and social-analyst-critic Cornel West has given a helpful commentary on the importance of hip-hop and rap, and what they can offer in the way of challenging not only the black community and wider culture, but young people.

Need for Mass Civil Disobedience

By the mid- to late 1960s, it had become clear to Martin Luther King that the nonviolent demonstrations that worked so well throughout the South were not adequate for the economic and other facets of the struggle that lay ahead. This was because of the systemic nature of the problem, and also because it had to be attacked outside the South. King had known for a long time that the methods of nonviolence had to be adapted to the local situation, and that the difference between South and North would necessarily mean that adaptations needed to be made to the types of nonviolence to be implemented.

Without question, Martin Luther King was wedded and devoted to nonviolence like no other person in the movement, indeed, in the world at that time. Some of the youthful movement activists were committed to it, but there were times when they wondered whether all the suffering that accompanied nonviolence was worth it, a point that Dave Dennis raised after the murders of Chaney, Schwerner, and Goodman. Indeed, after only a few weeks in Mississippi, one of the student volunteers wrote family and friends to say that some of them were close to advocating guerrilla warfare like some of the longtime local activists; that some of them "don't buy this nonviolent stuff." And further: "After facing a few bombings, beatings and jailings some of the summer volunteers felt like throwing a few bombs back themselves . . ."[51] No matter how bad things got, however, Martin Luther King did not waver in his commitment to nonviolence as a way of life. So entrenched was racism and the refusal of local, state, and national political leaders to grant civil rights and full equality of opportunity to blacks, that King came to believe that the only way to break through was to unleash mass civil disobedience campaigns, not least the Poor People's Campaign. Mass civil disobedience "is

---

51. Martínez, *Letters from Mississippi*, 167.

militant and defiant, but not destructive,"[52] King said. It is essentially a move from protest—important as that is in the early stage of social struggles—to "the stage of massive active non-violent resistance to the evils of the modern system."[53]

Significantly, King held, part of this effort toward nonviolent mass civil disobedience will be dependent upon the forming of deeper and broader alliances between young people in various groups. He was aware that there had been breakdowns in the coalitions formed between black and white youths during movement years. This was the result of a number of factors, not least the rising level of distrust between the two groups, and black youths' desire to work solely among themselves for a period in order to work on developing their own power base. Nonetheless, King still believed that in the long run the two groups would be stronger and more effective in civil rights work if they reunited in an alliance in common cause, rather than remain separate. Today, such coalition-building will be a huge task. But as intimated before, young people's commitment to and use of the various social media technologies, as well as their willingness to be informed by the sociopolitical insights of select hip hop artists, can be a significant means for such work.

Young people have their work cut out for them today, and it is work that they themselves will have to do. Many black youths naïvely think that their right to vote is guaranteed. And yet, time and again attempts are made to alter the Voting Rights Act, especially before major elections, thus putting in jeopardy the voting rights of blacks. Moreover, black youths will have to wise up to the fact that continued efforts to revoke Affirmative Action lessens their own life-chances in education and employment. These and other issues,

---

52. King, "The State of the Movement," 5.
53. Ibid., 8.

for example, what to do about immigration laws, are reasons young people need to get involved in carrying the struggle forward.

I happen to think that young people today are much more creative than my generation. During a question-answer period at a fiftieth-anniversary celebration of the 1963 "I Have a Dream" speech at Christian Theological Seminary in Indianapolis on April 12, 2013, a young seminary graduate from Garrett Evangelical Theological Seminary inquired as to how we might go about trying to get more young people to attend such events, if for no other reason than to learn about this period of history and to appropriate the lessons gleaned therefrom. He was concerned that so few youths were in attendance, even though some participants suggested that their attendance was desirable, and that this was something that planners of similar future events should work on. The young man went on to say that most young people probably would not have much appreciation for the general format of most events like the one in question, where there would be formal lectures and panel discussions, especially those that exclude youth. I reminded him that he and a few others of his generation were in attendance at the event, and that the place for future planners of such events to begin was with them. The youths may have to instruct us, I said, and our job will be to listen patiently, and take seriously the suggestions they make. Moreover, I said to him in private, they should even be offered leadership roles in the planning of similar future events. What I tried to impress upon him, when the event was over, was that it is not enough for young people to voice their concerns and to criticize only. They must also be willing to do what young people did in movement days, namely to jump right in and begin making their own contributions. In short, I said, they had to be willing to do the work, and to realize that there may be no immediate gain. They would have to be willing to keep their eyes on the big picture, and persevere.[54]

Without question, one of the aims of the mass civil disobedience project known as the Poor People's Campaign in 1968 was to disrupt the halls of Congress and the federal government; to essentially shut down the government until the legislative and executive branches both heard and responded positively to the demands of the several thousands of poor people camped out in Washington. Indicators are that something of this sort, on an even more massive scale, is needed today, in order to arouse the conscience of the nation, and more specifically that of elected officials and corporate executives of the large financial institutions. Of course, if such an event is to be consistent with King's approach, it will have to be based on nonviolence, which means that would-be participants will have to be trained in the ideology and techniques of nonviolence.

An Anvil or a Hammer

Many persons' personality is such that they tend to allow others to mold and shape them. This, we have seen, was not the way of the youthful civil rights activists, who took their lives and future into their own hands and molded them according to their own ideals and expectations, which were generally consistent with those of the Constitution. They were unwilling to leave such an important task in the hands of others, regardless of race-ethnicity and age. In this regard, they were at one with Martin Luther King who, quoting Henry Wadsworth Longfellow approvingly, said that "in this world a man must be an anvil or a hammer."[55] As free, autonomous beings, human beings can choose to be one or the other. The person with

---

54. Upon exchanging email addresses I promised to contact the young man to explore these things further. He welcomed that. I emailed him twice within a two week period. I received no response from him, which caused me to wonder how sincere he was about the question he raised during the discussion period.
55. Quoted in ibid., 11.

character will likely choose to be a hammer that shapes society and others around her, rather than an anvil on which she herself is forcibly molded in the image of someone or something else. "We must be hammers shaping a new society rather than anvils molded by the old," said King. "This not only will make us new men but will give us a new kind of power. It will not be Lord Acton's image of power that tends to corrupt, absolute power that corrupts absolutely. It will be power infused with love and justice that will change dark yesterdays into bright tomorrows."[56] One has to be intentional about this, since most people do not just fall into being molders and shapers of society.

To be a hammer that molds a society based on the beloved community ideal means that young people cannot continue making the mistake of burying themselves in computer games and social media conversations hour after precious hour each and every day. We have already begun to see a generation of children who seem addicted to computerized games and such, and would, if left to their own choosing, do nothing but plant their faces in the screens of iPhones and other computerized hardware every day of the week, and not for authentically educational purposes. This tendency has already reached epidemic proportion, and is not, by any stretch of the imagination, conducive to the work of fighting for freedom and liberation.

Young people who are interested in their future and a desire to contribute toward the formation of the good society and a life worth living will need to figure out how best to use computer technology and social media to advance the cause of the type of society that their predecessors struggled and sacrificed to attain during movement years. Although every citizen has a stake in such work, none have more of a stake than youth. However, since vast numbers of youths in every community know little or nothing about the contributions

56. Quoted in King, "The State of the Movement," 11.

of their youthful predecessors of the movement years and what this can mean for them today, it should be stressed once again just how important is education as a significant part of the remedy. Whether in the home, school, church, or a combination of these, young people need to be taught this history and given opportunities to discuss and think about its implications for their own lives and the type of society they wish to live in. It will be recalled that during the Montgomery bus boycott, the Children's Crusade in Birmingham, and other civil rights campaigns, black children and youths demanded that their teachers give time, space, and energy to discuss those local campaigns and implications for their ongoing education and day-to-day living. They wanted to know whether their education had any meaning for the struggle and the type of society being sought. But for an exception here and there, most of the teachers did not honor the students' demands, and yet this did not deter or discourage the students from joining the ranks of the demonstrators. There is no reason to believe that most teachers—at whatever level—would not respond similarly today should students demand that classroom time be given the social issues that have an immediate effect on them, for example, black-against-black violence and homicide among young black males. However, historically, there has always been a minority of wise, creative, and courageous teachers at all levels—in schools as well as religious institutions—who have understood the importance of helping students make the connections between what they are being taught and what is actually happening in their daily lives outside school and church. Today's youth will themselves have to decide whether it is in their best interest to be a hammer, or the anvil they have been to this point.

Index

Abernathy, Ralph, 23-24, 37, 41, 47, 88, 104, 115, 229, 242, 248, 255, 256, 267
Adams, William James ("Will.I.Am"), 309
Alabama Christian Movement for Human Rights (ACMHR), 69, 99, 101, 136
Alabama State College 80
Albany, Georgia campaign, 13, 99, 116, 126, 260
Albany State College, 116
Alcorn A & M, 283
Allen, Louis, 170, 204, 205
Alvarez, Carmelo, 272n2
American Nazi Party, 229n20
Anderson, Bailey Reign, xxxvii
Anderson, Jade, xxxvii
Anderson, Raven Lynn, xxxvii
Anderson, Sierra Lynn, xxxvii
Angelou, Maya, 101, 140n112

Anniston, Alabama, xxiv, xxix-xxx, xxxvi, 5, 54, 68, 69, 199, 221
Ansbro, John J., xxxiv
Aron, Drewey, 38
Arsenault, Raymond, 92, 95

"bad faith", 131n93
Baker, Ella J., 6, 65, 66, 162, 165
Baker, Simeon, 76
Baker, Wilson, 221, 222, 223, 225, 245, 257, 258
Baldwin, James, 201
Baldwin, Lewis, V. 198, 199n117, 255n84, 309n50
Baltimore Afro-American, 115
Baptist Youth Fellowship (BYF), 25
Barnett, Ross (Governor), 266
Barry, Marion, 63, 64, 66
Bell, Derrick, 276
Beloit College, xxiv

Bennett College, 56, 58, 84, 261
Bennett, Lerone, 132
Bergman, Walter, 68
Berkamp, Will, xxxv
Berkowitz, Abe, 143
Bertocci, Peter A., 290, 291
Bethel Baptist Church, 70, 99
Bevel, James, xviii, xxx, xxxi, 4, 14, 33, 107, 108, 109, 110, 111, 121, 122, 152, 166, 167, 168-69, 218, 231, 232, 267
Billups, Charles, 140
Birmingham Bar Association, 144
Birmingham Civil Rights Institute, 279
Birmingham News, 106
Birmingham Southern College, 142
Bishop, Jim, 138
Black CNN, 309
Black Consciousness Movement, 34, 298, 306
Black Power Movement, 298, 306
Blackwell, Unita, 211, 214
Blair, Ezell (aka Jibreel Khazan), 55, 56, 58, 61
Blake, John, 205
"Bloody Sunday", xvii, xxxii, 240, 245, 246, 248, 252, 253, 259
Blumberg, Rhoda Lois, 112
Blumstein's Department Store, 1

"Bombingham", 97
Boesak, Allan, 147n132
Bond, Julian, 154, 171, 221, 306
Booker T. Washington High School, 32, 46
Boston University, 23, 290
Boutwell, Albert, 112
Bowers, Sam, 188, 189
Boynton, Amelia, 221, 228
Boynton, Samuel, 221, 226, 227
Boynton vs. Virginia, 67
Bradley, Mamie, ix, 149
Bristol, James, 7
Brookings Institution, xi
Brown, Alexander, 123
Brown Chapel AME Church, 238, 249
Brown, Jerry (Governor), 180
Brown, Michael, 309n50
Brownlee, Henry, 118
Bureggemann, Walter, 147n132
Bryant, Carolyn, ix, 20
Bryant, Roy, ix, x, 20, 149, 159
Bryant, C. C., 174
Buckham, John Wright, 285
Burks, Mary Fair, 24
Butler, Mac, 256

Cagin, Seth, 158
Carey, Archibald James, 103

INDEX

Carmichael, Stokely, 217, 260, 261, 267, 306
Carson, Clayborne, 27, 182
Caston, Billy Jack, 170
Chaney, Ben, 194
Chaney, Fannie Lee, 194
Chaney, James, xxvii, 157, 158, 184, 185, 188, 189-91, 192-94, 200, 204, 205, 214, 282, 283, 292, 311
Character, 297-98
Children's Crusade, xxxi, 114, 120, 124
Christian Theological Seminary, 147n132, 312
Chuck D, 309
Civil Rights Bill (1964), 51, 147, 200, 233
Clark, Jim, 223-25, 227, 228, 230, 236, 237, 242, 244, 245, 246, 258, 266
"Club from Nowhere", 44
Cobb, Charles, 14, 177
COFO, 176, 178, 182, 189, 200, 291
Coleman, James P. (Governor), 160
Collins, Addie Mae, 145, 240
Collins, Leroy, 248, 249, 250, 251, 253

Colvin, Claudette, xxi, 28, 29, 31-36, 298
Coming of Age in Mississippi, 44
communal singing, 118
Connor, Eugene Theophilus ("Bull"), 68, 71, 98, 100, 111, 122, 123, 125, 126, 127, 130, 132, 133, 135, 223, 236, 245, 246, 266
Cooper, Jerome, 144
CORE, xxix, xxxi, xxxvi, 5, 53, 54, 56, 67, 151, 162, 177, 204
Cotton, Dorothy, 103n20, 105n23, 111, 117, 118, 125, 229
courage, 289-98
Courts, Gus, 159
Cox, W. Harold, 254
"creative minority", 11
Crozer Theological Seminary, 26, 27
Cultural centers, xxxii
Curry, Izola Ware, 1

Dahmer, Vernon, 189
Davis, Jim, 279
Day, Keri, 309n50
D-Day, 114, 121, 122, 130
Dennis, Dave, 167, 176, 179, 180, 181, 194-95, 204, 205-206, 207, 220, 208, 311

DeBerry, Roy, 161
Dee, Henry Hezekiah, 191
de la Beckwith, Byron, 145
Democratic Convention (1964), 180
Dexter Avenue Baptist Church, 20, 23, 24, 25, 33, 44, 53, 273
Dialectical Society, 81
Dixon, Rebecca, 80
Doar, John, 250, 255
Dostoevsky, Fyodor, 279
Dray, Philip, 158
Dream Defenders, 305
Drew, John, 135n101
Drew University, 189
DuBois, W. E. B., xix
Durgan, Andrew, 246
"Dynamite Hill", 97

Ebenezer Baptist Church, 24, 286
Ebony, 76
Edmund Pettus Bridge, vii, 241, 248, 252, 258
Edwards, Charles Marcus, 191n95
Elliot, J. Robert, 254
Ellis, Talbot, 108
"EL-P" (Jaime Meline), 309
Emancipation Day, 229, 230
Engel, William P., 143
Eskew, Glenn, 130, 143
Eubanks, Thelma, 201, 203

Evans, Glenn, 130
Evers, Medgar, 145, 149, 155, 204
Evers, Myrlie, 149, 155
existentialist, 131
Extremist for Love, xxxv

Fairclough, Adam, 144
Farmer, James, xxx, xxxvi, 18, 19, 67, 72, 93, 195, 277
Farris, Christine King, 246, 286n17
Faubus, Orval (Governor), 266
Faulkner, William, 93, 94
Featherstone, Ralph, 174-75
"fill the jails", 124
First Baptist Church, 24, 88
First Union Baptist Church, 194
Fisk University, xxiv, 54
Florida A & M University, 80
Forman, James, 30, 50, 125, 140, 141, 220 256, 260, 306
"Four Points for Progress", 135
"Freedom Fighters", 124
Freedom Party, 176
Freedom Ride, xxiv, xxv, xxix, xxx, xxxvi, 5, 8, 54, 67-68, 69, 70, 73, 88-96, 134, 279
Freedom Schools, xxxii, 175, 179, 201
Freedom songs, 118
Freedom's Daughters, 74

Freedom Speech Movement, 210
Freedom Summer, xxvii, xxxi, 8, 15, 117, 153, 154, 176-88, 204, 211, 214, 267, 283, 290

Gadson, Mary, 145
Gandhi, 11, 41, 72, 82, 106, 124, 124n77, 229
Gardner, Edward, 99
Garrett Evangelical Theological Seminary, 312
Garrow, David J., 29
Gaston, A. G., 113
Gaston Hotel, 103, 103n20, 122, 143
"generation of integration", 77
George A. Towne Elementary School, 2
George, C. H., 99
Georgia State Prison, 65
Gilmore, Georgia, 44
Gitin, Maria, 199n117, 260
"God intoxicated", 286
Gonzalez, Juan, 272n2
Goodman, Andrew, xxvii, 157, 158, 184, 185, 188, 189-91, 192, 193, 196, 200, 204, 206, 214, 282, 283, 292, 311
grace, 297
Graetz, Robert S., 31, 37, 42, 50-51

Gray, Fred D., 32
Gray, Victoria, 204
Gregg, Richard, 92
Greensboro *Champion*, 58
Guyot, Lawrence, 207

habit, 292-97
Halberstam, David, 124
Haley, Alex, 260
Haley, James O., 144
Hamer, Fannie Lou, 179, 182, 187, 211
Harvard University, 186, 201
Hayes, Curtis, 172
Hendricks, Audrey Faye, 124
Henry, Aaron, 176
Hermann, Susan, 75
Hermey, Louise, 189-90
Highlander Folk School, 71, 101, 142, 165
Hip-hop, 309, 309n50
Hodes, Bill, 182
Holiday, Billie, 152
Holt, Len, 140
Horton, Myles, 101, 101n14
Hotel Albert, 229
Howard, Princella, 49, 231
Humor, 255, 255n84, 256
Hurley, Ruby, 155
Hurst, E. H., 170

If Your Back's Not Bent, 105n23, 117
Independence Quarters, 158
Isasi-Díaz, Ada María, 272n2

Jackson, Jawana, 7
Jackson, Jimmy Lee, xxvii, 240, 250, 259
James, William, 292-96
"Jesus of the movement", 171
Jet, ix, x, 149
Jewish rabbis, 143-44
John Birch Society, 222
Johns, Ralph (aka Ricardo Raffles), 57, 58, 59
Johns, Vernon, 273, 274n3
Johnson, Frank, 248, 249, 250, 252
Johnson, Geneva, 29
Johnson, Lyndon Baines (President), 233, 234, 250, 251, 253, 256, 258-59
Jones, Charles, 167
Journey of Reconciliation, 68
Junker, Débora, 272n2
Junker, Tercio, 272n2

Katzenback, Nicholas, 257, 258
Kelsey, George, 3, 27
Kennedy, John F., 65, 94, 98, 133-34, 165, 171

Kennedy, Robert, 75, 93, 94, 112, 133, 165, 171, 174, 254
Kiddieland, 115
Killen, Edgar Ray, 191
Killer Mike (Michael Render), 309
Kilpatrick, James, 86
King, A. D., 111, 145
King, Coretta Scott, 1, 65
King, Delia, 104
King, Edward, 64
King, Edwin, 176
King, Lonnie, 88
King, Martin Luther Jr.: Afrikan heritage, 299; bombing of Sixteenth Street Baptist Church, 145-46; Chaney, Goodman, Schwerner, 158, 197-98; encouragement of students, 77-88; Emmett Till, 159-60; faith in God, 281-82; Freedom Rider, 75-77; freedom songs, 118-19; Mississippi, 157-64; racism in Congress, 146; radio and Children's Crusade 120; the Press, 129; "turnaround Tuesday", 248-54
King, Martin Luther Sr. ("Daddy King"), 75
King, Mary, 190, 192
King Papers Project, 27

INDEX

Klibanoff, Hank, 48, 127
Knight, Timothy, 309n46
Knudson, Albert C., 285
Ku Klux Klan, 40, 43, 44, 110, 152, 155, 160, 167, 216, 271
Kunstler, William, 195

Lacey, Joseph, 39, 40, 143
Ladner, Joyce, xi
Lafayette, Bernard, 4, 152, 156, 166, 167, 168-69, 218, 219, 220, 221, 226-27, 231
Lafayette, Colia, 219, 226, 231
Lake, Tim, 309n50
Lane, T. L., 99
Lawrence, Charles, R. 102
Lawson, James, 4, 59, 73, 86, 152, 161, 164
Lee, George, 159
Lee, Herbert, 170, 172, 173, 204, 205
Lelyveld, Arthur, 153, 196
"Letter from Birmingham Jail", 106
Levine, Ellen, 34
Lewis, Jewel, 25
Lewis, John, xxiv, 4, 68, 72, 74, 75, 94, 152, 156-57, 195, 203, 231, 236, 237, 242, 245, 249, 252, 256, 264
Lewis, Rufus, 220

Litigation approach, 52
Liuzzo, Viola, 257
Long, Carolyn, 64
Long, Worth, 221
Long, Wylma, 64
Longfellow, Henry Wadsworth, 314
Lord Acton, 314
Lowenstein, Allard, 176, 206, 213
Lowndes County (Alabama), 12, 261, 263
Lucy, Autherine, 127

Madison, James, 137
Manis, Andrew, 136
Marable, Manning, 120
March on Washington, 20
Marshall, Burke, 133, 140, 222
Marshall, Thurgood, xvi, 52, 113
Martin, Larry, 202, 203
Martin, Trayvon, 272
Martin, Yancey, 41, 42
Mason Temple, 256
mass civil disobedience, 310-14
Mays, Benjamin E., 3, 27, 274n3
McAdam, Doug, 212-13
McCain, Franklin, 55, 57, 58, 61
McCormick, Michael Brandon, 309n50
McDew, Chuck, xxxi, 167, 173, 174

325

McKissick, Floyd, 59
McNeil, Joseph, 55, 57, 58, 61
McNair, Denise, 145, 240
Meline, Jaime ("EL-P"), 309
"Messiah complex", 18
Milam, J. W., ix, x, 20, 149, 159
Miles College, 102, 114
Millard, Richard M., 291
Miller, Orloff, 249
Mississippi Democratic Party, 181
Mississippi Freedom Democratic Party, 157
"Mississippi Goddamn", 156
Mitchel, J. Oscar, 64
Montgomery Advertiser, 41
Montgomery Improvement Association (MIA), 40, 42, 44, 48, 49
Moody, Anne, 44, 45, 46
Moore, Amzie, 163, 169, 175
Moore, Charles Eddie, 191
Moore, Douglas, 81
Moore, William, 145
moral jiu-jitsu, 92
Morehouse College, 3
Morgan, Juliette, 41
Morgan v. Virginia, 102n17
Morsell, John, 52
Moses, Bob, xxxi, 107, 157, 162-64, 167, 169-76, 179-81, 185, 186-87, 203-206, 211, 220, 230, 231, 292
Mother's Day Massacre, 68, 88
Mott, Stephen Charles, 297
Mount Nebo Church, 158
Mount Zion Baptist Church, 188
Mullings, Leith, 119
Myrdal, Gunnar, 128

NAACP, x, 24, 52, 53, 55, 66, 79, 89, 150, 151, 155, 174, 177
NAACP Youth Council, 55
Nash, Diane (Bevel), xii, xviii, xxii, xxiii, xxiv, xxix, xxx, xxxvi, 4, 54, 72, 73-74, 75, 76, 86, 94, 107, 108, 166, 167, 220, 267, 277, 278
Nashville Student Movement, xxiv-xxv, 64, 72, 154, 164, 231
National Association of Radio Announcers, 120
National States Rights Party, 229
Neal, Claude, 19, 20
Nesbitt, Geraldine, xxi, 32, 298
Newsweek, 114
New York Times, 132, 264
Niebuhr, Reinhold, 101n14, 137, 277
Nixon, E. D., 47
Nobel Peace Prize, 228, 233
Nonviolent High School, 174

Norman, Silas, 221
North Carolina A & T, xxix, 55

Obama, Barack Hussein (President), 230, 307, 307
Oates, Stephen B., 28
O'Brien, Fran, 212
Olsen, Lynne, 74
Operation Freedom Vote, 179, 290
Orris, Peter, 186

Parchman State Penitentiary, xxix, 157, 166
Parham, Grosbeck Preer, 108, 109
Parker, Mack Charles, 159
Parks, Rosa, x, 28
Patton, Gwendolyn, 14, 32, 70, 71
Payne, Milton, 131
Peck and Peck Department Store, 70
Peck, James, 68, 70
"People to People Tour", 157
personalist, 131, 290
person intoxicated, 286
Phillips, Rebecca J., 309n47
"pied piper", 7
Pitts, Lucius, 102, 135n101
Plessy vs. Ferguson, 17
Poor People's Campaign, 311, 313
Post-traumatic stress disorder, 208

Powledge, Fred, 52, 61, 90, 258
Price, Cecil, 158, 190
Pritchett, Laurie, 126, 223, 225, 266
Proctor, Samuel DeWitt, 26
Project Alabama, 221-22
Project C ("confrontation"), xxx, 102
"Prospectus for the Summer", 177
Pruitt, G. E., 99
Public Enemy, 309

Quinn Chapel AME Church, 103

Rabbinical Assembly, 143
racism in Congress, 146
radio and the Children's Crusade, 120
radio announcers, 120
Raines, Howell, 41, 69, 177, 205, 206
Rauschenbusch, Walter, 12, 27
Raymer, George, 208
Reagon, Bernice Johnson, 116, 117
Recinos, Harold J., 272n2
Reconstruction, xv
Reddick, L. D., 22
redemptive suffering, 82
Reeb, James, xxvii, 241, 250, 259
Reese, Frederick, 246, 247

Reeves, Jeremiah, 36-38, 48
Render, Michael ("Killer Mike"), 309
Reynolds, Isaac ("Ike"), 111, 184
Richmond, David, 55, 58, 61
Rich's Department Store, 63, 64, 82
Roberson, Bernita, 105, 106
Roberson, Houston Bryan, 24
Roberson, James, 70
Roberts, Gene, 47, 127
Robertson, Carol, 145, 146, 240
Robey, Lucinda B., 99
Robinson, Jimmy, 56, 229
Robinson, JoAnn, 24, 25
Robinson, Ruby Doris, 30
Rustin, Bayard, 198n115, 264

Sartre, Jean Paul, 131n93, 288
Savio, Mario, 209, 210
Schwerner, Anne, 193-94
Schwerner, Michael, xxii, 157, 158, 184, 185, 188, 189-91, 192-94, 202, 204, 205, 214, 282, 283, 292, 311
Schwerner, Rita, 186, 202
SCLC, xxx, xxxi, 10, 13, 53, 66, 151, 177, 253, 264, 265
SCOPE, 198, 199n117, 267
Scott, Rick (Governor), 305
Seale, James Ford, 191

second great awakening, 254
Seigenthaler, John, 75
Sellers, Clyde, 43
Selma Freedom Day, 224
Sermon on the Mount, 229
Shambry, Henry Lee, 131
Shaw University, 6, 62, 65-66, 83, 164
"shero", 140n112
Shields, Roy, 217
Shores, Arthur, 113, 135n101
Shuttlesworth, Fred, 69, 71, 74, 99, 100, 111, 126-27, 135, 137, 141, 142, 267
Shuttlesworth, Patricia Anne, 101
Shuttlesworth, Ricky, 70, 101
Shuttlesworth, Ruby Fredericka, 101
Simone, Nina, 156
Simkins, George, 55, 56, 60
Simpson, Euvester, 202, 203
sit-ins, xxix, 5, 8, 54, 88-96
Sixteenth Street Baptist Church, 112, 123, 145
Smiley, Glenn, 47
Smith, Ervin, xxxiv
Smith, Kenneth, xxxiv
Smith, Lillian, 100
Smith, Mary Louise, 28
Smith, Nelson, 99
Smith, Ruby Doris, 74

Smyer, Sidney, 144
SNCC, xvii, xxviii, xxxi, xxxvi, 6, 13, 63, 66-67, 83, 151, 154, 162, 165, 177, 178-79, 204, 222, 253, 264, 265
Social and Political Action Committee (SPAC), 24, 25
social gospel, 12
socio drama, 59, 229n20
"songs of Zion", 119
Soracco, Frank, 243
sorrow songs, 119
"soul of the movement", 118
Southern Christian Ministers Conference (Mississippi), 159
Spain, David, 190
Spelman College, 74
Spencer, Benjamin, 262
Stanford University, 176, 179, 201
Stembridge, Jane, 63, 192
Stewart, Shelley ("the Playboy"), 122
Stone, Herman, 99
"Strange Fruit", 152, 153
Stride Toward Freedom, 92
Sweeney, Dennis, 213
Sweet Honey in the Rock, 116

Tabernacle Baptist Church, 226
talented tenth, xix
Tallahatchie River, ix, 21

Tarver, Judy, 114, 124
Taylor, Fred, 46, 47, 48
Temporary Student Nonviolent Coordinating Committee, 66
The Brothers Karamazov, 279
The Philosophy of Personalism, 285n15
This Bright Light of Ours, 199n117
Thomas, Frank, 147n132
Thomas, Hank, 69
Thrasher, Thomas, 42
Till, Emmett Louis, ix, x, xi, xii, xiii, 20, 21, 22, 44, 45, 46, 159, 239
Tillinghast, Muriel, 155, 214
Tougaloo College, 176
trait, 290
Tri-State Defender, 47
Travis, Brenda, 172, 173
Trinity Lutheran Church, 31, 42
Truman, Harry S., 85
"Turnaround Day", 250
"turnaround Tuesday", 248-54, 256
Turnbow, Hartman, 154
Turner, Albert, 240, 242, 245
Tuskegee University, 263

Union Theological Seminary (Virginia), 63
Unitarian Universalist, xxvii

University of Alabama, 127
University of California (Berkeley), 209-210
Urban League, 66

Vanderbilt University, 156
Vann, David, 126
Varela, Mary, 221
Virtue, 290-91
Vivian, C. T., 152
Voter Education Project (VEP), 164, 172
Voting Rights Act (1965), xxxii, 51, 147, 221, 257, 258, 259
Voucher, 226

Walker, Alice, 120-21, 273
Walker, Wyatt, 6, 111, 121, 123, 125
Wallace, George (Governor), 244, 257, 266
Wares, J. L., 113
Washington, Booker T., 109
Watkins, Hollis, 172, 178, 209, 210
Watson, Bruce, 197, 210
Wayne State University, 68
Webb, Sheyann, 237-39, 242-44, 247, 263, 264
WENN radio station, 123
"We Shall Overcome", 117

Wesley, Cynthia, 145, 240
Western College for Women, 182, 186, 202
West, Cornel, 310n50
West, Rachel, 238, 239, 243, 244
"whisper campaign", 122
White Citizens Council, 43, 44, 110, 160, 167, 216, 222
White Knights (KKK), 188
White, "Tall Paul" Dudley, 120, 122, 123
White, Viola, 29
Wilbur, Susan, 75
Wilcox County (Alabama), 198, 260-61, 291
Will.I.Am (William James Adams), 309
Williams, Hosea, 198, 238
Williams, Samuel, 27
Wilson, L. Alex, 47, 48
Wingfield, Katie, 29
Withers, Ernest, 47, 48
Wolff, Miles, 59
Woman's College 84
Women's Political Council (WPC), 24, 25
Woolworth, xxix, 57, 58, 172
Wright, Frank, 202
Wright, Judy, 202
Wright, Mose, 21

X, Malcolm, xvi, 113, 267

Yale University, 176, 179, 201
Young, Andrew, 104, 105n23, 111, 138, 222, 224, 228, 248, 250, 251, 255, 256, 267
Younge, Sammy Jr., 184n72
Youth Leadership Conference, 62
Youth March for Integrated Schools, 1

Zellner, Bob, xxxi, 167, 173, 185, 265
Zepp, Ira Jr,. xxxiv
Zimmerman, George, 272, 305
Zinn, Howard, 96, 148
Zwerg, Jim, xxiv, xxv, 94, 185, 196, 203, 204, 265, 277-80

www.ingramcontent.com/pod-product-compliance
Lightning Source LLC
Chambersburg PA
CBHW071147070526
44584CB00019B/2686